ROBBING

YOU

BLIND

ROBBING YOU BLIND

PROTECTING YOUR MONEY FROM WALL STREET'S HIDDEN COSTS AND HALF-TRUTHS

Moneymaking Strategies for Today's Investor

Mark Dempsey

William Morrow and Company, Inc. New York

It is the policy of William Morrow and Company, Inc., and its imprints and affiliates, recognizing the importance of preserving what has been written, to print the books we publish on acid-free paper, and we exert our best efforts to that end.

Library of Congress Cataloging-in-Publication Data

Dempsey, Mark, 1962–
Robbing you blind : protecting your money from Wall Street's hidden costs and half-truths; moneymaking stratgies for today's investor / Mark Dempsey.—1st ed.
p.   cm.
Includes bibliographical references and index.
ISBN 0-688-17034-X (alk. paper)
1. Finance—United States.   2. Stock exchange—United States.   I.Title.
HG181.D364 2000
332.63'22—dc21
99-047463

Printed in the United States of America

First Edition

1   2   3   4   5   6   7   8   9   10

BOOK DESIGN BY CHERYL L. CIPRIANI/BROOKLYN BAUHAUS

www.williammorrow.com

*This book is dedicated to my parents and
to the memory of Sarah and John.*

T he genesis of this book came from a confession I made at a lunch with a friend and fellow stockbroker whom I will call Charles Green. Charles was working for Merrill Lynch, and we were having the standard corporate lunch at which most of the world's problems are generally solved shortly before the check arrives.

Our meeting was initially scheduled as a brainstorming session on how we could convince our clients to invest their money in a bearish market. We, like most brokers today, were under a lot of pressure, because stock prices were declining and financial markets overall were in a tailspin. In the early nineties there were few compelling reasons to invest in the stock market, but our livelihoods depended on convincing our customers to invest their money. Each of us had tough commission goals to achieve and we were both hard-pressed to accomplish them.

Even though it was a difficult time to be a broker, I had enjoyed a great deal of success. I had been part of the money-managing flock for close to three years and my client base spanned ten states. I had raised roughly $10 million, opened three hundred different accounts, and generated thousands of dollars in commission, all for one of the largest full-service brokerage firms on Wall Street. Needless to say my firm was pleased with me and periodically showered me with a wide variety of gifts, such as sports tickets and exotic day-trip getaways. I should have been happy, but I was absolutely miserable. I needed a friend to talk to and Charles was it.

In this book I will describe how Wall Street cheats investors, but at lunch that day I realized that I was cheating myself by not listening to myself. Muting your conscience can be hazardous to your health! The danger occurs when that little voice inside your head tells you that something is wrong, then you quickly ignore it. Instead, you listen to the conventional chorus that sings the praises of what success ought to be and you surrender yourself to being a person you are not.

My conscience was definitely bothering me that day and this feeling was soon confirmed when lunch was served. My order of salad with no dressing did not look tempting, but it is the best food for the calorically as well as the morally challenged. Charles's plate, on the other hand, was teeming with onion rings and one large hamburger just they way he liked it—rare. He seemed to savor the moment before his first bite, disregarding all the unhealthy consequences that result from killing the innocent.

It was time to make my confession, so I began slowly. "Charles, I have to tell you something. I'm thinking about leaving the business. I'm pretty unhappy."

Charles gazed at me with utter disbelief. He took another bite of his hamburger and responded with the standard line that managers and brokers in the securities business use so often. "Unhappy, how the heck can you be unhappy? What other business can you be in where the sky's the limit? You can make as much money as you want and you can come and go as you please. Look at you, you're doing great. You drive a sports car, you live in a great place, and you make good money. What more do you want? What's there not to like?"

I meekly said, "Well, I guess my conscience is bothering me a little bit. You know, I can't believe how some of our clients are treated and I guess I don't feel good about what I do anymore. I used to think that making money was the end-all, but I guess I've had a change of heart. If the average investors only knew what really goes on behind the scenes with their money, they'd think differently about having us manage it."

Charles's only response to my bold confession was a blank stare and a gaping mouth. His deer-in-the-headlights look was very unlike this man, who was never at a loss for words or a quick retort. I had taken him totally by surprise, but a few moments later he was ready to give his "enlightened" response.

"Mark, the average investor doesn't give a damn what goes on behind the scenes. Look," Charles said as he tapped his wristwatch, "the little guy only cares about if the 'clock' works. He doesn't care about the inner workings of the clock, he doesn't care who made the clock, and he certainly doesn't want to repair a damaged clock himself. All the little guy cares about is if we make him money, and everything else is mere commentary."

I apparently had greater faith in the individual investor than Charles did, but if I couldn't appeal to his sense of decency, then I would have to bring in a higher authority. I knew that Charles was a faithful churchgoer. I have often noticed that the voice of good conscience is heard thunderously on Sunday in the pew, but rapidly diminishes to a mere murmur as the workweek progresses. Charles was not unaware of this phenomenon, but I thought that introducing a little Scripture into the conversation might have a positive effect. There didn't seem to be any harm in at least driving home a point with the aid of a biblical verse or two. Although I was certainly no angel myself, and my Sunday-school attendance had ended many years ago, this did not deter me from making my case with a touch of spiritual righteousness. Even thinking of a biblical reference at that moment somehow renewed my faith in the miraculous, if not in the possibility of divine intervention.

"Charles," I began, "do you remember the story in the Bible about the poor widow?" He gave me a puzzled look. "You know, the one about a woman who made a small offering to the temple's treasury after a number of rich men had made much larger donations before her. Jesus said that the woman had given more than anyone, because she had given all that she had. Charles, the woman in the story is kind of like the majority of our clients. Average investors don't have a lot of money, but they give us all that they have. Don't you think that they should be treated more fairly and with a great deal more respect than they are at present?" Surprisingly, he was unmoved by my little homily, and my future career as a financial evangelist seemed to be on hold. Nonetheless, I continued. "You might be right that the little guy doesn't care about the inside of the clock, but that's because he's never had an opportunity to know how he's being mistreated. It's not that he doesn't care to know, it's simply that he's never had an opportunity to know."

I had finally made my full confession, and I was looking for some spark of goodwill from Charles. Unfortunately, though, his faith seemed to be based only on the 80/20 rule. "Mark, you know that we get 80 percent of our business from the top 20 percent of our clients, so how can we possibly afford to attend to every Tom, Dick, and Harry on our books?" he said. "I have to do what's best for my business and for my family." With that, Charles was ready to end our lunch.

We parted as friends, and two months later I was fired from my job for not "meeting the firm's production standards." This is just a fancy way of the firm saying that I had not generated enough commission to earn my keep. I didn't feel like being a stockbroker anymore because I had become disillusioned with a business that saw people—clients and brokers alike—as disposable items and routinely sacrificed the needs of less wealthy but hardworking people to the interests of their wealthier counterparts. Being fired is indeed an emotional experience, but the lesson for me was that losing your job is, finally, less important than losing your soul. While I might have lost the desire to be a broker, I had gained the desire to become a better person.

Charles is still working hard as a broker for another firm, where he has more than doubled his business. He still believes that the average investor could care less about how Wall Street secretly mistreats him and he keeps reminding me of that one big clock that the eyes of all, at least in his mind, middle-class investors seem to be trained on. I am still betting that Charles is wrong and that you will not only care about the problems that I discuss here, but that you will do something about solving them.

The Wall Street that I will talk about in this book is not primarily focused on stocks, bonds, or the standard eye-catching, multicolored investment charts. Nor is it concerned with the volatility of financial markets, interest rate moves, or the inner workings of complex derivative products. I will not be offering you a magic formula that will make you an instant multimillionaire, though the information I present is the key to your future investment success. My concern here is with what investing is truly all about—people's lives and their futures. This book is about how investors are treated by those who are given the responsibility of managing their money and protecting their interests. At the present time such middle-class investors represent the majority of accounts on Wall Street, and now more than ever these people depend on their investments both to ensure their future financial independence and to maintain their current economic status.

CONTENTS

Preface   vii

Part One: Broken Promises:
When Wall Street Does Not Keep Its Word

Chapter 1   Pitching the American Dream to the Middle Class   3

Chapter 2   Rich Man, Poor Man: The Haves and Have-Nots of Wall
             Street—Whom Does Wall Street Care About?   23

Chapter 3   The Power of Information: The Rich See the Light and
             the Middle Class Is Kept in the Dark   52

Part Two: Selling the American Dream: What Wall
Street Wants You to Buy but Doesn't Want You to Know

Chapter 4   Salespeople, Sales Training, and Sales Contests:
             How Wall Street Does Business   73

Chapter 5   Going Undercover: In Search of a Financial Advisor   89

Chapter 6   Discount Brokers and Day Traders: Dirty Deeds Done
             Often and Cheap   115

Chapter 7   Mutual Fund Mayhem: Hidden Truths and
             Hidden Fees   130

Chapter 8   Initial Public Offerings: A World of Payoffs,
             Privileges, and Penalties   151

Chapter 9   Retirement, Savings, and Your 401(k)   166

Part Three: Getting Smart About Wall Street

Chapter 10   Asleep on the Job: Regulatory Agencies and Other
              Industry Watchdogs   185

Chapter 11   Settling Disputes Wall Street's Way: High-Powered
              Lawyers and Sleeping Solomons vs. the Investor   197

Chapter 12   Journalists: The Oft-Misinformed Oracles of Delphi   214

Chapter 13   Investment Experts: The Pied Pipers of Wall Street   229

Chapter 14   What Every Investor Needs to Know:
              Expert Redefined   240

Acknowledgments   251

Notes   253

Bibliography   261

Index   265

Part One

BROKEN PROMISES: WHEN WALL STREET DOES NOT KEEP ITS WORD

CHAPTER 1

PITCHING THE AMERICAN DREAM TO THE MIDDLE CLASS

The entry of the middle class into the world of investing has been a fairly recent phenomenon. The transformation of this class from savers to investors was spurred, in great part, by the creation of a number of innovative financial products in the 1970s. Such products as money market accounts, asset management accounts, and mutual funds were designed to capture the assets of the middle class and to make investing as convenient as possible. In the securities business there is an adage that says, "He who has the most assets wins," and what Wall Street saw in the middle class was a newfound market, rich in assets and with unlimited potential. When I refer to Wall Street in these pages, I mean the business of buying and selling securities and the companies that offer financial services to the general public. Targeting the middle-class market reduced Wall Street's dependence on the money class—i.e., the very wealthy—and gave it a fertile new market, one that was rich in commissions, account fees, and interest payments.

The assets of the middle class have been the cornerstone of Wall

Street's rapid growth in the last quarter of the twentieth century. These assets gave Wall Street the necessary building blocks to transform the securities industry into the mega-business it is today. For example, industry leader Merrill Lynch, which has over $1 trillion under management, generates the bread-and-butter commissions and fees from the 85 percent of its accounts that contain less than $250,000.[1] These accounts, for the most part, represent the millions of middle-class investors who do business with the firm. Merrill Lynch could not support its army of fifteen thousand brokers without middle-class investors. Charles Schwab, the leading discount firm, is in a similar situation. Only a little over 5 percent of its 2.2 million customers are viewed as "Signature Gold," clients who either have $500,000 in assets or do at least twenty-four trades a year. But it's the other 95 percent, the collective little guy, that make Schwab the powerhouse it is today.

Wall Street's concerted effort to popularize stocks and bonds among members of the middle class helped to further its own interests, but unfortunately the interests of average investors have been sacrificed along the way. The majority of this middle-class market were people who were new to investing, people who could easily be persuaded by Wall Street's promises and temptations. But such get-rich-quick scenarios never became realities; all they did was lure many first-time investors to Wall Street. When one carefully examines the methods that Wall Street used to capture the assets of middle-class investors, one sees again and again a history of promises that were made only to be broken.

Wall Street's sales pitch to middle-class investors about the virtues of owning stocks and bonds has been incredibly successful. In the early 1930s, only 1.5 million Americans held brokerage accounts,[2] but today 45 percent of American households, some 45 million families, own some securities.[3] This relatively new "silent" majority of investors continues to take a backseat to the interests of their wealthier counterparts, yet without middle-class investors, full-service and discount firms alike would not have the resources to attend to the needs of their rich customers.

Let's first take a brief walk down Wall Street and see how it all began. Our journey will take us back more than two centuries and will end when Wall Street finally comes to Main Street. As we take our brief stroll, we will focus only on some historical highlights because a more complete history is best left to academics and scholars. My focus will be on the way Wall Street has treated average investors.

A BRIEF WALK DOWN WALL STREET: SETTING UP SHOP

Wall Street has become synonymous with free enterprise and the epitome of American capitalism. The street itself is rather short and narrow, with such familiar historical landmarks as Trinity Church, the New York Stock Exchange Building, and the old U.S. Subtreasury Building, where George Washington was inaugurated in 1789. Wall Street takes its name from a wall built in 1653 by Peter Stuyvesant that was used to protect the Dutch colonists. Stuyvesant was the fourth and last director general of the Dutch colony of New Netherlands, which later became New York. It seems ironic that Wall Street, a seemingly open market today, got its name from a wall that had been built with the dual purpose of protecting those inside and preventing ousiders from entering. Perhaps history is being a little too generous in disclosing the nature of Wall Street's initial intentions.

From its earliest beginnings in the late eighteenth century, Wall Street catered to the interests of only a select few. The first traders on the scene came in two varieties—auctioneers and dealers. The auctioneers set the prices for the securities and the dealers haggled among themselves. In those days trading securities was an outdoor activity in which traders literally stood outside, weather permitting, and conducted their affairs. There was not a formal place of business per se and few traders adhered to any code of ethics. More often than not, traders preyed upon one another, as some do today. An investors' guide from the period notes the comments of one anonymous observer who told of a trader who had been victimized by his fellow traders: "It had one good effect . . . that such an insight into the business disgusted him . . . and induced him to seek an honorable independence, which he has since acquired in a more respectable employment."[4] There were few standards of fair play and little organization in the early days of Wall Street, but some improvements were eventually made.

In May 1792, the auctioneers and dealers met under a buttonwood tree (now 68 Wall Street) and signed the Buttonwood Agreement, a document that established a formal exchange for the buying and selling of securities. Members decided to move their business indoors into a more private setting, free from the eyes of nonmembers. Only twenty-four brokers forged the agreement and these twenty-four constituted their market—not a free market opened to everyone. Entry into this esteemed club was permitted by membership only and the cost of admission was $25,[5] a hefty sum in those days, which successfully kept membership low. The traders agreed on set commissions on all of their trades so that the cost of doing business would be fixed. This practice of fixed commissions became a standard on Wall Street for the next 183 years.

In 1817, the dealers who had signed the Buttonwood Agreement decided to organize themselves further. They established the New York Stock and Exchange Board, the first organized stock exchange in the country and the precursor of the New York Stock Exchange. The members met daily and stated their prices on various issues, but trading was still by membership only. In 1800, there were only 335 corporations in the United States,[6] and by 1818 the new stock exchange listed only 29 domestic companies and a handful of foreign issues.[7] The forerunner of the New York Stock Exchange was up and running, but those who could not afford membership into this exclusive club had to find other ways to seek their fortunes.

Nonmembers found themselves doing business outside along the curb of Wall Street. These curbside brokers specialized in stocks not traded on the exchange, and organized themselves and adhered to their own standards. This organization led to the New York Curb Market, the forerunner of the American Stock Exchange. These curbside brokers conducted their business outdoors for nearly one hundred years, until they moved into their permanent indoor facilities during the early 1920s.[8]

THE CRASH OF 1929

The catastrophic stockmarket crash of October 1929 was one of the first signs that middle-class investors would have to endure hardship of a different kind than the brokerage firms who sold them the securities. The crash of 1929 left thousands of average investors ruined, but no major firm was forced to liquidate.[9]

The roaring twenties was a time of great prosperity in America, and Wall Street was enjoying an unprecedented bull market. The stock market had rapidly matured from the clubbish atmosphere of the 1800s to a multibillion-dollar business in the early part of the twentieth century. Around this time few Americans had brokerage accounts, but stocks were a household word among the middle class who could not afford to buy them. Nonetheless, the euphoric atmosphere of the day contributed to frantic buying, and the chance to live on easy street proved to be far too tempting for many middle-class people to stand idly by and watch. Wall Street had the solution to the problem and offered investors the chance to buy securities on margin. Margin is the down payment needed to secure a loan from a broker to buy securities, and in some cases the margin requirement during these years was only 3 percent.[10] This small sum made investing appear affordable to ordinary wage earners and gave them an open invitation to speculate in the stock market. In other words, the dreams of instant wealth that Wall Street conjured could now come true for the middle class as well as the rich by investing as little as 3 percent of their own money and borrowing the rest from the broker. By allowing investors to buy on margin, brokerage firms reaped the benefits of the commissions on the stock trades as well as the interest they charged customers on the money the customers borrowed. Buying on margin gave fresh new assets to an already inflated market, and by August 1929, approximately 300 million shares of stock had been purchased on margin.[11] The bubble was about to burst.

In September, some investors began selling their shares, believing that stock prices had hit their high.[12] This caused stocks to decline, a fact that especially hurt those who had bought on margin because they owed their broker the amount of the original price of the stock—even if that stock was worth only half or a third as much as they had paid for it. On Tuesday, October 29, the frantic selling reached a peak and over 16 million shares changed hands.[13] By the end of the year stock values had declined by $15 billion.[14] At the worst period of the crash, the Dow Jones Industrial Index had lost about 50 percent of its value and thousands of margin accounts were wiped out.

The crash of 1929 was a defining moment for thousands of middle-class investors who had learned the true cost of investing on Wall Street. Many who lost it all resorted to petty crimes in order to provide for their families; others simply committed suicide. *Variety* got it right when it ran a headline that summed up Wall Street's performance at the time: WALL STREET LAYS AN EGG.

Surprisingly, though, the egg Wall Street laid did not land on the faces of any of the major brokerage firms, not one of which was forced to go out of business. Rather, it was the many middle-class investors who had entrusted their money to the brokerage houses who suffered the most. Most firms did not encounter devastating losses because brokers had sold their own inventories before they liquidated the stock positions of the their customers.[15] Many brokers had anticipated a market downturn and were ready to sell their securities quickly. Brokerage firms were also given extended grace periods by their banks, which allowed them time to recoup their losses and to repay the banks without fear of financial collapse. Unfortunately, brokers did not extend the same professional courtesy to their customers, who were forced to pay their loans off without delay or have their accounts liquidated.[16]

The crash showed that the interests of the middle-class investors were dearly compromised and this message should not be forgotten today. If brokers of that day had investors' best interests at heart, they would never have allowed their customers to buy so heavily on margin in the first place. They would have made efforts to sell their customers' stocks as the market spiraled downward, instead of holding them while they sold out their own stock positions. The lesson that the crash has for us today is that even if an investor's portfolio is soaring in value, as most were before the crash, the investor's interests must take precedence. It's not always the conditions of financial markets that bring investors to ruin, but rather the priorities of the people who manage the investor's money. This competition of interests will be a recurring theme in this book, and it is one the federal government addressed after the crash of 1929 when it created the Securities and Exchange Commission.

WALL STREET GETS A POLICEMAN

The 1929 crash was a catalyst for legislators to rein in the free-wheeling ways of Wall Street and to put a stop to some of the abuses that trampled upon the rights of average investors. Samuel Untermyer, a lawyer at the time, summed up the public's general feelings about Wall Street when he called for tougher industry regulations: "Some day when there is a real investigation of the history of the Stock Exchange we shall get a picture of the means by which billions of dollars have been literally filched from the public through the machinery of that institution that is still permitted to remain beyond official government regulation, supervision and control, and above and beyond the law."[17] After more than two centuries of little or no regulation, Wall Street was finally having to answer to Washington; the Roosevelt Administration's New Deal legislation would lead to better treatment of investors. In his inaugural address, Franklin Roosevelt proclaimed that "the money changers have fled from their high seats in the temple of our civilization. We may restore that temple to the ancient truths."[18] Restoring the public's faith in Wall Street would take time, especially because Wall Street was not willing to end its long-established sales practices overnight. A 1939 Roper Poll found that "people did not trust the hot tips that they got from brokers. They were convinced that brokers foisted bad stocks on clients. Fifty percent of those polled said that rich customers got better treatment than the less affluent."[19]

At the time people were not sure that government regulation was the cure for Wall Street's moral ills. Some conservative legislators believed that the laws of the free market had a built-in mechanism for justice that would correct any wrongs, and thus the only rule to abide by was the survival of the fittest. In their view, any kind of regulation would only hinder Wall Street's ability to operate efficiently. Others took a more cynical position and believed, as did Republican Congressman Fred Britten of Illinois, that any legislation designed to interfere with the "natural" workings of the financial markets was nothing more than an attempt to move the country toward socialism. "The real object of this bill," said Britten, referring to the Securities Act of 1933, "is to Russianize everything worthwhile."[20]

Fortunately, Congress took the middle class's interests to heart and passed legislation that somewhat restrained Wall Street's ability to take advantage of them. The legislation certainly did not spell an end to abuses, but it was the first time the federal government publicly acknowledged that that there were problems in the securities industry that needed to be addressed for the good of the nation. The first major piece of legislation was the Securities Act of 1933, which regulated the way new issues of corporate securities were brought to market and sold to the public. The law required investment bankers to be truthful in their dealings and to disclose fully all relevant information about such securities.

Later that year the Glass-Steagall Act was passed. Congress had concluded that one of the causes of the 1929 crash was that commercial banks engaged in investment banking and used the funds from their depositors to make risky investments. The act erected a wall between commercial and investment banks, so that the deposits of individuals could not be blatantly misused again. The act forbid commercial banks from underwriting securities and prevented investment banks from opening deposit accounts or making commercial loans.

A year later the Securities Act of 1934 was passed; this legislation created the Securities and Exchange Commission, which would be made up of five commissioners (no more than three of whom may belong to the same party) appointed by the president and approved by the Senate. The Maloney Act, an 1938 amendment to this act, provided for the establishment of a national self-regulatory body of broker/dealers. With this, the National Association of Securities Dealers (NASD) was born. The act also instituted a number of reforms that sought to protect the interests of investors. For example, the margin requirement on most securities was set at 45 percent, thus making it more difficult for brokers to convince investors to overextend themselves. As the years went by, additional legislation was enacted that sought to protect the rights of investors, and for the first time ever Wall Street had some rules to play by. These rules formed the foundation of the SEC's promise to protect the rights of investors. As we shall see, the agency has broken this promise many times over.

A CHAMPION FOR THE MIDDLE CLASS

If I could pick the guests at a fantasy dinner, Charles Merrill, the cofounder of Merrill Lynch, would certainly be high on the list. A feisty, colorful character who never let a good time pass him by, Merrill didn't fit the mold of the conservative financial professional who sits quietly gazing over company reports and stockmarket charts. Merrill lived life to the fullest and by most accounts was a womanizer, a lover of fine spirits, and a constant partygoer.[21] One company publication said that he had "the physique of a Plymouth Rock rooster, the savvy and courage of a horse trader, and the soul of a poet."[22] This larger-than-life characterization mirrored Charlie Merrill's own propensity for bragging and hyperbole. "Good Time Charlie Merrill" was indeed an original.[23]

The son of a doctor, Merrill grew up in a number of small towns in Florida. He dropped out of Amherst College because of financial troubles and was later a newspaper reporter for the *West Palm Beach Tropical Sun* and a semiprofessional baseball player in Mississippi. He attended law school at the University of Michigan, but got tired of the classroom regimen and soon quit. "I didn't know what I wanted to do, except that it had to be exciting,"[24] said Merrill, and in 1914, after finding out that he wasn't cut out for working for others, he decided to open his own brokerage firm with only $6,000 in his pocket. He was twenty-nine years old.[25]

What is so noteworthy about Charles Merrill's career is how quickly he saw the middle class as a potential new market and the measures he took to capture its business, years before doing so was fashionable. A true visionary, Merrill saw the unlimited potential of middle-class investors and almost single-handedly brought Wall Street to Main Street. While his contemporaries saw Wall Street as a high-expense, low-volume business that catered to the wealthy, Merrill believed that the keys to its future success lay with the middle class.

He worked toward achieving this goal up until his death in 1953. The middle-class market was a tough one to crack simply because most middle-class investors knew nothing about investing. A Roper Poll sponsored by the New York Stock Exchange soon after World War ll discovered that most respondents believed Wall Street was home to some of the nation's top thieves, crooks, and villains. Interestingly, a great number of the respondents thought the "stock" market was a place where cattle were sold.[26]

Merrill tried to offset this perception by treating his customers fairly. For example, he strongly believed that brokers should be paid a salary instead of having to survive solely on the commissions on their trades, and during his tenure as head of Merrill Lynch, he enforced this policy. He recognized that making money on commissions throws brokers into an inherent conflict of interest with their customers. Merrill also lauded the virtues of long-term investing and was known to go into a rage if he ever discovered that one of his employees had made a trade purely for the sake of a quick profit.[27]

Investor education was also a top priority throughout his professional life. He believed that the only way to convince the middle class about the merits of investing was to teach them. He devised a nationwide investor education program that included the mass distribution of literature that helped average investors take the first steps into the world of investing. "It was probably the biggest job in mass education that's ever confronted any business at any time in the history of this country," he said.[28] In 1955 alone, the firm distributed 11 million pieces of investment literature; and Merrill Lynch conducted seminars, lectures, and even investment courses for women.[29] Merrill was a great believer in mass marketing and advertising at a time when advertising of any sort was, in his competitors' eyes, a breach of good taste. All of this was designed to reach out to the middle class by making them more knowledgeable about the virtues of long-term investing.

Shortly before his death, he delivered a speech to the firm's partners in which he criticized the securities industry for its refusal to accept many of his ideas. He was concerned about the industry's reluctance to pay salaries to brokers instead of relying on commissions. He thought that the industry had failed the middle class by its continued belief that capturing the business of wealthy clients was the key to success in the brokerage business.[30] At the end of his life, Merrill still believed what he had said in 1911: "Having thousands of customers scattered throughout the United States is infinitely preferable to being dependent upon the fluctuating buying power of a smaller, and perhaps on the whole, wealthier group of investors in any one section."[31]

At the time that Merrill made his speech, there were only 6.5 million individual investors, who accounted for a mere 4 percent of the country's population.[32] The middle class just wasn't ready to experience all that Wall Street had to offer. But Charles Merrill was a visionary, a man who was ahead of his time, a man who saw that the future of Wall Street lay in the middle class. He would eventually be proven right.

MAYDAY

May 1, 1975, or Mayday, as it is still known on Wall Street, was a historic day, the beginning of a new era. It marked the end of fixed trading commissions. Today, we take for granted the many pricing alternatives full-service and discount brokerage firms offer, but until Mayday, Wall Street had operated under a fixed commission system. For over 180 years, if you wanted to buy securities, it didn't matter which brokerage firm you went to, because the commission amount had already been established, with no room for negotiation. Rates, of course, increased over time, but according to the NYSE's Rule 390, as it was called, all firms that bought and sold securities on the exchange were required to be member firms that adhered to the set pricing guidelines.[33] Wall Street had not changed its business practices since the days of the Buttonwood Agreement, but its clublike atmosphere had become outdated and no longer fit the rapidly changing securities industry of the 1970s. Fixed pricing was a cherished certainty in an uncertain business, but through government pressure and the trading clout of primarily large institutional customers who demanded lower commissions, this safety net was removed.

While middle-class investors eventually benefited from these reforms, Mayday was not meant to protect the interests of the middle class. Small investors did not have the clout to cut deals or to negotiate commission discounts with Wall Street. Although the government pressured the NYSE to begin price discounts, it didn't do so out of concern for the average investor. The average investor did not have a voice on Capitol Hill, but the lobbying efforts of large pension funds, mutual fund companies, and institutions were readily heard.[34] The price discounts these big players enjoyed had to be made up for somehow, and it was the middle-class investors who were expected to do so. For example, on Mayday, Merrill Lynch actually raised the commissions it charged individual investors, even though it had previously announced that it would negotiate commission rates with its large institutional clients.[35] For middle-class investors, Mayday was more of a distress call than a show of support from the government or Wall Street. It made middle-class investors realize that Wall Street readily gave commission discounts to wealthy clients, who allegedly "earned" them, instead of to the many smaller investors who rightfully deserved them.

WHEN WALL STREET FINALLY COMES TO MAIN STREET

The early seventies marked a new era for Wall Street, an era in which brokerage firms, full service and discount alike, began to aggressively market their wares to the average investors. This was the time when Charlie Merrill's vision finally became a reality, though I can't imagine that Merrill would have considered the loyalties of the brokerage firms, once the assets of middle-class investors had been successfully captured, anything other than misplaced. Wall Street came to Main Street bearing gifts that would transform millions of savers into active investors. Here were a few of the main products that introduced average investors to Wall Street:

Money Markets: A money market is a near-cash investment that is a mutual fund. Unlike the mutual funds that contain stock and bonds whose price fluctuates every day, money markets invest only in such short-term securities as T-Bills and have a constant net asset value of 1 dollar per share. The SEC requires that money markets have maturities of thirteen months or less and the average maturity of the entire portfolio cannot be more than ninety days.[36] The companies that own and operate money market funds make their money by imposing administrative and management fees; total expenses for a fund can run as high as 1.86 percent of assets.[37] As of this writing, the average yield on money market accounts is around 5 percent and the total amount invested in these accounts, which of course fluctuates daily as investors buy and sell their shares, is a staggering $1,307 trillion.

The first money market fund on record was the Reserve Fund, begun in 1972 by Henry B. R. Brown and Bruce R. Bent. It took the SEC two years to approve this highly innovative new investment vehicle that we take for granted today. Both Brown and Bent had worked in the insurance industry and saw an opportunity to capitalize on the high inflationary times of the seventies and the dismally low interest rates that banks were paying depositors.[38]

Ever since 1933, the Federal Reserve had controlled the interest rates that banks paid to customers through Regulation Q. Prior to the crash of 1929, banks competed for business by offering high interest rates, rates that ultimately caused many of them to foreclose. Banks had placed depositors' money at risk by promising interest rates they could not pay. In the early seventies, inflation was roughly 5 percent, but average bank deposits were earning 4.5 percent, and thus the government was causing depositors to lose money as the invisible hand of inflation steadily ate away at their purchasing power.[39]

Brown and Bent came up with a way to circumvent Regulation Q by creating a mutual fund that invested in short-term debt securities that paid a higher rate of interest than the banks. Their Reserve Fund invested in T-Bills and "Jumbo" CDs (CDs that are valued at $100,000 or more); this was a safe bet for investors who wanted to preserve their capital and get a higher rate of interest than they would find at a bank. A money market fund was ideal for middle-class people and it would serve as the first stepping-stone in the transformation from savers to investors. Such funds provided the best of both worlds: not only a higher rate of interest but also a principal that did not fluctuate in value. James Benham, a former stockbroker independently involved in creating the money market fund, said he came at it "from the perspective of the little guy."[40] And Wall Street was striving to market to the little guy.

Today, virtually every brokerage firm offers a money market fund, of which there are now approximately 1,025 in existence. They are wonderful tools that can help brokers accumulate cash that can later be used to make investments. Money market accounts help in the never-ending quest to bring new money in the door. Once cash sits soundly in a money market account and clients can see the relatively low interest rates they are receiving, a financial consultant can more easily persuade them to take on more commission-worthy investments. Moreover, money market funds provide brokerage firms with an additional income stream on idle cash deposits, income that they would not otherwise have.

When I was a broker, I got a computer printout of the cash deposits in my clients' money market accounts every day. Management often reminded the brokers in my office that cash was not king—investments were. The computer pointed out clients who had cash deposits that were seen as a commission opportunity waiting to happen. The equation was simple: money markets lead to investments and investments lead to commissions. Even if I wasn't successful in convincing my clients to invest their cash, all was not lost, because at the end of every month I received a check for each of my clients' money market funds. The fee was shared with my firm and extracted from the true yield of the fund. None of my clients ever bothered to ask me about this fee and I, like all of my broker colleagues, never felt obligated to tell them about it. In short, the brokerage industry adopted money markets to help them harvest the assets of average investors. While this was happening, another product was about to be born, and this product would go way beyond the most optimistic of expectations.

Mutual Funds: No investment has captured the attention of middle-class investors like mutual funds. In 1924, MFS Investment Management invented the first such fund, called the Massachusetts Investors Trust (MIT). In 1928, Scudder pioneered the first no-load fund, but it wasn't until 1981, when Fidelity placed an up-front charge for purchasing shares in the Magellan fund, that American investors saw their first load fund. At the end of World War II, all mutual funds combined held $1 billion,[41] but today there are over seven thousand funds with over $5.6 trillion under management. Through slick, multimillion-dollar advertising campaigns and the sales efforts of thousands of financial advisors, mutual fund companies have popularized their products to the middle class. Mutual funds promised the middle-class investor clear-cut directions to the Promised Land, where their dreams of the milk of double-digit portfolio performance and the honey of superlative professional money management would be realized. Since most average investors were convinced that they could not effectively manage their own money, mutual funds provided a convenient way for them to confidently hand over their assets to professional money managers, who, supposedly, knew more about the business than they did.

In return for this professional management, mutual fund companies received a variety of fees for their expertise. Management fees, administrative fees, and loads were all part of the price that investors had to pay for the privilege of participation in the mutual fund industry. And, you may ask, what did middle-class investors get for their money? The answer: funds that for the most part did not perform as they had been expected to perform. According to Lipper Analytical Services's most recent five-year survey, 94 percent of mutual funds do not outperform the S&P 500 index,[42] even though these funds continue to charge their shareholders millions of dollars in fees. Promises of performance have been weighted down with unnecessary expenses, elaborate marketing costs, and the liabilities incurred by excessive trading—all of which have all been paid for with the middle-class investors' money. The average investor's blind belief in the mutual fund industry's false-bottom advertising slogans, instead of a faith in his own ability to manage his money, has helped make the mutual fund industry into the giant enterprise it is today. While mutual fund companies continue to pick the pockets of middle-class investors, their shareholders still wait patiently to see the vaunted promises of performance fulfilled.

Today, the single largest mutual fund is Fidelity Magellan, which began in 1963. During much of this time, it was managed by stock-picking legend Peter Lynch, who began his tenure as the fund's manager in 1977 and who was able to produce double-digit returns that were an industry exception. Fidelity's chief, Edward (Ned) Crosby Johnson III, the son of Fidelity's principal owner, Edward Crosby Johnson II, believed that people would be willing to submit to higher fees in order to have their money managed by Lynch, so in 1981 he tacked a 2 percent up-front load onto the Magellan fund. A year later he increased the load to its current level of 3 percent.[43]

At the time many in the industry saw load funds as a rather risky business. After all, who would want to fork out an up-front load when they could choose from a number of no-load rivals? But Johnson guessed right that investors would interpret the fee as somehow ensuring top performance they could not find elsewhere. In reality, the 2 percent load, much less the 3 percent load, was not necessary to the fund's overall success, nor did it ever aid Peter Lynch in his stock-picking ability. However, the additional load provided Fidelity with another income stream that helped to make Ned Johnson one of the wealthiest men in America.[44] Not only did it give the company the money it needed to further its own interests, but middle-class Americans were willing, indeed eager, to foot the bill. The addition of the load helped create the illusion that Magellan was better than its competitors, and so, somewhat ironically, more money flowed into Magellan once it became a load fund.[45] The standard pitch from load advocates was that you got what you paid for in life, and mutual funds were no exception. Did that truism end up applying to Magellan? The answer is no, but Fidelity's pitch convinced hundreds of thousands of people to invest in the fund and today Magellan is the largest single mutual fund, which, as of this writing, has $100 billion under management.

Magellan's performance over the last ten years, however, tells quite a different story. The fund's performance shows that investors could have done better with a low-cost, S&P 500 index fund that invested in the market itself, instead of pinning their hopes on Fidelity's brand name or the personality of one of its fund managers. From 1989 to February 1999, the Magellan fund beat the S&P 500 index only four times—four out of ten—and these results do take into consideration the high cost of the up-front load. Fidelity's Web site (www.fidelity.com) offers the data on load-adjusted returns:

Fidelity Magellan Load-Adjusted Returns	S&P 500 Performance
(as of 12/31/98)	
1 year 26.62%	28.58%
3 year 22.37%	28.23%
5 year 19.75%	24.96%
10 year 19.53%	19.21%

From this chart, it seems safe to assume that Fidelity's first-class sales and marketing efforts have paid off handsomely. The firm is the number-one provider of 401(k) accounts, the second largest discount brokerage firm, and the third largest provider of 403(b) retirement plans for not-for-profit institutions in the United States. The company manages over $900 billion in assets.

When I was a broker, I remember talking to one of my colleagues who handled primarily high-net-worth clients. I told him of my success in convincing many of my clients who were middle-class investors to invest in mutual funds. Mutual funds paid me a great commission and a quarterly annuity in fees, which I shared with my firm. After listening to what I said, my colleague paused, then said, "You know, wealthy people don't buy mutual funds. Wealthy people don't come to brokers to buy mutual funds, they come to us to buy individual stocks. That's where the smart money is and don't you forget it." As it turns out, he was right.

Asset Management Accounts: Most investors today take for granted the conveniences of an asset management account. These accounts are multipurpose brokerage accounts that combine the characteristics of a checking account with those of a brokerage account. Asset management accounts are hybrid accounts that come complete with an interest-bearing money market, check-writing privileges, and even a debit card that can be used practically anywhere in the world. In one account, investors can trade and monitor their securities, write checks, use a debit card, and even borrow money, using their securities as collateral. Asset management accounts have been extremely effective tools in garnering the assets of the middle class. They are an open invitation to investors to consolidate their cash and securities under one roof in order to experience all of the conveniences of one-stop shopping. Most firms today offer an asset management account, but the first firm to come up with the idea was Merrill Lynch. They called it a "cash management account," or CMA.

Merrill Lynch invested millions of dollars in developing the CMA account, which it unveiled at a press conference in 1977. Initially, most of Merrill's senior staff were vehemently opposed to this new invention, which they thought had absolutely no practical use. It was their view that the account would not generate new commissions, nor would it give Merrill's brokers any measurable competitive edge.[46] This turned out to be a shortsighted view and one that was quickly dismissed by then-CEO Donald Regan, who, one day, after listening patiently to Merrill's top managers state why the CMA account would be an embarrassing failure to the firm, said, "I appreciate your recommendations, but there has been a vote taken here today, and it's one to nothing. I'm the one, and you guys are the nothing. We go forward."[47]

Regan spearheaded the effort to make the CMA a reality because he saw its ultimate value as an effective asset-gathering tool, ready made to capture the dollars of middle-class investors. "For the first time," says one Merrill executive, "we got a true picture of our customers' assets."[48] The account would be successful not only in consolidating assets, but in facilitating and simplifying the buying and selling of securities, since cash deposits were, in effect, just waiting to be drawn from the CMA's money market account. In the end, Regan's view prevailed and the CMA attracted billions of dollars in new assets from stock certificates, cash, mutual funds, et cetera. Today, such accounts are brokers' principal tool in the effort to attract new retail customers.

When I was a broker, management made selling my firm's asset management account a top priority. Brokers throughout my firm competed for prizes in sales contests that rewarded them for selling the account. The prizes included TV sets, trips, and even money, and whoever sold the most was in the firm's good graces whether the clients needed the accounts or not.

The asset management account, from which the fees provided a multimillion-dollar yearly annuity to the firm, became the backbone of its business. This was income that my firm could count on regardless of market conditions. Also, the asset management account went further than a standard account in protecting the firm's interests, because it contained an arbitration clause. Investors who opened an asset management account automatically signed away their rights to settle any dispute they had with the firm in court and agreed to have their disputes settled at an industry-sponsored arbitration hearing. Finally, the account was ideal in terms of cross-selling opportunities. Many of my clients who opened an asset management account also let me manage their retirement accounts, business accounts, and so on. With some luck, shortly after the account was opened, I was able to convince my clients to recommend that their family members and friends open up accounts with me as well. I could see how asset management accounts furthered the interests of my firm, but I was not always convinced that they furthered the interests of my clients.

Individual Retirement Accounts: IRAs also helped to popularize stocks and bonds with the middle class. While IRAs were not an invention of Wall Street, they were a natural haven for such products as mutual funds and stocks, products that Wall Street wanted to sell to the middle class. According to an Investment Company Institute report in 1997, 42 percent of IRAs were invested in mutual funds and 38 percent of all IRAs were held at brokerage firms. The ICI estimates that the total IRA assets as of the end of 1997 were $1.948 trillion, $739 billion of which was held in brokerage accounts.[49] Who were the principal buyers of IRAs? you ask. The answer: the middle class. A 1995 ICI study showed that households with IRAs had median incomes of $48,000 and median financial assets of $44,500.[50]

In 1974, Congress established the IRA, but it wasn't until a tax bill passed in 1981 that investors were granted a tax break for contributing to such accounts. The bill made it possible for anyone setting aside $2,000 in this tax-deferred account to receive a $2,000 deduction from their taxable income. Years later, as part of the Taxpayers' Relief Act of 1997, the Roth IRA or, as some called it, the American Dream IRA, came into existence. The Roth IRA, unlike its predecessor, allowed after-tax contributions that grew tax-free. Through an IRA the government was trying to give the American public an incentive to save their money, but Wall Street saw the IRA as an ideal opportunity to convince people to invest their money. IRAs were the first vehicles of choice for many middle-class investors who wanted first to test the investment waters before exploring the many other opportunities offered by Wall Street. Invest in the future was Wall Street's plea to the middle class.

Most of the retirement accounts that I managed were put directly into mutual funds. IRAs invested in mutual funds were referred to internally as "buried money," and the lack of attention that these accounts received by my fellow brokers matched the name perfectly. Brokers refer to them as buried money because once the initial trade has been made, there are rarely any additional commission opportunities to be had, unless the customer adds fresh money. Accounts with the least commission opportunities generally received the least amount of attention. Moreover, management frowned on trading in a retirement account, so the conventional wisdom was that mutual funds provided the best investments to the customer long-term. They were also the best investments for the brokers short-term, due to the loads and fees charged the customer.

While it's true that Wall Street successfully pitched investors on the benefits of retirement accounts and on the merits of long-term investing, it is also true that the securities business is a "now" venture. Wall Street is more concerned with what happens today and worries about the future later. Brokers attend to what will make them successful today, rather than focusing on investments that will make their clients successful tomorrow. Sadly, the commission goals most brokers have to achieve take precedence over customer service. Wall Street succeeded in getting the middle class to invest their money for the future, but it is my fondest wish that the financial industry will make a better effort in investing in their clients, so that their clients' futures will no longer be neglected.

CHAPTER 2

RICH MAN, POOR MAN: THE HAVES AND HAVE-NOTS OF WALL STREET—WHOM DOES WALL STREET CARE ABOUT?

The companies that manage your money want you to know they care about you and that your account is important to them. Before most people make their investments, they purchase the satisfaction of knowing that the company managing their money cares about their interests. Only then are they comfortable enough to make their initial investments. Wall Street's brand of care is never oversold, but all too often it is overbought by investors. Care is such a valuable commodity, but it always seems to be in short supply. The reason for the imbalance between supply and demand in this regard rests with Wall Street's continued practice of making care in its purest form available only to its best customers, those of high net worth or frequent traders. What many investors don't realize is that most of the companies charged with managing other people's money care very little about the assets of individual, middle-class investors. Their focus is on serving their wealthy clients who have substantial portfolios that produce large commissions.

Daily attention to investments ultimately rewards the investor, and those accounts that are not given this attention ultimately suffer from neglect. It's the higher level of service, the specially crafted products, and the many perks bestowed on wealthy investors that cast a shadow over the interests of small investors. Financial markets are ever changing, yet the attention given to the vast majority of accounts held at brokerage firms and mutual funds is stagnant. How can financial companies lead average investors to believe that they really care about them when they show them so little attention? How can average investors ever hope to make the maximum return on their investments if their money is with companies that care so little about them?

You may find it hard to believe that your investments are being neglected when you think of your broker's friendly personality or when you review your mutual fund statement. The picture that I draw here will be of the securities industry in general, and it is not a pretty one. It is one that the securities industry would rather you not see, but it is one you must know about in order to protect your own interests.

THE BEST THAT MONEY CAN BUY

I wanted to test my theory that most brokerage firms and mutual fund companies give special treatment to their high-net-worth clients, so I called a number of them. The companies ran the gamut from full-service to discount firms to load and no-load mutual fund companies. There are, of course, hundreds of companies that fall into each category, but the ones that I chose are leaders in the industry and home to millions of investors' accounts. The business practices discussed here are not limited to the companies featured, and my critical remarks should not be taken as an indictment of any organization. The brokerage firms and mutual fund companies I discuss below are representative of the securities industry in general, and this discussion is not meant to be a negative commentary on the policies of any one company.

I told each of the company representatives that I was calling on behalf of my father, who was concerned about the amount of attention that he was receiving from his current broker. I informed each representative that my father's assets were between $500,000 and $3 million in value. When I was a broker, I fielded a number of inquiries from sons and daughters who called on behalf of their parents. But this time I was calling as a typical shopper who was in the market for a financial advisor. Each representative was chosen at random and I did not know any of them personally. I never disclosed my background as a broker, but my professional background and past sales experience were invaluable resources in this exercise. After they told me about their various customized programs designed for their wealthy clients, I asked them to explain to me how they would service my father's account. What special precautions would they take in order to ensure that my father's account would be made a top priority and how could they make these assurances when they had so many other accounts to manage?

I was very surprised by the candor of many of their replies and by the willingness of the representatives to admit that their primary concern was high-net-worth customers. Below is a summary of the conversations that I had with each representative and each story is revealing in its own way. Notice the standard rule under which each representative operates: the accounts that mean most to the firm receive the most attention and care—not those accounts that mean most to the customer. For example, a general rule of thumb is that an elderly woman's life savings of, let's say, $40,000 would rank well below that of a multimillionaire's portfolio of $500,000. This would be the case even though the millionaire's half-million dollars might represent only a small percentage of his entire net worth. But when the widow opens her account, she is never given this information and where her account ranks in importance remains a total mystery.

I have changed the names of the persons that I talked with, which is the standard precaution taken to protect the innocent. I claim that the representatives are innocent, because the problems I describe here are inherent in the securities industry—not the result of any one person's character. Moreover, some of their remarks might be construed by some readers as a confession, and if these pages do serve as some sort of confessional, then the confessor's true identity must be kept secret. I have not changed the name of any of the companies the various representatives worked for, but my remarks concerning the representatives should not in any way reflect upon their employers. I make this disclaimer out of fairness to the companies, who cannot fully control what their representatives say, especially when their salespeople think that they are vying for new accounts with substantial assets.

FULL-SERVICE BROKERAGE FIRMS

Today, the majority of individual brokerage accounts in the United States are held at full-service firms. Full-service brokers pride themselves on the advice they offer and the special services that they provide to their clients. This is what lures investors to the doors of name-brand, full-service firms.

Merrill Lynch: The very first call I made was to a local Merrill Lynch office. Most full-service firms like Merrill Lynch randomly assign a different broker each day to handle inquiries from the general public. These calls are referred to as "BOD" or broker-of-the-day calls. My call was routed to Mike Reynolds, who had a pleasant personality and was eager to talk to me about my father's account. After we exchanged the customary pleasantries, he told me about Merrill Lynch's Priority Client Program.

He said that Merrill Lynch made a distinction internally between high-net-worth and non-high-net-worth clients. Accounts of high-net-worth investors were labeled "Priority Clients" and those customers had to have at least $250,000 under management to be worthy of the designation. There were two additional tiers of distinction. Clients with at least $1 million in assets were labeled "Premier Priority Households," and those with $2 million or more, Merrill's crème de la crème clients, received the distinguished "Premier-Plus Households" title. Immediately it seemed to me that customers whose assets totaled less than $250,000 were automatically tossed into Merrill's nonpriority category, regardless of their particular financial situation. Assets alone determined who was a member of the Priority Client Program.

Wouldn't every Merrill Lynch customer want her account to be made a priority regardless of her assets or net worth? And how many investors would feel comfortable paying yearly account fees and full commissions on their stock trades and so on if they knew that Merrill

Lynch did not consider their accounts a priority? The cornerstone of the full-service brokerage industry, in which Merrill Lynch is the leader, is that customers receive a higher level of service than they normally find at a discount firm. This is a promise that full-service brokers make every day to their clients, but apparently it is kept only for those clients the firm considers a priority. This was certainly true when I was a full-service broker and it is common throughout the industry.

Reynolds was happy to answer my questions about the services that my father would receive as a Merrill Lynch Priority Client. He gave me an overview of the services, then followed up by sending me a nice glossy brochure that discussed what the firm had to offer in greater detail. The Priority Client brochure begins by saying, "You will enjoy convenient access to comprehensive planning, personalized service and investment alternatives designed to achieve your financial goals and to exceed your expectations of quality." I have summarized some of the exclusive services mentioned in the brochure:

- Customized comprehensive statements that are distinct from what regular customers receive.

- "A cap on annual fees for the CMA (cash management account), individual retirement accounts and other central accounts in your household."

- "No application fee or annual fee for our Equity Access home equity credit line ($50,000+)."

- Access to Priority Phone. The service gives Priority Clients "twenty-four-hour-a-day, year-round access to information about [their] account, stock and mutual fund quotes, key market indicators, and the ability to buy and place orders after market hours."

- Subscription to the Priority Client Newsletter, which "offers timely commentaries and insights on asset management, investments, credit management, transition planning, tax planning, and financial services."

Next, I asked what kind of service my father would receive as a Priority Client and whether Reynolds's smaller accounts would compete for his attention. Reynolds made his position very clear very quickly. "The small individual is really not worth it," he said. "It's people like your father who are the ones that are going to appreciate my service and refer me to other clients like themselves who can help my business." I had to give Reynolds an A-plus for honesty. One of the keys to becoming a successful broker is getting as many referrals as possible from your existing clients. Generally, rich people know other rich people, and Reynolds let me know why it was in his best interests to manage clients of high net worth, instead of wasting his time on smaller investors.

I then pressed Reynolds for information about how he prioritized his clients and how he could assure me that my father's account would be a top priority. He told me that 65 or 75 percent of his day was spent on high-net-worth clients. I told him that this was great news, but I wondered how did he service his smaller clients when so much of his time was spent with his Priority Clients? "A person who has $20,000 is about a ten-second decision for me," he said. "I will plug the account into two or three mutual funds and sit back and watch it. I'll give them a call maybe once a year or so." He also told me that Merrill did not want brokers spending their time with smaller accounts but, to my amazement, stopped short at disclosing Merrill's internal pay structure. What he didn't tell me were facts I already knew about how the firm compensated their brokers and how the firm's compensation discouraged them from giving attention to smaller accounts. For example, in 1997, Merrill instituted a new policy for brokers who had been with the firm for six or more years according to which they were compensated only on client assets that exceeded $100,000 invested with the firm.[1] A year later Merrill instituted a company-wide policy, irrespective of a broker's tenure, which eliminated commissions for transactions in client accounts that had less than $20,000 in assets.[2] In addition to these policies, Merrill tied their brokers' bonuses, which ranged from 4 to 6 percent of annual gross production, to winning contest points for capturing the assets of wealthy individuals. Brokers received one point for each new and existing Priority account and two points each for opening a Premier or Premier-Plus account.[3] Reynolds was trying to tell me that Merrill's internal pay structure generally rewarded brokers for managing larger accounts. Since there was no monetary reward in place for acquiring smaller accounts, I need not worry.

Reynolds also offered additional evidence that he was the right broker to manage my father's money. For example, he told me that he would throw in Merrill Lynch's financial plan (the "Financial Foundation") for free, which was a $250 value. He also said that it would not be a problem to negotiate a reduced commission on all of my father's stock trades. His offer was enticing, but unlike Merrill's Priority Clients, few if any average investors ever get an opportunity to obtain a free financial plan or a substantial discount on their stock trades. Finally, he gave me absolute proof of his dedication and loyalty. While we were talking on the phone, he told me that he had asked his assistant to take messages from two existing customers who were not Priority Clients. Reynolds had placed the interests of his two other clients on hold while he explored the prospect of managing another Priority account with me.

Salomon Smith Barney: Nancy Myers at Salomon Smith Barney explained that the firm had two programs designed for high-net-worth individuals. The Preferred Client Services required at least $500,000 in assets and the Select Client Program was for investors with $1 million or more in assets. She said it would be okay for me to swing by her office and pick up the brochures about the programs, which I did.

The brochures detailed all of the conveniences offered to their high-net-worth clients and stressed the importance of these special services. According to the introduction to the Preferred Client brochure, "At Smith Barney we believe clients of distinction should receive distinctive services. . . . 'Preferred Client' designation provides clients with a range of special benefits, services and recognition, *at no additional cost.*" Some of the services include:

- Comprehensive statements.

- Round-the-clock Internet access to the customer's account.

- Membership in the Preferred Client Service Center, which features twenty-four-hour access to account information, "stock quotes by Touch-Tone phone," and "knowledgeable service representatives."

- "Complimentary Financial Planning Services" that will help maximize the potential of the customer's investments.

- "Selected fee waivers and other special offers."

According to the closing paragraph of the brochure, "The level of service and information we provide to our clients is as important as the investment products that we offer." I could not agree more, but it seems that you have to have at least $500,000 to experience the highest level of service that Smith Barney has to offer.

The "Select Client" brochure offered even more services for those with $1 million or more. On the first page, it says, "Smith Barney recognizes that substantial, high net worth investors require—and indeed should demand—an enhanced array of services that enable them to make intelligent, informed decisions. . . . As evidence of this belief we have designed a package of services available exclusively to our most valued clients." I have summarized some of the exclusive services they offer:

- "Waiver of fees": All administrative, legal transfer, wire funds, and safekeeping fees will be automatically waived.

- "Toll Free Client Service Center: A special toll-free number is available exclusively for Select Client use from eight A.M. to eight P.M. Eastern time. . . ."

- "Preferred Lending Rate": The service offers a reduced lending rate if you want to buy stocks on margin or borrow money and use your securities as collateral.

What struck me was how much more average investors would benefit from these services than their wealthy counterparts. For example, many middle-class customers would welcome the opportunity to have some of their fees waived or to be allowed to borrow money at a reduced rate. How many investors who might be worried about their investments after a market downturn would be comforted by an after-hours call to a Smith Barney representative? How many average investors who are saving for their futures would benefit from a free financial plan that normally costs them hundreds of dollars? The benefits of all of these services middle-class investors would notice, but the cost savings to high-net-worth individuals are negligible.

I reviewed all the materials that Myers left me at the desk, but soon came to realize that she had given me more information than I needed. When I looked in her packet, I noticed that she had enclosed a "Financial Consultant Fact Sheet" for Salomon Smith Barney's "High Net Worth Fixed Income Program." I could not believe my eyes. This fact sheet is for brokers' eyes only and shows why the firm likes their brokers to sell the product.

The program is for investors who have at least $500,000 in fixed income assets (i.e., bonds) invested with the firm. The piece clearly states some of the special benefits provided to customers, like conference calls and client meetings with bond analysts, but it's the right-hand side of the one-sheet that explains why the broker should sell the product:

WHY SHOULD I USE THE FIXED INCOME HIGH NET WORTH PROGRAM?

1) To increase your production [that means commission] in both the taxable and tax-exempt fixed income markets.

2) To gain access to an excellent prospecting tool and source of referrals.

3) To give you a competitive edge in capturing new fixed income assets, and to bring more of your existing clients' assets under your control.

The fact sheet and the other materials in the packet convinced me that the representatives at Salomon Smith Barney focused on acquiring the accounts of wealthy people instead of the accounts of average investors who would benefit from most of their special programs.

PaineWebber: Of all of the brokers I talked with, I most enjoyed speaking with Matt Johnson at PaineWebber. After our conversation I almost wanted to open up an account with him and I could see why he was a successful broker who had been in the business for eight years.

Johnson told me that PaineWebber referred to their top, high-net-worth clients internally as "Premier Clients." To be part of this elite group, a person had to have had at least $1 million in assets invested with the firm. Johnson explained that Premier Clients had a higher-level relationship with the firm. "It all comes down to a service question and it comes down to a relationship," he said. To Johnson, full-service firms basically offered the same products and his hand-delivered letter to me drove this point home. The letter begins by saying that every full-service firm has basically the same investment products and services to offer. What distinguishes one firm from another is the level of commitment shown toward the high-net-worth investor by those handling the account. He claims the broker who demonstrates, through attention, service, and support, that he truly values the investor's business is the broker who will successfully gain that investor as a client. He closes by pledging that Paine-Webber, his support staff, and of course he himself will take the necessary steps to gain and maintain my father's satisfaction for many years to come. I told you that he was good salesperson, and he's right when he says that service and attention are the keys to effectively managing money.

I wanted to find out how Johnson would make sure that my father's account would be a top concern when he had so many other accounts to manage. I asked him directly if my father's account would be a priority and he said, "There is no doubt about it that the account would get more attention." He also said that he talked only with his high-net-worth clients and delegated the smaller clients to his support staff. His support staff included a secretary, a sales assistant, and two or three interns from a nearby university. He justified his actions by saying, "I can't afford for a subordinate to make a mistake or to lose a million-dollar account and that's why I take care of my high-net-worth clients directly."

There are many full-service brokers like Johnson who have been in the business for some time and whose clients have become victims of their success. These brokers can't possibly manage all of their clients personally, so they hire a support staff that attends to the needs of average investors. If what Johnson said is true, that service and attention are the key elements for successful investing, then how can the majority of clients benefit from quality service when their accounts are being looked after by his sales assistant? It still amazes me that clients who continue to pay for full service get little or no service from some of the most successful brokers in the business. I suppose that the insights and money management skills of a sales assistant or a college intern are sometimes the best that money can buy unless you have a million dollars or more to manage.

A. G. Edwards: A. G. Edwards must have been having a fire sale the day I called or maybe my contact at the firm, Joe Wilson, was just in an exceptionally good mood. After Wilson realized that I was calling on behalf of my father, who was a high-net-worth prospect, he told me that he generally gave his high-net-worth clients discounts on their stock trades. He explained, "Full-service commissions are extremely expensive and I give a 40 percent discount across the board to my best clients." He felt the fees the firm charged were too costly and took too big a bite out of the return on investment. Wilson was offering full service at discount prices, which is common for brokers to offer to their wealthy clients, but rarely do average investors enjoy these same privileges. Full-service brokers justify their fees by telling the majority of their clients that they get what they pay for. But by that reasoning, wealthy clients should feel shortchanged when they get double-digit commission discounts and automatically have other fees and expenses waived.

When I asked Wilson how he would manage my father's account, he was most helpful. He stated the standard 80/20 rule and offered it as his guiding management principle. "I spend 80 percent of my time on the top 20 percent of my clients," he said. "The top 20 percent are the clients that I concentrate on. They are the ones that pay my bills." This is a rule that brokers learn quickly in brokers' school and it is written in stone in sales training manuals at most firms. Wilson assured me that my father would be in the top 20 percent of his clientele, and that I had nothing to worry about.

Finally, I asked if A. G. Edwards had any special program for high-net-worth individuals that would give them more personalized attention outside of his outstanding service. Sure enough, the firm did have such a program. Wilson told me that A. G. Edwards sent investors who had $3 million or more invested with the firm on an all-expense-paid trip to their corporate headquarters in St. Louis. There they met the very people who help manage their money. They could see whomever they pleased, including analysts, research personnel, retirement professionals, and so on. The trip would be capped off with a personal visit to Ben Edwards III himself, who is a direct descendant of the firm's founder. It seems that at A. G. Edwards, as at most other firms, they give greater attention and a higher level of service to those customers that they care about most.

DISCOUNT FIRMS

Every time I turn on the television I see another ad for a discount brokerage firm that assures me that commission discounts are what investing is all about. On the surface, the companies seem like true democracies, offering all of their clients basically the same services. But when you probe a little deeper, you see that this is not the case. Some discount firms do offer a level playing field, but many others roll out the red carpet when wealthy investors come knocking.

Charles Schwab: Charles Schwab is the number-one discount broker, with an impressive 28 percent market share of the on-line trading business. Schwab's co-CEO David Pottruck has said that "the industry is rife with double standards,"[4] and when I examined what Schwab had to offer their wealthy clients, I saw how right he was.

I walked into a nearby Schwab office located in a strip mall just north of Dallas and was greeted by Katherine Morris. She welcomed me and asked me to have a seat at her desk. I told her I was there on behalf of my father and that I was looking for a brokerage firm that offered services specially designed for high-net-worth individuals. I let her know that what mattered most to my dad was personalized service. She then began to explain how Charles Schwab could best address my father's needs.

First, she told me about Schwab's "Priority Customer Program." Charles Schwab, like Merrill Lynch, labeled their high-net-worth customers as "Priority Clients," and just as with Merrill Lynch there were levels of distinction. First-tier or Priority Clients had to have at least $500,000 in investable assets with the firm. The second level required customers to have at least $1 million in their accounts. Schwab referred to the members of this select club internally as "Priority Gold" customers.

Morris assured me that as a Priority Client my father would receive a higher level of personalized service than an ordinary customer of the firm. There were other perks as well, like having access to a private Web site that featured complimentary research reports, stock trading tools, and a list of companies that would match my father's investment profile. Priority Clients were also given a special toll-free number that routed their calls to trained professionals who could help them make investment decisions. "Having your father's calls directed to a team that would be familiar with his account would be far more preferable than calling one of our regular customer service reps," she said, "because sometimes people have to wait a long time just to get through." Finally, as a Priority Client my father could participate in private conference calls with such leaders from the business world as Jack Smith, CEO of General Motors, and Michael Armstrong of ATT. One business leader per month would be featured on each call and participants could pose questions to them. If they missed the call, they could listen to a recording of it on a private Web page on the Internet.

All of these conveniences were intended to ingratiate Schwab with their high-net-worth clients and to make them better informed and educated at the firm's expense. When I asked Morris why Schwab automatically deemed accounts with assets of $500,000 a priority, and one that necessitated personal attention, she answered candidly, "If we didn't provide some personalized services for our high-net-worth customers, they might take their assets elsewhere."

Next, she told me all about the services offered to Priority Gold customers. They receive all of the above services plus some additional ones. First, they get a 20 percent discount on all of their stock trades that are executed either by a Schwab representative or via Touch-Tone phone. Priority Gold customers were also the first to be included in all initial public stock offerings (IPOs) and the firm had agreements with investment banks that included CS/First Boston and Hambrecht and Quist. Customers could also take advantage of financial planning services, retirement specialists, customized statements, and unlimited complimentary research reports from such companies as First Call, Argus, and Standard and Poor's. Customers who were not Priority Gold Clients could still receive the research reports from the two investment banks, but they would be charged $49.95 a month. Finally, Priority Gold Clients would also be invited to participate in special events with leaders in the business and investment communities. Morris said it best after I told her that I was very impressed with all of the services that Schwab provided their high-net-worth clients. "That's just the way the world works," she said. "He who has the gold rules!"

A few months after my visit, I learned that Schwab had made some changes to their programs designed for high-net-worth individuals. It turned out that the company had renamed these programs rather than changing their substance. The first alteration had to do with retitling the programs that granted most favored status. The new batch of services was called "Schwab Signature Services," and according to the introductory material, "Schwab Signature Services rewards our most valued clients with special service and extraordinary benefits. A higher level of service for valued clients." There were now three levels of service, and a combination of assets and a minimum number of trades per year would allow some customers to get the best that the firm had to offer. The current guidelines are as follows:

Service Class	Minimum Assets	Minimum Annual Trades
Signature Services	$100,000	12 (1)
Signature Gold	$500,000	24 (2)
Signature Platinum	$1 million	48 (3)

(1) and $10,000 minimum balance
(2) and $25,000 minimum balance
(3) and $50,000 minimum balance

The new class/service structure gives greater emphasis to trading and commissions—the lifeblood of any brokerage firm. It's good that Schwab reduced the minimum balances, but tempting their customers to trade by giving them research and special services troubles me. As we shall learn in Chapter 6, some studies have shown that the more investors trade, the more they stand to lose. These studies have caused me to wonder about the integrity of any brokerage firm that gives their customers an incentive to trade when it is not necessarily in their customers' best long-term interests to do so. There is little difference between offering customers an incentive to trade and offering full-service brokers prizes and exotic trips as rewards for their commission production, because both reward systems don't have the customer's interests in mind. Investors who have less than $100,000 in assets and prefer a conservative buy-and-hold strategy will not be rewarded by all of the perks granted to those customers who have larger accounts or trade more often. It's ironic that long-term investors may not have access to many of Schwab's services that might protect their holdings long-term.

Signature Gold and Platinum customers still receive most of the perks, which include the opportunity to participate in initial public offerings and double-digit discounts on their stock trades. Gold and Platinum customers also have access to a small team of brokers who are familiar with their accounts, while Signature Services customers can call upon a senior representative who, I was told, was more knowledgeable than the typical customer service representative. It really doesn't matter if customers are referred to as Priority, Signature Gold, Priority Gold, or Signature Platinum. What matters is that the majority of Schwab's customers are not given the same privileges, perks, and personal attention that other customers enjoy.

Even at a discount firm like Charles Schwab, the importance of personalized attention cannot be undervalued for the average customer. In the August 26, 1998, edition of *The Wall Street Journal,* Charles

Schwab took out three full-page ads; the first page asked this question in big bold type: HOW CAN YOU HEAR FIRSTHAND FROM MANY OF AMERICA'S LEADING CEO'S ABOUT WHERE THEIR COMPANIES ARE HEADED? Page two had this full-page headline: HOW CAN YOU ENJOY THE ADVANTAGES OF WEB INVESTING WHILE GETTING THE PERSONAL SERVICE AND HELP YOU NEED? On the last page, of course, was the answer: INTRODUCING FULL-SERVICE ELECTRONIC INVESTING FROM CHARLES SCHWAB. The ad says that the people at Schwab "believe that all the technology in the world is often no substitute for the personal interaction that takes place between an investor and a skilled representative." This all sounds good, but you can't tell from the ad that it would have taken at least $500,000 (now $100,000) or a good amount of trading per month to get the personal service and help the ad lauds. A casual reader of the ad might conclude that Schwab offered these services to everyone.

Charles Schwab himself is a proponent of the personal touch. He is quoted in his company's Specialized Service brochure as saying, "Of course you need quality information, easy access and a good price. But you also need something more—objective assistance you can trust and specialized service you can rely on." If Schwab thinks that personalized attention is so important, why doesn't he offer it to the majority of his customers? I am sure that there are many first-time investors or elderly customers with Schwab accounts who would benefit from the services they provide only to their wealthy clients. Charles Schwab can afford to give their best customers a high level of personal attention, but given how important investing is to the average investor, how can Schwab not afford to give them the benefits of personal attention as well?

Quick & Reilly: Tom Miller, the office manager, told me why Quick & Reilly was the best firm for my father's account. He said Q&R, unlike Charles Schwab, believed in personalized attention; all investors got their own personal broker, instead of having their calls routed to a pool of representatives. He said that my father would get the attention his high-net-worth status deserved. That sounded fine to me, but I almost passed out after I asked him what level of attention my father should expect. "We do distinguish between the good guys and the regular guys," he said. "For our high-net-worth customers we take a bend-over-backward approach. I mean, let's face it, if there were two phones ringing and one person had one hundred shares to sell and the other person had ten thousand shares to sell, you know which one we would put on hold." Miller's blunt honesty seemed too much for me to take at the time, but I quickly asked him if he would send me some information on the company. Miller's information was not new to me, but I was surprised by his almost ruthlessly blithe frankness, especially in talking to a stranger on the phone. But in the heat of battle for large assets, brokers sometimes make statements that they later regret.

A couple of days later I received the packet of information I had requested. Enclosed was a small booklet entitled "Why Independent Investors Choose Quick & Reilly." On page two, the first paragraph says, "Ethics. Service. Value. Over the past decade these words seem to have lost their meaning." I couldn't have put it better myself.

Fidelity: Fidelity was next on my list and I called their 800 number. My call was answered by their call center in Salt Lake City, where the customer service rep told me about the "PAS" account, or Portfolio Advisory Services. This account required a minimum investment of $200,000 and I asked her to send me some information, which she said she would do. To my surprise, no more than ten minutes later I got a call from a local Fidelity office located about ten minutes away from my home. Senior Financial Representative Mark Thompson was on the phone and he invited me to visit him at his office to discuss the PAS account. Within one hour I was in his nearby Fidelity office talking with him and Chris Roberts, another senior financial representative.

Roberts took control of the meeting and explained that Fidelity had created the PAS account for their high-net-worth clients. The account is a fee-based, professionally managed mutual fund portfolio that assigns each client a dedicated "relationship officer," who acts as a liaison between the PAS investment team and the client. Prior to entering the program, all customers are required to fill out a questionnaire so that their investment needs can be properly determined. The account forces the customer to buy Fidelity funds, and if the customer has purchased mutual funds that the management team deem unworthy of the program, those funds have to be sold before the PAS investment team takes over. This seemed to me a hefty price to pay, especially for customers who had built up a great deal of equity in a mutual fund or for those who suffered a substantial tax liability resulting from such a sale. It seemed that if Fidelity was going to manage a mutual fund portfolio, then every mutual fund in the portfolio had to be blessed by the PAS team, whether the fund's performance had been a blessing to the customer or not.

The PAS account is an ingenious invention because it produces not one but two income streams from the same customer. It's true that the investor pays a flat fee for the PAS team's "expert" management, but she also pays all the fees associated with the expense ratio of the fund. These fees include the administrative costs, trading costs, and so on that are incurred by each fund. A double layer of fees would of course negatively affect any fund's value and would be a constant drag on the portfolio's overall performance. Fidelity does waive the management fees for each mutual fund, though, and gives the customer a .75 percent credit toward the overall PAS advisory fee.

The PAS account has some positives and negatives. Allowing customers access to a relationship manager who works with them is a positive, but I don't see why clients need to pay an extra fee for a team of people to manage their mutual funds. Mutual funds are long-term investments and have proven to give their shareholders rewards over time by virtue of buying and holding them—not by trading them. Moreover, the PAS account has two levels of trading for clients to contend with. First, there are all the trades executed by an individual fund's portfolio manager. Second, there is the trading of the PAS team, which includes the buying and selling of different funds within the customer's account. Both types of trades are taxable events, which could hurt the customer's overall performance.

I asked Thompson and Roberts if the PAS account was the best account they had to offer for wealthy clients. They assured me that it was and that they did not know of any other that would give my father the personal management attention he was looking for. I could not believe that a company as large as Fidelity had nothing other than the

PAS account to offer its high-net-worth clients. I thought that it would be worth my while to call Fidelity's main customer service line once more. My second call paid off, because that's when I learned about Fidelity's "Premium Services Program."

The Premium Services Program is designed to suit the needs of investors who own at least $750,000 in assets. This is an elite service group and entrance into the program is by invitation only, which would explain why I had initially found it difficult to get any information about it. I was trying to invite myself into a program that Fidelity did not advertise or make readily known to their customer base. There wasn't even a brochure on the program at any of the Fidelity offices I visited. A couple of service reps told me that Fidelity wanted to keep the number of people that entered the program low so that they could ensure their customers optimum service. Finally, my persistence won out and a local Fidelity representative agreed to send me some material.

Fidelity's Premium customers have a special customer service number they call to gain access to the Premium Services department. Customers are assigned to a select team of brokers, but they can at their choosing pick an individual broker within the team to take care of all of their needs. According to the Premium brochure, "Your Premium Services number connects you to a higher level of service." There is also a quote from a Premium Services representative: "We get to know our clients—how they like to conduct business—and I think that makes it easier and more comfortable for them." Well said. The representatives give customers the added convenience of one-stop shopping and there are a number of perks associated with the program as well. Premium Services customers get unlimited stock quotes from their customer service representatives, but regular customers get only one hundred free quotes per year. Premium Services customers are also the beneficiaries of stock discounts. All Internet trades for up to one thousand shares are only $14.95 per trade, which is a 40 percent discount compared with the fee for regular customers. Premium Services customers also get a 20 percent reduction for all of the stock trades that are made via the assistance of a Fidelity representative. Finally, Premium Service customers can receive research reports via fax, Internet, or mail and there is even an exclusive newsletter just for them; called *Perspectives,* it offers market commentary and insights on investment strategies.

As we have seen, Fidelity is a big believer in mutual funds and in some of their materials they tout the importance of investment research. Premium customers get a twenty-unit or twenty-dollar credit toward Fidelity's real-time research reports. These reports offer the latest news and analysis on a variety of companies and are authored by Fidelity's research staff. Regular customers have to pay the full price for each report, which is around $1 to $3, and they don't get any built-in credits.

The Premium Services Program gives Fidelity's best customers personal attention and lowers their cost of doing business via commission discounts and discounts on services. Trading costs and other fees, of course, add up over time and take away from the investor's overall return, and this is why many of Fidelity's customers who are not in the Premium Services Program would benefit from what it has to offer. The costs to an investor of not receiving personal attention can also increase over time, but Fidelity falls in line with the industry standard and offers only its wealthiest clients the highest level of personal attention and discounts.

MUTUAL FUNDS

Most people who have mutual funds sleep soundly at night knowing that their money is being professionally managed by some of the best money managers on Wall Street. Whether investors are partial to load funds or like the no-load variety, mutual funds seem on the surface to be the most democratic of investments, everyone receiving the same level of service regardless of personal wealth or the amount of money invested. As we shall see, some of the largest mutual fund companies offer special services and price breaks to their wealthy clients that average investors never get a chance to experience. The mutual fund industry has two faces, one that is held up for public view and a second, more private one.

LOAD FUNDS

American Funds: The American Funds family was founded in 1931 and today is the third largest mutual fund family. The fund group consists of twenty-nine mutual funds that are sold only through financial advisors.

American Funds follows the industry standard for load funds by charging the greatest load for the least amount of money invested in the fund. For example, if a person invested less than $50,000 in any of the American stock funds, he would have to pay a whopping 5.75 percent load, but if he invested $1 million in the fund, he would not have to pay any load at all. With a $40,000 investment in any one of the American stock funds, the customer would have to pay $2,300 out of his own pocket in commission, but for the wealthy investor, one with $1 million to invest, the fund company itself picks up the commission paid to the broker. The broker receives a 1 percent commission on a $1 million investment, or $10,000. The question that needs to be asked is, is it right for fund companies to charge the maximum commission to investors who can least afford to pay the full load, while at the same time waiving the load completely for their wealthy customers? The answer has to be no. In the mutual fund industry, standard rules of fair play apply to wealthy investors who can afford to purchase them, while average investors have to abide by practices that are blatantly wrong.

In addition to the price breaks that American Funds offer their wealthy customers, there are additional personalized services. I initially called the American Funds customer service line and asked if the company had any special programs for high-net-worth investors; the customer service rep told me in a rather soft voice that they had such a program but it was not one that they advertised and was only for their best clients. He gave me another toll-free number that connected me directly to the personal management division. Karen Miller, who is the chief administrative officer for this division, took my call.

Miller told me that I had come to the right place and confirmed that the company did indeed offer special services and gave a higher level of attention to their high-net-worth clients. Customers who had at least $3 million in assets with the firm did not have to talk to a customer service rep, but were assigned their very own personal investment counselor. This individual addressed the client's every need from tax planning to retirement counseling and offered her an additional level of service beyond what her broker gave. Also, the personal investment counselor served as the customer's direct contact with the fund's portfolio manager so that the customer could talk with the portfolio manager directly. Miller assured me that the personal investment counselor assigned to my region, who, by the way, lived in Los Angeles, would be happy to fly to Dallas and meet with my father to discuss his financial goals.

Then I asked Miller to tell me what was the greatest benefit of hiring the personal investment counselor. She said that the best chance for investment success was not with a fund manager who had to do what was best for the fund, but with a personal money manager who would do what was best for my father's interests. In other words, the interests of the fund itself might be contrary to the interests of the individual investors who have invested their money in it. This is a point that is often overlooked by many mutual fund investors, especially those who are strapped with paying capital gains taxes at the end of the year because the fund manager aggressively bought and sold securities in the portfolio. A buy-and-hold philosophy on stocks might serve many investors better, but many mutual fund managers cannot afford such a luxury when they are graded only on quarterly and yearly performance. The diversity of interests and goals that millions of investors bring to bear on a fund cannot be fulfilled by a single money manager, who must first attend to the interests of the mutual fund itself. The interests of the fund, like any business, is making money, but making money via fees and commissions has nothing to do with fulfilling the interests of shareholders, who primarily want capital appreciation.

Second, Miller said that unlike brokers, the personal investment managers were not compensated on transactions, so their interests and my father's interests would be one and the same. Miller's remarks surprised me, because American Funds are sold exclusively through financial advisors, many of whom are brokers, who may, as Miller implied, pose an inherent conflict of interest.

Alliance Capital: Alliance mutual funds are owned by AXA Financial and are the seventeenth largest fund family in the United States. The company manages benefit plans for thirty of the Fortune 100 companies and has over 118 funds in the group.

When I was a broker, I remember the local Alliance wholesaler often visiting my firm to pitch brokers on selling Alliance funds to their clients. This wholesaler was an aggressive, accomplished salesperson who believed in the merits of proactive salesmanship as the single most important factor in convincing customers to invest in Alliance funds. Alliance sponsored evening cold-calling sessions during which brokers in my office randomly called residents in high-net zip codes to pitch them on their funds. The brokers were rewarded with a free dinner and some nice prizes at the end of the evening, which typically ended around nine-thirty.

When I called Alliance, I first wanted to find out if they had any special programs for high-net-worth individuals, but I also wanted to see how aggressively they would try to capture my father's account. I called their standard 800 number and the representative told me that they did have such a program, but he wasn't sure exactly what it involved, so he told me that he would leave a message for a person named John, who could answer my questions. Ten minutes later John called and told me that Alliance had such a program, but if I wanted information about it, he would have to refer me to another person within the company. I decided to call the customer line again just to make sure I was getting the right feedback. When I did this, I was transferred to what I thought was a manager, who told me in no uncertain terms that Alliance did not have any programs specially tailored toward attracting wealthy investors. "We treat all of our clients the same," he said. I asked him if he was sure. "Yes," he said, "I'm sure."

Despite these assurances, about a half hour later I got a call from Mark Hughes at Alliance's Investment Managers' Services Department, who very willingly told me about the great services Alliance offered their high-net-worth customers. He told me that the company managed three separate mutual funds that required at least $500,000 as an initial investment. These funds were classified under three main broadbrush categories, such as equity, balanced, and fixed income, and they were in segregated accounts with a professional money manager assigned to each account. This was a private program for Alliance's best customers and the funds could not be tracked in the newspaper. Moreover, Alliance never advertised that such funds were even available. This might explain why some of the customer service reps that I spoke with did not even know of their existence.

Hughes told me that the performance of all three funds was spectacular. For example, the equity fund had beaten the S&P 500 nine out of eleven years and the balanced fund had never had a down year in its lifetime. The only fees associated with accounts invested in the funds was one hundred basis points or 1 percent a year, which went, in part, to pay for the personal money manager. The personal money manager worked for a company called Regent Investor Services, which was owned by Alliance. I thanked Hughes for his time and thought that was the last that I would hear from Alliance.

I was wrong. The next day I got a call from Howard Rosenburg, who was the senior portfolio manager at Regent Investor Services. During the half hour Rosenburg and I chatted, I listened to him explain to me the benefits of having a personal money manager as opposed to having just a regular mutual fund account. Rosenburg's presentation was compelling and he offered to fly from Manhattan to Dallas to meet with my father in order to explain to him firsthand all that Regent and Alliance had to offer.

Two days later my phone rang, and it was none other than the local Dallas Alliance sales rep wanting to talk with me about my father's account. I never returned his call, but I must say that Alliance's sales effort is a testament to persistence.

When I was a broker, my firm did some internal studies that showed what investors wanted most from a broker. Surprisingly, the key factor to a client's satisfaction was not investment performance. What investors wanted most was for their broker to stay in touch with them. People communicate with those whom they care about and most of all clients wanted a broker to care about them. The fine folks at Alliance certainly cared enough about the prospect of managing my father's six-figure account that they repeatedly called me and even offered to pay me a visit.

NO-LOAD FUNDS

Vanguard: Vanguard Funds is the second largest mutual fund company and was founded in 1974. The fund family comprises 102 funds, and as of this writing manages over $500 billion in assets.

Of all of the mutual fund companies I called, Vanguard had the most to offer high-net-worth individuals. I initially thought that since Vanguard was a no-load company, services would be tailored to average investors because cost-conscious average investors would most like such funds. I discovered that this was not the case and that Vanguard had basically three different programs that were well staffed to address the needs of wealthy individuals. Investors were not informed about any of these special services until they opened an account and the programs were not advertised or marketed to the general public, although I did discover some information about them on Vanguard's Web site. Once the account is open and the appropriate asset threshold is met, customers receive a call telling them that their account will be managed by one of the three special groups. If a customer has $250,000 to $1 million in Vanguard mutual funds, then she is placed in the "Voyager Group." Assets totaling $1 million to $5 million place the customer in the esteemed "Flagship" category, and assets of $5 million or more boost the customer into the distinguished "Flagship Plus" league.

As a Voyager customer, my father would receive special privileges not available to ordinary customers. For example, all Voyager customers can call a personal representative who is familiar with their account, instead of calling Vanguard's regular customer service number. At the time of my inquiry, Vanguard had fifteen Voyager representatives who handled about four hundred to five hundred individual accounts and customers were welcome to discuss a variety of financial matters with their representative, like retirement planning or the benefits of a Roth IRA. Also, the minimum investment amounts for additional accounts were lowered for Voyager customers. A $3,000 minimum was lowered to $1,000 and for UGMA (accounts that are used to gift assets to minors) the minimum was only $500. This made it easier for Voyager customers to open accounts for their children and grandchildren than for regular Vanguard customers. Some fees were waived as well, such as IRA custodial fees, low balance fees, and so on, and all Voyager customers received a 10 percent discount on all of their broker-assisted stock trades if their brokerage account was held at Vanguard.

Flagship and Flagship Plus customers received all of the services of their Voyager counterparts, but with a somewhat higher degree of customer service. For example, Flagship Plus reps had around one hundred to two hundred customers apiece and each rep was responsible for filling out and processing all of his customers' paperwork personally. In addition, Flagship and Flagship Plus customers were sent special advanced editions of *In the Vanguard,* the company's newsletter, customized statements that could collectively show the total household assets, and 25 percent off all of their stock trades in a Vanguard brokerage account.

Vanguard was definitely in the vanguard when it came to providing conveniences to its wealthier customers. Double-digit discounts on stock trades, lowered investment minimums, the waiving of certain fees, free products, and personalized service all made for an open invitation to wealthy investors, but excluded average investors.

T. Rowe Price: T. Rowe is a name-brand no-load fund company that was established in 1937. It's the nineteenth largest mutual fund company and actively manages eighty funds.

T. Rowe Price has an entire department, called the "Personal Services Group," set up to address the needs of wealthy individuals. I left a message with one of the main customer reps and about an hour later Stephen Wilson contacted me. The conversation I had with Wilson told me a lot about the importance of personalized service and attention, even when the customer owns nothing but shares in mutual funds.

Wilson said that customers with $250,000 plus in assets are transferred to their own client manager in the Personal Services department. These managers all have college degrees, are registered representatives, and some have taken advanced training courses and are charter mutual fund advisors. At the time of our chat, the company had eighteen client managers with four hundred to five hundred clients apiece. Wilson assured me that the higher level of service I was interested in would not be a problem because only 20 percent of the client base called on a frequent basis.

I asked Wilson how important it was to have a personal manager attend to an investor's account as opposed to one of the many customer service representatives. He said, "Well, you don't want your father calling 1-800-Guess-Who, do you?" Clearly, Wilson had a sense of humor, but then he told me on a more serious note: "I would say that it is critical because the client manager knows what your options are and knows the funds inside and out." He went on to say, "I think most people would rather have a personal contact. The customer service reps are around twenty-two years of age, just out of college, and you know most people don't know a thing at that age."

T. Rowe Price also offers preferred customers some perks. For example, they receive a quarterly newsletter called *Take Note,* which discusses, among other topics, retirement issues, estate planning, and the company's current view on financial markets. Preferred customers also receive a quarterly audiocassette series that features interviews with some of the portfolio managers and a preview of new mutual funds before they are opened to the general public. How much would T. Rowe Price preferred customers be charged for all of these additional perks and extra personal attention? "The service is free," Wilson said.

On Wall Street a distinct line is drawn between the rich and the poor and the haves and the have-nots. Labels for wealthy clients like Priority, Premier, Preferred, and Platinum help foster a class system that treats average investors like second-class citizens. This is a long-established hierarchy, and a very rigid and clear-cut one. The contrast between the treatment of wealthy clients versus that of average investors is disturbing. I don't blame financial services companies for looking after their rich customers, but to deny services to middle-class investors who would benefit from them is not right. I am not arguing that restricting certain services to wealthy investors is unfair, because a one-size-fits-all definition of fairness escapes me, but it is my belief that such restrictions are "objectively" wrong. When a wealthy investor comes knocking, Wall Street celebrates the occasion, orders complimentary gifts, and issues price discounts. But when the average investor comes to Wall Street, there is no fanfare and he is not allowed to take part in all of the perks and privileges that are given freely to his wealthy counterparts.

Wealthy investors receive a higher level of service simply because of the worth of their assets, not because their accounts necessarily warrant the attention. I hope that the examples I have provided in this chapter prove to you that the level of service that an investor receives is dependent on what the account means to the brokerage firm or mutual fund—not on what the account means to the investor. Investors who have given Wall Street all that they have should be the true Premier Clients and they are the ones who justly deserve to be the financial services industry's top priority. Investors like the elderly lady who hands over her life savings to a broker, or the single mom who invests in one mutual fund to help send her son to college, or the husband and wife who are counting every penny toward their retirement should be the financial services industry's top priority. These are the real preferred customers who need the highest level of service and personal attention, but unfortunately Wall Street has lost sight of this fact. When it comes to average investors, Wall Street's well of good conscience has run dry, yet for the interests of wealthy investors, its well, and its cup, runneth over.

DON'T BE SHY WHEN DEALING WITH YOUR ADVISOR

• Always ask your advisor for commission discounts, reduced minimum account balances, and lowered fees before you open your account. Commission stock discounts of 20 to 40 percent are well within the range for most brokers to give you without management approval. Keep in mind that fees and account balances and so on are products of a negotiation and products of a negotiation are negotiable.

• Client referrals are the lifeblood of an advisor's business. The best time for an advisor to ask for a referral is at the time that you open your account, but refrain from doing so until you are happy with your own account performance. Let your advisor know that treating you well will be good for your investments and for his business as well.

• Family and friends who have investments with your advisor can come in handy. Make the advisor aware of your relationship with his other clients so that you will benefit from it. Capitalize on the cumulative assets of the group so that the advisor will think that losing your business may jeopardize these other accounts.

• Be proactive in calling your advisor. When you call your advisor, it distracts him from his other clients, but if he is often unavailable to take your call, then find another advisor immediately.

CHAPTER 3

THE POWER OF INFORMATION: THE RICH SEE THE LIGHT AND THE MIDDLE CLASS IS KEPT IN THE DARK

On Wall Street the most valuable commodity is information. Investors have won and lost fortunes based solely on the quality of information and advice they receive. What's going on at Company X, where will interest rates be in June, what about Company Y's earnings forecast is all information that many investors crave and are willing to act upon with a buy or sell order. It's what investors think they know about tomorrow's investment climate that makes them react today, and the path between today's certainty and tomorrow's uncertainty is littered with Wall Street's finest forecasts, speculations, and prognostications.

Wall Street's information purveyors come in all shapes and sizes, from the mighty, six-figure-income analysts who sit securely on their perches thirty floors up to the garden-variety stockbroker who works the street persuading middle-class investors about the next sure thing. Wall Street is home to basically three types of people who have information to offer: those who know, those who think they know, and those who don't have a clue, but say that they know anyway. It's hard to tell who is in the know and who is just pretending, but many investors take comfort in the fact that any information, real or somewhat counterfeit, is better than no information at all.

As a general rule, people communicate or share information with those they care about, and Wall Street is no exception. In the last chapter, I showed that Wall Street primarily cares about its wealthy customers, who receive a greater level of service and discounts. Here I will show that wealthy customers are generally better informed because they have access to information denied to most average investors. In most cases, wealthy clients are the first to know about news that will affect their investments, and average investors, if they have an opportunity to be informed at all, are generally the last. An obvious example of this principle playing itself out is the full-service broker, whose job it is to take a proactive stance in providing his clients with information that could affect their holdings.

THE RICH MAN'S INFORMATION SOURCE: FULL-SERVICE BROKERS

The job of a full-service broker is a tough one because full-service brokers serve two masters—their wealthy clients, and the clients who truly need professional advice but don't have enough assets to capture the broker's undivided interest. As we saw in the previous chapter, it is in the best interests of brokerage firms and their brokers to serve the needs of their high-net-worth customers.

Most brokers are not as well informed as their clients might think. When an investor opens up an account with a full-service broker, she expects the broker to be a professional schooled in the fine art of investing. The customer also assumes that the broker has her best interests at heart and will be the full-time caretaker of her portfolio. Most investors are simply overwhelmed by the number of investment choices and look to their full-service broker's expertise to guide them safely through the many pitfalls that investing presents.

What most people do not realize is that there is no minimum

education requirement to become a broker and that many full-service brokers are poorly trained. Believe it or not, when a broker passes the industry entrance exam, it does not mean he knows how to manage money; it simply means that he has figured out how to pass the exam. There are no questions on the exam that, if correctly answered, would make a broker an accomplished money manager. The securities industry does not require full-service brokers to have a college degree, a high-school diploma, or even a GED in order to manage someone else's money. If the industry thinks educating brokers is so important, then why isn't there a minimum education requirement? These low standards beg the question. Anyone in good legal standing who can pass the test can become a broker. Just ask my good friend and coworker whom I will call David. One week he was selling ladies' underwear and a few weeks later he was managing other people's money for one of the largest firms on Wall Street. David is still a broker today, and as far as I know, he has no desire to get back into the lingerie business. I know another broker who is a vice-president at a firm where he actively manages his clients' money. What I bet is that his customers don't know that he declared bankruptcy in 1990 and was sued for $108,000 for fraud in 1985. These examples should give you the incentive to check out your own broker's credentials, unless you would like to have your money managed by an erstwhile ladies' underwear salesperson or a broker who has gone belly-up.

Don't count on your broker being an encyclopedia of investment knowledge either. It's true that when I was a broker, my personal box was stuffed daily with my firm's best research, but I was advised by my sales manager to throw most of it in the garbage and never to read it during market hours. To read research information during market hours was considered a cardinal sin because it took away from the time that I would have to generate commissions. Even today, years after I left the securities business, I vividly remember my sales manager waving his finger in my face and admonishing, "Mark, remember your job is to sell—not to do research!"

As a broker, I was always stunned to see that most clients would rather have their investment advisor give them almost any answer to a question than an honest admission of ignorance. Investors don't pay the person who manages their money to be ignorant; they rely on the expertise of brokers because they know very little about investing themselves. A sobering study by the National Association of Securities Directors proves this point. The study showed that 63 percent of Americans know the difference between a half-back and a fullback, but only 14 percent know the difference between a growth and an income-producing stock. Another study showed that 78 percent of Americans can name certain characters in sitcoms, but only 12 percent know the difference between a load fund and a no-load fund. For a broker to admit her own ignorance can be a mortal wound to her client's confidence in her and may undermine her ability to persuade her clients to accept her investment recommendations. Brokers who give their clients bad advice or wrong answers would do well to heed Abraham Lincoln's advice: "It is better to keep your mouth shut and appear stupid than to open it and remove all doubt."[1]

The fact that brokers are not generally Ph.D.s or wellsprings of information is not my main concern, rather it is what brokers do with the vast resources of information at their disposal. After all, you don't need an advanced degree in astrophysics to realize that a flaming meteor in the sky is barreling toward the earth with a force that might devastate a town. In this scenario, you would naturally think that a community message would be sent out to ensure everyone's safety, but if a stockbroker headed the town's communication services, he might call his clients in the high-net-worth zip codes first to save them from the blast. The broker's clients in the middle-class neighborhoods might never get a call and would experience the full force of the meteor's impact.

How does this story translate into a real-life situation? Let's say that AT&T has fallen in early-morning trading by five points as a result of a bad earnings report issued the previous day. Accomplished full-service broker Lester Reynolds is ready to call his clients with the untimely news. Reynolds hesitates to make the calls because he had picked AT&T just last week as a near-term winner and had recommended the company to many of his clients. He takes a deep breath, swallows his pride, and moves slowly toward his computer. He pulls up a list of clients who currently hold AT&T in their portfolio and this is what he sees:

Mr. Dobbs	10,000 shares
Ms. Owens	8,800 shares
Mr. Nickles	8,500 shares
Mr. Taylor	7,400 shares
Ms. Beavers	7,000 shares
Ms. Eisenberg	5,800 shares
Mr. Thorn	5,700 shares
Mr. Horner	4,650 shares
Ms. Estes	4,600 shares
Mr. Lancaster	4,500 shares
Ms. Akard	3,400 shares
Mr. Stone	3,300 shares
Mr. Tanner	2,200 shares
Ms. O'Conner	1,000 shares
Ms. Noel	900 shares
Mr. Eden	800 shares
Mr. O'Malley	700 shares
Ms. Kellog	700 shares
Mr. Dante	600 shares
Average Investor	250 shares

Which client do you think he will call first? Customer Dobbs, Reynolds's most wealthy client who has the greatest number of shares, will undoubtedly get the first call. Reynolds will then proceed to call the other clients in descending order, according to how many shares they own. Why? Because the sooner Reynolds calls Dobbs, the sooner he can protect his client's downside and generate a nice commission for himself. The more shares Reynolds sells, the more money he makes, and the less Dobbs stands to lose. It might take Reynolds hours, perhaps even days, to contact all his clients. By the time the average investor gets a call, the stock may have hit its lowest value. This is the so-called full service that many average investors pay for when their broker manages money for wealthy clients as well.

In addition to this problem, the broker may have other matters to attend to. While he is calling his clients about AT&T, his assistant might tell him that another client is in the lobby waiting to see him. Meanwhile, his other two phone lines are ringing, and he has just been informed that his firm has downgraded Yahoo. He remembers that he has a lunch appointment at noon and a client meeting at three P.M. He needs to buy 500 shares of Ford for Mr. Peters, sell some bonds for Ms. Philips, and put in a limit order to buy 1,500 shares of Microsoft for Mr. Thomas. He needs to prepare for an investment seminar he is giving that evening, and for an early-morning retirement breakfast he is attending the following morning.

It's easy to see from this typical scenario why brokers have to focus on their wealthy clients and why the needs of smaller investors get lost in the daily frenzy. Remember, a broker can talk to only one client at a time, she can manage only one account at a time, and while she is informing her best customers about the latest market news the majority of her customers, especially small investors, are kept in the dark.

The way many full-service brokers selectively divvy out their firm's research is also a problem. Full-service firms invest millions of dollars in their research departments and pride themselves on their quality research, but few brokers make their smaller clients privy to their firm's research reports. The reason for this is that it's in a broker's best interest to send research reports only to those clients who have the most available cash in their accounts so that they can buy the stock that the firm is recommending. In order to justify a stock's purchase or sale, brokers will make good use of their firm's research reports to entice their customers to make a trade that will generate a commission. Those customers who can afford to buy the stock or who are thinking about selling the stock are the ones that the broker will generally want to bless with the firm's latest research findings. Rarely do brokers send research reports to customers who cannot afford to buy the stock or to those clients who don't want to sell their holdings. On Wall Street, cash buys more than stocks and bonds, it also buys information, and information is the most powerful asset money can buy.

Finally, full-service brokers have a difficult time minding their stores. It's crazy to think that your broker is the full-time guardian of your portfolio when he is either entertaining his clients on the golf course or engaged in a three-hour lunch with one of his wealthy clients. It's no secret in the brokerage business that the road to increased commissions and greater assets is not found by gazing at a computer screen all day or wading through volumes of information via the Internet. No, brokers are hunters of customers rather than gatherers of information and they have to constantly be out of the office in search of fresh, new business if they hope to achieve their ever-increasing commission hurdles. The best targets for the hunt are, of course, the elephants or wealthy clients who will provide a large bounty of commissions, assets, and fees.

WHEN COMPANIES TALK BEHIND YOUR BACK

The telephone has proven to be a marvelous invention, but I wish companies would use it more often to communicate with all of their shareholders. Every year hundreds of publicly traded companies host conference calls to announce their quarterly earnings or to make special announcements regarding their businesses. This is an opportunity for the company's management to inform participants about the latest company news, and an opportunity for participants to ask management timely and perhaps insightful questions about their operations. Listening to how management responds to questions can give participants added information about the company that printed materials may not reveal. It's when management has to give impromptu replies that a company's true financial situation can best be discovered. When it comes to conference calls versus the standard press release, hearing is often better than reading.

Companies that do host conference calls typically invite only a select few to hear them. Analysts who are friendly to the company, institutional investors, and wealthy individuals who have large equity positions in the company are the typical invitees. Average investors are generally shut out and left wondering on the sidelines. On Wall Street, ignorance is not bliss, and not having access to the important information shared during these conference calls can have negative consequences to individual investors. A few examples will serve to prove my point.

Dell Computer: In July 1998 PaineWebber hosted a conference call for Dell Computer and invited only analysts and large institutional investors. During the call, Dell's chief financial officer announced that average PC selling prices could fall for the quarter ending that month. This was definitely bad news since it could affect Dell's overall earnings and thus the value of the company. Before the call, Dell's shares were up 1.4 percent for the day, but after the call shares tumbled 5⅛ and the stock lost 4.4 percent of its value.[2] The selling pressure on the stock more than likely resulted from the listeners to the call who were made aware of Dell's gloomy predictions for the quarter. The analysts and large institutional shareholders were the first to hear the bad news and were probably the first to protect their money. But the millions of average investors who own Dell stock, many of whom also buy Dell's products, didn't find out the bad news until after the market closed, or the next morning.

Monsanto and American Home Products: In June 1998, Monsanto and American Home Products, two pharmaceutical giants, announced that they would merge. The merger was valued at $33.6 billion, but on October 13 of that year it was called off because of what some analysts say was a clash over how the executives would run the company.

On the day the merger was canceled, it was the hot story on CNBC, but commentators seemed frustrated that they could not confirm the report. One of them even said that there was "a campaign of misinformation" under way to conceal news about the two companies. But CNBC did report that the principal investment banks covering both companies had mysteriously downgraded both companies just before the market opened. The firms involved were Cowen and Company, Salomon Smith Barney, Lehman Brothers, and Wertheim. Their lowered opinions on both companies most likely were the result of the failure of the merger, but how they'd gotten the news before it was released to the public remained a mystery. Rumors circulated about a conference call selectively informing key analysts and institutions, which gave them the opportunity to sell their shares before the average investor could do so. What was the effect on each company's stock after news became available? Monsanto plummeted a whopping 26.6 percent, or 13.37½ points, and American Home Products fell 10 percent, or $5.

Walt Disney: When Disney announced its fiscal second quarter in 1998, it chose to inform only a few analysts. The entertainment giant hosted a conference call during which it recommended that key analysts lower their expectations for the second quarter but did not release this information to the general public. The stock slid 2.8 percent on the day of the call. Disney's defense was that it did not consider this news to be "material" enough to report.[3] It appears that Disney's "it's-a-small-world philosophy" has at times crept into its method of announcing quarterly expectations, but it is hard to imagine why the company thought that lowered revenue or an earnings projection was not signficant enough to many individual investors who own the stock.

General Motors: GM made a handsome profit when it delayed informing the public about plans to buy back $4 billion worth of its stock. The auto giant selectively informed securities analysts about its intentions more than one hour before it informed the public. Between the time that GM had made the announcement to analysts and the time the news got to the public, GM's stock rose from 60⅜ to 62½.

It was clearly in General Motors' interest to keep their plans quiet until they had actually bought the stock at the market price. If the company had made a public announcement, investors might have bought additional shares, which would have ultimately increased GM's buyback price per share. When General Motors was asked about this, they said the delay was unintentional and due to a "technical glitch."[4]

These are just a few examples of how companies selectively inform analysts and institutional shareholders but don't inform the public. Arthur Levitt, head of the SEC, has frowned on this practice and has framed his critique as an ethical issue that all publicly traded companies should address. In March of 1999, the SEC announced that it would take close to a year to explore ways to force companies to disclose information to all investors at the same time. These invitation-only meetings have been going on for decades and are a true disservice to most investors, but why the SEC waited so long to address this problem boggles the mind. I am glad to see that the agency has finally gotten around to giving it the attention it deserves, but waiting till the twenty-first century is a clear sign of a bureaucracy at work. I have nothing but admiration for the SEC's public relations efforts, but only a modicum of thought will lead a rational person to conclude that making financial information available to all investors at the same time is more an ideal to be wished for than a goal to be achieved. Levitt says, "Ethically, it's clear: If analysts or their firms are trading— knowing this information, and prior to public release—it's just as wrong as if corporate insiders did it."[5] I agree with him, but when it comes to money and ethics, corporate America's definitions of right and wrong are often blurred or written with pencils that have oversized erasers.

On December 9, 1998, the NASDAQ seemed to come to the rescue of the average investor when it announced an arrangement with Internet broadcaster broadcast.com to give the top one hundred NASDAQ-traded companies an opportunity to broadcast live four quarterly earnings conference calls a year. This was to be a pilot program that would begin in 1999. Alfred R. Berkeley III, president of the NASDAQ, said the initiative "will help to level the playing field for individual investors by giving them access to the same information previously available only to a select few on Wall Street. We would like to see Internet broadcasting become a standard corporate communications tool for public companies in the near future, and are pleased to experiment with this new technology in partnership with broadcast.com."[6] At first glance, I thought that the NASDAQ had successfully dismantled the traditional barriers to information, but further reflection soon proved otherwise and I realized that broadcasting a conference call on the Internet does not level the playing field for investors. First, many investors do not have an Internet connection and only a fraction of those who do will have the computer capacity to permit a quality listening experience. Moreover, most investors would be at work while the call was taking place and thus would not be able to act on the information. Curiously, Berkeley stated that he was pleased by this "new" technology, but a cursory glance at the broadcast.com Web site showed that the NASDAQ had been broadcasting their market updates for years. One has to wonder why this important fact was not included in the press release.

Todd Wagner, then CEO of broadcast.com, lauded the move by saying, "NASDAQ's endorsement brings the investor relations process one step closer to providing timely and 'full disclosure' of corporate information to investors of all sizes, from the individual investor to a large institutional firm."[7] Once again this statement sounds better in the abstract than in the concrete. If a person stands alone in the woods and shouts all of his personal secrets only to the trees, has he fully disclosed this information? No. To fully disclose information, there must be a large enough audience to hear it. Currently, millions of investors are not huddled around their computers waiting for the next earnings release, so it's hard to imagine how the term "full disclosure" can be fairly applied to Internet broadcasting.

Though Internet broadcasting does not open the floodgates of information, it does provide a practical way for companies to market themselves on-line. Keep in mind that the NASDAQ is heavily weighted toward high-tech companies and holding conference calls on the Internet may serve some purpose for investors, but they also allow companies, especially high-tech companies, to address marketing and public relations concerns. The Internet space is valuable real estate for many high-tech companies and broadcasting their conference calls in this way gives them, as well as NASDAQ, an additional multimedia presence complete with a highly trafficked site like broadcast.com. It also gives NASDAQ top-of-mind awareness with an Internet audience, which is more than likely smitten with high-tech companies and in many cases is one keystroke away from purchasing NASDAQ companies via an on-line broker. Who would argue the truism that most investors buy what they know, and what better way to get a potential investor to know more about a company than to broadcast their earnings call on the Internet?

Please don't think that I have critical remarks only for Wagner and Berkeley. Seven months after they made their announcement, only fifteen companies accepted their free offer (some of which already held open calls),[8] but I commend them for their forward thinking concerning Internet broadcasting. As more and more people go on-line, the

Internet might someday serve as an effective means of leveling the playing field for investors. I look forward to that day, but that day is not today!

Regardless of whether a company broadcasts its quarterly earnings calls or not on the Internet, it's up to shareholders to demand as much information as possible from the companies they invest in. Unfortunately, the possibility of full disclosure seems remote because current securities laws do not require companies to disclose important information that could negatively affect the company's stock. Take for example K-Tel, the Minneapolis-based company best known for its TV ads of goldie-oldies music collections. The company received a letter from NASDAQ informing it that due to its lack of assets it might be delisted from the exchange. K-Tel had the letter two or three weeks before letting the public know. The reason: the company thought being taken off NASDAQ was not a material event. Well, if being taken off NASDAQ is not a material event, what is? When investors finally did hear about the news, the stock plunged 32 percent in one day.

Currently, the SEC does not require companies to disclose the following: restructuring charges, fraud or embezzlement convictions, government fines convictions, government investigations, and top executives' serious health problems, among other factors.[9] Moreover, as of this writing, I cannot point to one example of the SEC fining or punishing a company that has selectively disclosed information at the individual investor's expense. It appears that it's going to be up to individual shareholders to pressure companies into being more forthcoming and to demand that they be treated fairly.

Not only do publicly held companies hold conference calls that shut out average investors, but many mutual fund companies are guilty of the same practice. It's very common for mutual fund portfolio managers to host closed-door teleconferences that selectively inform analysts, financial advisors, and wealthy individuals about the latest news on the funds. The managers take calls from call participants and update them on the fund's current holdings, investment strategy, outlook for the future, and so on. Representatives from such mutual fund companies as Montgomery Funds, Neuberger Berman, Franklin Templeton, Aim, Oppenheimer, Putnam, Kemper, and Invesco all freely admitted to me that they hosted portfolio manager conference calls to which individual investors were not invited. I had to ask myself what was the big secret contained in these calls and why couldn't most individuals who had their hard-earned money invested in these funds listen in? It seems to me fundamentally wrong to enlighten analysts, brokers, and select wealthy individuals, but not to do the same for average investors who would certainly benefit from this information.

ELECTRONIC COMMUNICATIONS NETWORKS AND AFTER-HOURS TRADING

Consider the plight of first-time investor Mike Paine, who had recently invested $25,000 in the company Better Pies Inc. Paine was your typical nice guy, a fair-minded fellow who always looked for the best in people before making a decision. He bought Better Pies several months ago after a tip from his neighbor Joe, who worked as a stockbroker. Better Pies had a thriving business in the Midwest and prided itself on its fifty-year-long tradition of making some of the tastiest frozen pies known to mankind. Paine and his family had enjoyed Better Pies for years and their refrigerator often held all twelve delectable flavors. Before making his investment, Paine called Better Pies' investor relations department and inquired about the company's financials. After about a week of intensive research and soul-searching, he decided to make his investment. In Paine's mind, there was no better pie, thus there could be no better place to invest his money than the company that made them.

Paine's investment in the company was a substantial one for him. He earned $40,000 a year and his $25,000 investment represented the results of a stringent ten-year savings plan. He knew about the risks of the stock market, and while the daily gyrations of the major indices did not concern him, the daily value of his one investment caused him quite a bit of worry. He often obtained stock quotes on Better Pies throughout the day; he periodically tuned in to CNBC for news on the company; and he paid close attention to any press releases the company issued. In one release he noticed that the company planned to report its earnings after the market closed the following Tuesday. Paine called the Better Pies' investor relations department to verify the report and they told him the press release would go out on Tuesday evening and the earning results would be published in the paper the next day. However, Paine didn't know that on Tuesday at four P.M. Better Pies was hosting a conference call for some analysts and select individuals to discuss the company's earnings and its outlook for the near future.

Tuesday arrived and Paine was in good spirits. He checked the price of Better Pies throughout the day and the stock seemed solid. But the conference call told quite a different story. Management spun a sad tale of decreased earnings and advised those on the call to lower their expectations for the company for the next two quarters. Profits had slid by 35 percent and overall revenues were off by a whopping 40 percent. Unlike the stockholders who heard the call, Paine slept soundly that night, knowing that he had made the right decision in investing in Better Pies. The stock closed up one-eighth.

When Paine woke the next morning he opened his paper and saw the bad news about Better Pies. The dismal earnings report took him totally by surprise and he thought that the negative article would send the stock plummeting to a fifty-two-week low of 14. Paine panicked, wanted out of the stock, and made the decision to sell all of his shares immediately. At five minutes before the opening bell, he was poised by his computer, and after the first minute of trading he got his first real-time quote on Better Pies. The stock was down 30 percent and Paine saw his once-in-a-lifetime investment drop by $7,500. How could this be? he asked. How can the stock open 30 percent down after only the first minute of trading? To safeguard his principal he sold all of his shares of Better Pies, took the $7,500 loss, and vowed never to invest in the company again. The only pie at the time of Paine's sale was the one on his face, but his loss and bad luck were not his fault. Paine was just another victim of after-hours trading.

Wall Street's traditional hours of operation are from 9:30 A.M. to 4 P.M. ET, but that's not when the trading ends for large institutions, wealthy people, and a handful of investors who actively trade after-hours. In the example above, the investors who were aware of the conference call decided to sell their shares of Better Pies before the market opened the next morning and it was those sell orders that made the stock open 30 percent down. This select group is able to communicate through a number of electronic communications networks (ECNs) that allow them to buy and sell shares of stock, a phenomenon that may ultimately affect the stock price the following day. One of the main ECNs is Instinet.

Introduced in 1969, Instinet is owned by Reuters and is used primarily by institutions. Investors can trade both listed stocks (those that trade on the New York Stock Exchange) and stocks on the NASDAQ, and on average 170 million shares trade per day. Currently, some 17 percent of stock trades are executed via ECNs[10] such as Instinet, but unfortunately, most individual investors do not have access to this private marketplace. Most full-service brokerage firms don't give their clients access to the after-hours market and only a few discount firms like Jack White, J. B. Oxford, and Muriel Siebert & Company offer the service. In the summer of 1999, Datek Online became the first on-line broker to offer after-hours trading, which they did with little fanfare. A couple of other Internet-based companies (Wit Capital and Market XT) announced in 1999 that they would offer after-hours trading on-line, but their success or failure remains to be seen. After-hours trading allows institutions and select individuals to act on information that most investors don't have at that time and to trade when most investors cannot. Ninety percent of earnings releases and 60 percent of corporate announcements occur after hours,[11] but most investors cannot act on this information and thus are at a competitive disadvantage. In the private arena of after-hours trading, few average investors have a voice and they are at a distinct disadvantage, especially if the stock that they are holding falls on bad news.

Tom O'Brien, owner of Tiger Investment Group, based outside of Boston, has experienced the effects of after-hours trading firsthand. Tiger trades securities on the company's behalf and it also provides financial services to individual customers. In addition to his entrepreneurial duties, O'Brien cohosts a weekly radio talk show called *After Hours Trading*.

I initially thought that I would impress O'Brien with my knowledge and with some examples of the way that after-hours trading is detrimental to an individual's financial health. I told him about 3Com being down 13 percent and RJR Nabisco sliding 7 percent in after-hours trading, but I quickly realized that his in-the-trenches view was far more insightful than mine. After I shared my examples with him, he said, "That's nothing. Let me tell you about Oxford Health Plans." As O'Brien recalled the story, Oxford had announced some internal accounting mishaps that cast doubt on the company's revenue and profit. This sent a shock wave through Wall Street and blocks of the shares were sold in after-hours trading. On October 25, 1998, the stock was at 73, but the next morning it opened up at 38 and it closed that day at 24. O'Brien was unfortunately a buyer of the stock at 38 and I guess that's why this particular company had left such an indelible mark on his memory. All professional traders remember their profitable trades as well as their not-so-profitable ones. When I asked him if investors without access to after-trading were at a disadvantage, he said, "Oh sure, they are at a great disadvantage, because by the time everyone else reads the news the next day about the stock in question, the stock's price could be a lot lower."

After-hours trading via ECNs is inconsistent with the SEC's rules for fair and open markets. In January 1997, the SEC's order-handling rules forbade private markets (markets that do not allow all investors to buy and sell securities) and better pricing (better than what an investor would receive on the open market) for the buying and selling of stocks,[12] but not until almost two years later did the SEC cast its eye on the private markets that ECNs posed. On December 3, 1998, the SEC announced that private markets, like Instinet, would have to publish their stock quotes for all investors. Moreover, each market would have to become either a market participant and register as a broker/dealer, or become a separate market and register as an exchange. It took the SEC three years to write these rules and they did not take effect until 1999. SEC officials said the new regulations were "truly of landmark proportions,"[13] but as far as I'm concerned they're a nonevent. While it's true that the ECNs have to publicly state their bids and offers, many average investors won't necessarily have access to these alternative markets. Under the new guidelines, ECNs will be allowed to establish their own trading rules and certain criteria such as credit-worthiness and minimum assets for customers. These self-imposed standards will more than likely prevent many average investors from participating in these alternative markets. Moreover, the new regulations do not address the problem of most investors being locked out of after-hours trading. A private market is still a private market unless "all" investors have access to it. On this issue the SEC has made a fine public relations effort, but the net effect for average investors is still minimal.

To some market watchers, it appeared that in May of 1999 the NASDAQ was going to help level the playing field for average investors. Its board of directors announced that it had unanimously approved a proposal to extend its hours, running from 5:30 P.M. to 9 P.M. or 10 P.M. ET, Monday through Thursday, and only the NASDAQ 100, or the mostly widely traded stocks, would be able to be traded. Name-brand firms like Charles Schwab and Merrill Lynch lobbied for longer hours that would help their bottom lines, and in some press reports the move was seen as a convenience to investors who would want to trade from their homes. Louis Thompson Jr., president of the National Investor Relations Institute, lauded the move by saying, "After hours trading is a way to begin to level the playing field,"[14] but it is hard for me to imagine why when it is filled with additional risks that may plague average investors—risks such as a low liquidity, predatory professional traders, volatile price fluctuations, and larger spreads between the bid and the ask price, all of which could cost investors dearly. Moreover, investors need to learn about the "Wild West" nature of after-hours trading. NASDAQ should have addressed all of these problems before they made the decision to approve a proposal for extended trading hours. This reasonable precaution would have helped to ensure that the interests of investors would be protected.

A few days later the New York Stock Exchange announced that it would delay its plans for after-hours trading till the second half of the year 2000. Initially, the exchange planned to trade only five hundred of its most liquid stocks, leaving the majority unavailable to most investors. Richard Grasso, the NYSE's chairman, said that the Exchange had a "large challenge to educate"[15] investors about the differences between after-hours trading and the regular trading session. Grasso made a valid point when he said, "Whatever the competitive arguments in favor of extending trading hours the overriding interest should be protection of the public interest and the integrity of the marketplace."[16] The NYSE's decision to delay the extended session was sound, but for those investors who are anxious to trade late into the night, be careful about what you wish for. Don't get caught up in the "cult of equities" that will force you to spend more time glued to a computer screen and less time with your friends and family. While it's true that brokers on Wall Street have to trade to live, the average investor might have many a sleepless night when he chooses to live to trade.

TAKE MEASURES TO BE IN THE KNOW

• Participate in as many company conference calls as you can for the companies you own. If you can't hear the live call, contact the company's investor relations department and ask if you can hear the replay. A valuable on-line resource for upcoming conference calls is www.bestcalls.com.

• Take it upon yourself to keep abreast of the latest financial news. A daily effort to stay informed will help you learn as you go and will increase your ability to be self-reliant.

• Staying glued to twenty-four hours of televised financial news may make you better informed, but it will not make you better educated about financial matters. Some financial "news" reporting today is not that far removed from a multimedia calculator in which minute stock price changes fill the airways when more important concerns should be being addressed.

• Use the Internet, but be selective about which Web sites you use. Here are a few sites I would recommend: www.cbsmarketwatch. com (free), www.cnbc.com (free), www.cnnfn.com (free), www.wsj. com, and www.nytimes.com (free).

Part Two

SELLING THE AMERICAN DREAM: WHAT WALL STREET WANTS YOU TO BUY BUT DOESN'T WANT YOU TO KNOW

CHAPTER 4

SALESPEOPLE, SALES TRAINING,
AND SALES CONTESTS:
HOW WALL STREET DOES BUSINESS

In most businesses, salespeople are easy to identify, but not on Wall Street. When you walk into a car dealership and see a mass of white shirts and friendly smiles headed your way, you can be sure that the sales team has noticed your arrival. Spotting salespeople at a nearby retail store will also prove easy. They are the ones who constantly roam the floor asking customers if they can help them and are generally met with the words "No, just looking, thanks." With practically every product or service, a consumer knows beforehand that she is going to discuss her purchase with a salesperson, and she readies herself for her once-in-a-lifetime offer.

Once a customer knows this, he is better prepared to safeguard his interests and to proclaim that the salesperson is not going to take advantage of him. The sales profession's reputation precedes the salesperson, and savvy consumers may vow that no matter what special offer or sales pitch the salesperson uses, they are not going to fall victim to it. They know that salespeople work on commission, have to meet commission goals and win sales contests, but they promise themselves they'll resist any sales pressure. Yet few investors apply this rationale to their stockbroker. They instead take an enormous leap of faith and act on the broker's advice. Most investors do this because they do not realize that brokers are also salespeople who work on commission and have commission goals to meet and sale contests to win. The principal question that you must ask is, Do you want your money managed by a salesperson? If the answer is yes, then you may want to skip this chapter, but if the answer is no, then read on.

The heart and the soul of Wall Street is selling, and in this chapter, I will describe sales training, sales contests, and the professionals who try to sell you. My focus will be on full-service brokers at such name-brand firms as Morgan Stanley Dean Witter and Prudential and also those in the securities area of your local bank. These sales professionals primarily deal with individual investors and are paid handsomely for their investment recommendations. The first topic is where brokers come from and what skills brokerage firms look for when they hire so-called financial consultants.

RECRUITING NEW BLOOD: WHEN
WALL STREET NEEDS A FEW GOOD PEOPLE

Seventy-five percent of all brokers leave the brokerage business within the first five years and this high turnover rate prompts brokerage firms to always be in search of new sales talent. Firms use a variety of methods to lure new blood into the business that range from career seminars to on-line chats to the standard classified ad. A quick scan of the classifieds in my local paper (*Dallas Morning News*) showed what firms were looking for in new hires. Smith Barney's ad is in bold, eye-catching type and paints the job of being a full-service broker as one with "no limits, no boundaries, no barriers, no nonsense." The fine folks at Smith Barney want you to know that "a career at Smith Barney will allow you unlimited opportunity to achieve earnings that are as impressive as your abilities. If you are looking for an environment where you can surpass your current boundaries, there is no place like Smith Barney."

Morgan Stanley Dean Witter also uses classified ads to search for new brokers. One of their ads, listed under "Sales Professionals," as was the Smith Barney ad, begins, "YOU WANT MORE CHALLENGE. FIND IT IN MORE PLACES." This statement is open to interpretation, and first it seemed to me to be an invitation to look at other ads, but as I read further I got a clearer picture of what they were looking for: "Ambition. Tenacity. The desire to achieve more in your career. If you have what it takes to establish yourself professionally, we have the means to help make it happen."

A classified ad for Prudential Securities also wants sales professionals. Prudential's ad for new brokers begins by offering the answer to one of life's great questions. The invitation to join the firm begins with this bold headline: FIND OUT HOW MUCH YOUR DETERMINATION AND AMBITION ARE REALLY WORTH. It's not clear when this will be revealed, but Prudential implies that it will be at some point. The ad concludes, "There is a lot to be said about a career where the compensation is limited only by your work ethic and ability." I'm sure it's true, there's a lot to be said about such a career, both good and bad, and the final judgment will probably have a lot to do with whether you are a broker or a customer.

The Internet has also been a fine recruiting ground for brokerage firms. For example, Merrill Lynch's Web site offers an open invitation for new recruits to join the firm. Merrill's pitch goes like this: "Like many other successful individuals, you may be coming to a point in your career when you know it's time to make a change. Perhaps you are in search of greater financial rewards or new challenges, or maybe you would simply like to be your 'own boss.' " You might never know from Merrill Lynch's posting that selling is required to become one of their financial consultants. Jim Lusk, then senior director of Merrill Lynch Private Client Human Resources Division, clarified this matter in an on-line chat sponsored by the firm. This question was posed to him: "You call them financial consultants, but how much of their work is actually advising and consulting and how much of it is sales?" Lusk replied, "Sales is an inseparable part of the financial consultant's job. It takes a good salesperson to win the right to advise clients and prospects on investment choices and plans."

Ads like these speak to a salesperson's desire to make money and to be successful. I have never seen an ad sponsored by a brokerage firm entitled "Wanted: Investment Professionals" with an invitation like this: "If You Genuinely Care About People and Making Money for Investors, Then We Want to Talk with You." Surely this ad would catch the interest of a few talented good-natured individuals, but unfortunately it would not attract the kind of person brokerage firms really want. Brokerage firms want people who can sell their products and generate commissions. A broker's success in making his clients money is of no concern to the firm. One of the things many salespeople find most attractive about the securities business is that theoretically it doesn't put a cap on their income. The more commission the merrier is the industry's chant, and brokers are internally judged by how much commission they generate from their clients' assets. In other words, how much money the broker makes *off* his clients is what his employer cares about—not how much money he makes *for* his clients.

Noticeably absent is some sort of standard for rewarding brokers who make money for their clients. Every day the commission that I generated was ranked against that of the other seventy-five brokers in my office, but never in my tenure as a broker was I asked how much money I made for my clients. I was judged every four months by the number of new accounts I opened and the amount of assets and commission I brought in. If I didn't meet minimum standards in all three categories at the time of the review, I might have lost my job. If I was successful, however, I received a cash bonus and was in the office manager's good graces. The bonus for meeting the goals in the first quarter was $1,000 and for each quarter thereafter it doubled, until the final quarter, when I had a chance to win $6,000.

This system is similar to the one most brokers use. It helps clarify why brokers have little choice but to generate commissions, particularly by paying closer attention to their wealthy clients.

Brokers can also inadvertently harm their clients' interests when they move to another firm, and an established broker is always being recruited away to another brokerage house. When this happens, your broker may say he made this move because it is best for his clients and ask them to transfer their accounts to his new firm. However, he may not tell them then that he has received a lump sum of money to ship off to the other firm. This is a standard industry practice and the broker's worth to his new employer is based solely on the amount of commission he has produced in the past year. On average, a broker who produces $300,000 in commission can receive an up-front cash bonus of 30 percent, or $90,000. Brokers with at least $500,000 in commission are fetching bonuses of 45 percent, or $225,000.[1]

To decrease the turnover rate of its largest commission-producing brokers, firms generally offer them incentives to stay. These perks range from discounted shares of the firm's stock to a deferred compensation program. One prevalent standard in the industry is to pay top producers a greater share of the commission that they generate. At most firms, the more commission a broker produces, the greater percentage of the commission he keeps for himself. This policy, of course, gives brokers an added incentive to retain their positions, but it also entices them to make investment recommendations solely for the purpose of generating fees and commissions.

Here are the maximum commission payouts from a number of leading brokerage firms in 1998, according to the magazine *On Wall Street:*

Brokers with less than $150,000 in gross production:
Smith Barney: 33% (40% for mutual funds, 46% for insurance)
Prudential Securities: 25% (27% for annuities, 50% for insurance)
+Merrill Lynch: 30% (all products)
*PaineWebber: 31% (40% for insurance)

Brokers with $500,000 in gross production:
Smith Barney: 39.5% (42% for mutual funds, 50% for insurance)
Prudential Securities: 40% (45% for annuities, 50% for insurance)
+Merrill Lynch: 36% (all products)
*PaineWebber: 41% (40% to 50% for insurance)

Brokers with more than $1 million in gross production
Smith Barney: 42.5% (44% for mutual funds, 50% for insurance)
Prudential Securities: 43% to 45% (48% to 50% for annuities, 50% for insurance)

[+]Merrill Lynch: 38% to 40% (41% for 2.5 million-plus producers)
(all products)
*PaineWebber: 43% to 45% (40% to 50% for insurance)
[+]varies depending on service
*add 1% for all business done in premium, fee-based accounts[2]

How can brokers make the best investment recommendations
when they are constantly concerned with hitting new and higher commission plateaus? This causes many brokers to recommend mutual
funds and insurance products that may not be the best investments for
their clients. Wall Street would be better off if brokers were given
greater monetary rewards based on the returns they made for their
clients. Money is not the root of all evil in the brokerage business, but
paying brokers on commission and giving them hefty bonuses based
solely on their commission production can be. This standard practice
is a disservice to investors. Christos Cotsakos, CEO of E*Trade, sums
up the industry's myopic view on commissions well when he says, "In
terms of its drive toward racking up commissions, this industry is as
crooked as a snake's eye. It looks at the customer more as a sheep to
be shorn, not as a client to be served."[3]

BROKER BOOT CAMPS AND SALES TRAINING: STOMACH IN, CHEST OUT, CONTRACT IN HAND

Most of the major investment firms spend millions of dollars per
year teaching their brokers how to sell their products. Alternately, the
amount of time and money spent in researching the inner workings of
investments and the latest money management techniques is kept to a
bare minimum. Indeed, I learned more about Wall Street and investing
by researching this book than I did in my three years as a broker. My
sales training, however, was second to none.

In addition to the weekly sales meeting in the office, I and the
other brokers were regularly flown to my firm's corporate headquarters
for heavy-duty sales training. Once we landed, we were whisked away

in style from the airport in a limousine complete with a well-stocked bar and a variety of tasty snacks. With suitcases in hand, we were each given our own room at the firm's private hotel facility. The complex was massive and included racquetball courts, gaming areas, a complete gym, full-length bar, and round-the-clock buffets that featured wall-to-wall choices of every imaginable entrée and dessert.

During most of the day I stayed quietly seated in the main lecture hall, where the firm's biggest commission producers told us how they had become "successful" brokers. They openly shared the sales techniques that had worked best for them and let us in on the emotional buttons to press when clients became difficult to sell. They could manipulate clients as easily as a potter molds clay.

The highlight came when we were broken up into smaller groups and videotaped while we pitched various products. About ten rooms were devoted to these mock sales presentations. Afterward we received feedback on our sales abilities from our peers and were critiqued by the firm's senior brokers. The firm spared no expense on this and even hired guinea-pig clients for us to practice on. These people ranged widely in age and occupation, but most of them were retirees (a prime prospecting category for brokers) or part-time workers. Each of them had memorized scripts that included their own fictional persona and financial profile.

Every broker then received a copy of his videotape and was asked to review it with his local sales manager. As I look back on my own video performance, I am reminded that not even one hour of my training was devoted to managing money. I wonder what customers of the firm would have thought if they could have sat in on some of the training sessions or played a part in the videotaping exercise. Surely they would have learned that the firm did not have their best interests at heart when it spent so much money on teaching their brokers how to sell their clients instead of trying to help them.

The firm wanted us to be sales machines and to be fully prepared to grind up any customer objections that might hinder the close of a sale. In doing so, they lost sight of what truly mattered to their clients, such things as integrity, investment knowledge, and goodwill. This is only one example of the way sales training takes the place of investment training, a common practice on Wall Street. The general consensus is that sales ability alone can make a broker successful. This is the same message that brokers receive at the granddaddy of sales instruction: the Million-Dollar Boot Camp.

THE MILLION-DOLLAR BOOT CAMP

I first heard of the Million-Dollar Boot Camp from a fellow broker and learned more about it in *On Wall Street,* a sleek-looking monthly magazine for financial professionals. The magazine has a circulation of ninety thousand and bills itself as the number-one publication in helping brokers build a more successful business. A reporter for the magazine, Tanya Bielski, wrote a first-person account of the most renowned sales-training boot camp. I have relied heavily on Ms. Bielski's article to describe the camp and used comments from brokers who also attended the seminar. I have also examined the sales brochure on the seminar in the effort to paint the fairest picture possible.

The Million-Dollar Boot Camp is hosted by certified financial planner Tom Gau, who resides in Torrance, California, a town outside of Los Angeles. Six to nine times a year, brokers and financial planners come from all over the country and pay $1,495 per person to listen to the wisdom of Tom Gau during his intense two-and-one-half-day sales training session. Major firms generally make up twenty-five percent of his attendees.[4] Gau is well known in the business and his credentials are second to none. He has claimed that he is the number-one commission-producing full financial planner in the United States and Canada.[5] Amazingly, he produces $5 million in annual fees from his financial planning business and around $800,000 a year from his broker-boot-camp seminars.[6] This stellar performance Gau claims to achieve by working only two weeks out of each month.[7] He supposedly meets eighty clients a week[8] and his work ethic runs only on high-octane adrenaline. Now you can understand why brokers would be willing to pay Gau $1,495 and why brokerage firms would encourage their financial consultants to attend and experience his "life-changing" philosophy.

The boot camp begins with Gau taking center stage to begin to rev up the troops. "I am SICK and TIRED of going to CONFERENCES and being told if I only WORKED harder, I'd GET more CLIENTS. That BOTHERS me," he yells,[9] and then launches into all the secrets and techniques that have made him such a success over the years.

1) *"Look to Be a Marketing Expert, Not a Financial Expert."* In Gau's opinion "most people do things back-assward,"[10] i.e., most brokers may be deluded into thinking that their investment expertise is going to win them clients. He instructs brokers on solid prospecting techniques and tells them to concentrate on marketing their businesses to the public instead of reading up on the latest investment news during market hours. The bottom line for brokers, Gau says, "is to get 'qualified' people walking through your door. Not people that are having financial problems, being hunted by the IRS, people with MONEY," he bellows.[11]

2) *Think of Your Client as "Raw Material" and Your Business as a "Client Factory."* How would you feel if your financial advisor thought of you as raw material? How would you treat someone if you thought this way? You must admit that this is not the most flattering theory for a broker to adopt about his clients, yet Gau preaches this philosophy seemingly without pause. In Gau's view, a broker's relationship with his client is based on the broker's ability to mold the client to suit the broker's desires and wishes. Think of it as a client factory, he says. "First, they're raw material, then a work in progress. Finally, they're a finished product."[12]

3) *"Confuse Your Clients with Facts."* Gau admits that most investors don't know much about investing, so he advises his audience to overwhelm their prospects with facts. Only when investors feel that they can't manage their own money will they seek out the services of a broker. Gau doesn't seem to be a pro-

ponent of investor education either. He tells brokers that they should never place *The Wall Street Journal* in their offices and advises them to opt for *People* instead,[13] because "clients could get nuggets of information from financial journals that are 'dangerous' to them."[14]

4) *"Mimic Your Client's Body Language."* People respond to others who generally speak and act in a similar way as themselves. This is the point that is driven home during the seminar given by Dr. Donald Moine, a psychologist and the author of seven books including *Unlimited Selling Power.* He says, "They will feel more comfortable doing business with us because we sound like them."[15] In other words, a broker should concentrate not so much on what he says, but on how he says it. Trust me, this is time-tested advice that works.

5) *"Make It Easy for the Client to Sign on the Bottom Line."* To get clients to agree with a broker's investment recommendations they must be in the habit of saying yes. The small yeses will eventually lead to the final yes, the one that allows the broker to manage the client's money. Gau instructs his audience to ask questions of their clients that have only affirmative answers so that they will begin the process of agreement. For example, "I do not want you to outlive your income,"[16] is an immediate agree. He also says to use stories that go for the emotional jugular to persuade prospects. For example, appeal to them with comments like "Your children will only be able to attend college when you put away two hundred per month."[17]

I called Gau's office about the Million-Dollar Boot Camp, but he was unavailable. I did come across his twenty-page booklet about the boot camp, though, which included some biographical information. It turns out that Gau had been selected by *Worth* magazine as one of the country's "Best 200 Financial Advisors" and had been quoted as a tax and financial authority in *Money* magazine, *The Robb Report*, the *Los Angeles Times*, and *Kiplinger's Personal Finance* magazine. I wonder if any journalists from any of the publications had sat in on one of Gau's seminars.

There were also a multitude of positive quotes from brokers and financial planners who had gone through the boot camps. Quotes like:

"Using just one idea from the Boot Camp, I made $60,000 in commissions in the first four days after returning to my office." —David Bach, Orinda, CA

"Shortly after the Boot Camp, I had my biggest disability [insurance] sale ever—a $12,000 premium which will increase over future years!" —Keith Johnson, Phoenix, AZ

"I was practicing as a Certified Financial Planner for four years and I hit a wall. I couldn't seem to raise my production any higher. Plus I was working like a dog. Then Tom Gau turned me on to his remarkably simple, yet effective techniques. Thanks to Tom, I'm now making four times the income that I did before. I've become one of the top producers in my broker dealer. And the best part is that now I get to go on four vacations a year!" —Ray Day, CFP, Palos Verdes, CA

Tom Gau's Million-Dollar Boot Camp is a bleak commentary on the securities industry as a whole. After all, Gau would not be in business if it were not for the support of brokerage firms. The SEC has turned a blind eye to the Million-Dollar Boot Camp as well. Seminars like these make for future victims, some of whom will probably be elderly investors.

SALES CONTESTS

Imagine discovering that the retirement investments you made at your broker's recommendation were tied to his winning a boat. Things like this happen all the time at many name-brand firms because the industry loves sales contests. Most full-service firms have them throughout the year, and for many brokers it's Christmas all year long as they aggressively compete to win the prizes from the firm's treasure chest. The contests basically serve two purposes. First, they motivate brokers to sell, and this clouds the real reason why many brokers make their investment recommendations. For example, does a broker recommend the firm's financial plan because she thinks it's a good idea for her client, or is she just trying to rack up some points in the firm's sales contests? Her customers don't know what her true intentions are. No regulation requires her to reveal that a sales contest is going on. Second, the contests are used by firms to grade brokers on their ability to sell the firm's products and services. How well a broker does in the firm's sales contest is his internal report card on his ability to push products, produce commission, and gather assets.

The key for a broker doing well in sales contests rests in large part on his commission production. I think a new world order or some cataclysmic event would have to occur before brokerage firms realize how sales contests can damage the interests of their customers. Running sales contests rips the words "buy and hold" out of the broker's dictionary and can transform well-meaning financial consultants into sales-contest fanatics. The interests of customers are sacrificed, and in so doing, Wall Street tramples upon the futures of its client base.

The top commission-producing brokers are held up as examples at their firms and become members of the firms' prestigious "recognition clubs." These clubs have been a mainstay on Wall Street for years. Once a broker becomes a member, the firm rewards him with a panoply of perks, which typically culminate at the end of the year in an all-expenses-paid luxury vacation to some exotic location. Below, according to *On Wall Street* magazine, are the membership requirements for the clubs at some major firms:

A. G. Edwards

Chairman's Club	$525,000 (annual gross production)
President's Council	$375,000
Crest Club	$250,000

Merrill Lynch*

Circle of Champions	$2.5 million (annual gross production)
Director's Circle	$1.75 million

Circle of Excellence	$1.0 million
Charles E. Merrill Circle	$800,000
Chairman's Club	$600,000
President's Club†	$500,000 (ten years)
	$425,000 (zero to nine years)
Executive Club†	$400,000 (six years)
	$360,000 (five years)
	$300,000 (four years)
	$250,000 (three years)
	$200,000 (two years)
	$125,000 (zero to one year)

Morgan Stanley Dean Witter

Chairman's Club	Top 150 brokers (gross annual production)
President's Club	Next top 400 brokers
Director's Club	Next top 40 brokers in each region

PaineWebber

Chairman's Council	$1.25 million (gross annual production)
President's Council	$750,000
Pacesetter Club	$475,000

Prudential Securities‡

Chairman's Council $2.4 million average gross production for past two years
President's Council $925,000 (straight annual commission)
Director's Council $575,000 (straight annual production)

Salomon Smith Barney

Director's Council	$1.35 million (gross annual production)
Chairman's Club	$1 million
President's Club	$600,000

*To qualify for any of Merrill Lynch's clubs the broker has to earn sixteen points in the firm's annual sales contests. The points are calculated in part on the number of financial plans the broker sells.

†Ranked by years of service.

‡To be a member of the Chairman's Club the broker has to have produced $500,000 in gross commissions in the preceding year.[18]

A Goldman Sachs broker who wanted to remain anonymous paints a standard picture of what it's like to go on one of the all-expense-paid trips: "They hired a banquet room for a bunch of us, and we had butlers, a private balcony overlooking the city, expensive cigars—everything," he recalls. "They really spent a lot of money on us."[19]

Here is a list of some of those wonderful destinations that brokers are just dying to go to every year. Again the source is *On Wall Street* magazine:

Firm	Year	Destination
Dain Rausher	1999	Sydney, Australia
	1998	Palm Beach, FL
	1997	Madrid, Spain
	1996	Los Cabos, Mexico
	1995	Rome, Italy
Merrill Lynch	1998	Caribbean cruise
	1997	Prague, Czech Republic
	1996	Ireland
	1995	Mykonos, Greece
	1994	Oahu, HI
Salomon Smith Barney	1998	Boca Raton, FL
	1997	Scottsdale, AZ
	1996	White Sulphur Springs, WV
	1995	Amelia Island, FL
PaineWebber	1998	Venice, Italy
	1997	Monte Carlo, Monaco
	1996	London, England
	1995	Rome, Italy
Prudential Securities	1998	New York City
	1997	Hong Kong[20]

If a broker realizes on December 15 that he is $10,000 in commission away from going on an all-expense-paid trip to Hong Kong, what do you think he does? Most likely he will find some way to produce the commission before the end of the year, even if it is at the expense of his clients' interests. Arthur Levitt, chairman of the SEC, acknowledges this problem, but has done nothing about solving it. At a Securities Industry Association seminar, he said, "It has probably not occurred to many of you that buying securities from some firms in the month of December may be riskier than at other times of the year."[21] Levitt is correct when he says that most investors are not aware of this problem, but they also don't know that this problem occurs, in part, because sales contests are held year round as well. Perhaps the SEC could put its best foot forward by letting all investors know the perils that await them from the sales contests that the SEC allows to take place every day.

I am at a loss to understand how Wall Street can conduct sales contests and sponsor recognition clubs when both of these inventions serve no practical purpose for investors. How is it possible for brokers to choose what is best for their clients when they have to contend with sales contests that may bring out the worst in them? What message does the SEC send when it casts a blind eye to the way firms motivate their sales forces? What effect do recognition clubs and sales contests have on brokers? A Morgan Stanley broker who wished to remain anonymous says it best: "You just get caught up in it. You become desperate for the glory."[22] All true, and while brokers become desperate for the glory, their clients become desperate to find a financial advisor who will not compromise their interests.

ALWAYS ASK ABOUT SALES CONTESTS AND INCENTIVES

• Ask your advisor to tell you about any and all incentives that he has been given in order to sell you certain products. The standard financial consultant response of "I don't have any incentives outside of my client's interests" is baloney, so don't believe it when you hear it.

• Inquire about your advisor's commission calendar. See if there is a direct correlation between when he gets paid and when he makes his recommendations to you.

• Base your evaluation of your advisor on your investment returns and the cost for his advice. An advisor's worth cannot be inferred from investment performance alone.

CHAPTER 5

GOING UNDERCOVER:
IN SEARCH OF A FINANCIAL
ADVISOR

Wall Street provides a wide selection of financial advisors, from brokers at full-service firms to bank salespeople and financial planners. All these professionals are good at selling their products and services to investors, and their sales pitches can be so effective that it's often hard to determine who is offering the best advice.

To investigate this field of advisors, I decided to conduct a search myself. I met with two bank salespeople, two full-service brokers, and two financial planners. The brokers and bank salespeople were from well-established firms and all of the representatives were chosen at random. Once again I have changed the names of the advisors, but the names of the firms have not been altered. Any remark or criticism I make about the advisors' recommendations should not be taken as a commentary on financial planners in general or any of the brokers' employers. I am concerned here with comparing investment advice and not with any particular company or profession.

I told each of the representatives that I knew nothing about investing and that I needed their expertise in order to invest my money wisely. I added that the money I planned to invest represented my life savings. Here is the information that I told each advisor about myself:

a) I had $125,000 in cash to invest.

b) My income for the previous year was $65,000.

c) I owed $12,000 in credit-card debt.

d) I was self-employed.

e) I considered myself a moderate-risk investor.

f) I was thirty-six years old.

I played dumb throughout their presentations and asked questions that would make them think I was a total novice at investing. Often feeling like the TV detective Columbo, I'd scratch my head and ponder what they told me, hoping they would think I was an easy mark. I did this to see if any of them would take advantage of my ignorance, and sure enough some of them did. The half-truths and misinformation that some of the salespeople told was most apparent when I asked them to explain how they differed from their competitors, and whom I should do business with. I was familiar with the sales techniques and pitches they tried to use on me, but if I hadn't been, they could easily have taken advantage of me.

BANK INVESTMENT ADVISORS

In some investors' eyes, bank salespeople are more credible than stockbrokers. Many elderly people mistakenly think that the person who sells investments at a bank offers the assurances, security, and promises of a federally insured banking account. This perception leads customers to believe that they can get better-than-CD returns at a bank with little or no risk. And unfortunately many bank sales professionals have capitalized on this misperception. For example, in May 1998, NationsBank was fined $6.7 million by three federal agencies for selling high-risk mutual funds as no-risk investments.[1] Many of the customers who bought these funds were elderly people, who ended up suffering substantial losses. The two banks I visited disclosed in writing or verbally that the products they were selling were not FDIC insured, like a bank account, and also let me know that there were risks involved, including the loss of my principal. This admonition is for the customer's benefit, but it had little effect on the way each representative tried to sell me their investment recommendations.

NationsBank: Mike Johnson, vice-president of NationsBank Investments Inc., was in his mid-fifties and had previously been a broker at Merrill Lynch for a number of years. He had seven hundred clients and managed around $50 million. Of all of the salespeople I visited, Johnson was the most accomplished and his pitch was well honed. I asked him to explain the difference between a bank salesperson, a broker, and a financial planner, and without delay he told me he was all of the above. Johnson was apparently every investor's dream because he represented the best in convenience and one-stop shopping: customers could get three sales professionals for the price of one. He then described his investment philosophy by pointing to an investment chart behind his desk. The chart showed the stock market's performance from the 1920s to 1995 and it had a line tracking the market's increase in value over the years. He said, "Think of that line as a train from San Diego to New York. You don't know where the train is going to stop, so you don't dare get off." With this he was "preselling" me on mutual funds and the notion of long-term investing. He then gave me some statistical data that showed why smart money remains fully invested and how market timing can have a disastrous effect on a person's portfolio. This was followed by a one-sheet on the benefits of long-term investment performance with large subheadings for growth and income. Next to "income," he asked me to write bonds, CDs, and savings. "Growth," he told me, means stocks. Although Johnson was doing 99 percent of the talking, he was trying to get me to interact with him. Sales 101 teaches that salespeople who can engage their customers and get them actively involved in the decision-making process dramatically increase their chances of closing the sale. The trick is to make customers think that the salesperson's ideas are their own, because people are less likely to object to ideas they've played a part in forming. Johnson had completed the presell portion of his presentation and now it was time to make his recommendations.

He concluded that the best investments would be mutual funds, which I expected. The task of choosing the right funds would be easy. He admitted that there were thousands of funds to choose from, but NationsBank had done all of the hard work for him and selected ten fund families. This was a wonderful sales tactic, because Johnson was turning a negative—in other words, a limited selection—into a positive. It is natural to think that a wider selection is better, but when customers shop for top-quality merchandise, many times they do so at stores with limited selection. The selection in Johnson's "store" was not only limited, but among the funds offered he had his favorites. He determined which fund to pick by looking at the age of the mutual fund manager. Johnson told me that the average age of a manager was twenty-six, but that he chose managers whose average age was forty-six. "Aren't you better now than you were ten years ago?" he asked. Of course I answered yes, but I am not so sure of the validity of this analogy. I have never seen a study showing that someone at age twenty-six could not manage a portfolio as well as someone at age forty-six. What matters is the perception of truth that Johnson was spinning and his reliance on commonsensical notions that may or may not be true, to help convince me which funds would be best.

Johnson finally recommended several funds. Unlike most of the other investment advisors I saw, he did not recommend any retirement accounts. I thought this was rather odd, because he told me at the end of our conversation that one of his specialties was retirement planning. Perhaps I struck Johnson as a person who wanted to work forever, but I never said that. He did say that I should pay off my credit-card debt and place all of my investments in a NationsBank Money Manager Account, which he said was going to "revolutionize the banking industry." This account is simply an asset management account, not unlike Merrill Lynch's CMA, created in the 1970s, which Johnson admitted he had sold as a broker for Merrill Lynch. After the deduction of $12,000 for my credit-card debt, I had $113,000 to put to work and here is how Johnson wanted to see the money invested:

Retirement Account Investment:
None

Nonretirement Account Investments:
MFS Investors Trust Fund (Class B)
Alliance Premier Fund (Class B)
MFS Emerging Growth (Class B)
Fidelity Advisor Growth (Class B)
Alliance Growth Fund (Class B)

He recommended that I split my money evenly among the five funds, investing $22,600 in each. The MFS Investors Fund, he said, was the very first mutual fund, which must mean that MFS knows what they are doing. I knew that longevity didn't necessarily equate with quality, but I also knew his statement would sound good to a novice investor. I asked Johnson why he had recommended Class B shares over Class A. He told me that Class A shares required a sales charge that would compromise my principal, but Class B would not. The funds, he said, compensated him and I would not have to pay him anything up front if I purchased the B shares. When I checked, I discovered that this was only partly true. There is no up-front load and he is compensated by the companies, but he didn't say that the investor ultimately pays his commission—not the fund company. Class B shares have higher operating expenses and their net return to the customer is generally lower than that of Class A shares. That difference, or the spread, is where the customer pays the salesperson his commission. The commission does not come from the principal; it is taken from the overall return of the fund. The standard commission paid on B shares is 4 percent and Johnson was looking to produce a $4,520 commission. It's true that in this life there is no such thing as a free lunch, but salespeople can easily persuade clients that there might be, because their commission is not fully disclosed in the mutual fund prospectus.

Johnson did admit that the operating expenses on Class B shares were more costly than those on Class A, but he argued that this should not be a problem for a long-term investor, because after a certain time the funds converted their Class B shares to Class A. Still, I asked myself why an investor should have to pay greater expenses for years, eroding his returns, when he doesn't have to. Wouldn't index funds or low-expense no-load funds be better choices? They lower the costs of investing without compromising investment performance. Johnson would not make as much commission on these products, however, so it is understandable why he and other salespeople wouldn't recommend them.

Another plus for the salesperson selling Class B shares is the deferred sales charge. All of the funds Johnson recommended could be transferred to most major firms, but Class B shares penalize investors for years, by making them pay a back-end load if they liquidate their holdings. This penalty could discourage Johnson's customers from switching to new funds in the future, thus providing some assurance to Johnson that the assets would remain at NationsBank. This is a wise move for any salesperson, but a rather risky purchase for someone investing his money with a salesperson he doesn't know.

After Johnson gave me his recommendations, we chatted about a few other things and I asked him about some of the awards that he had displayed on his wall and desk. I saw two Executive Member Awards from Alliance mutual funds for 1996 and 1997, a 1998 award from Federated Companies, the parent company of Fidelity, and NationsBank's honor of Highest in Cross-Referrals in 1996. Awards like these I had seen many times as a broker. They are given to salespeople who sell substantial amounts of product and they note strong sales ability—not investment expertise. Johnson was highlighting his sales success for all to see, but I noticed that the companies who gave him the plaques were some of the same companies who ran the mutual funds that he'd recommended I invest in. When I told him that I was impressed with his "credentials," he politely changed the subject and seemed not to want to call attention to his awards or his past sales success. I suppose he thought that I might conclude after comparing the plaques with his recommendations that he had tailored his advice to fit what he was good at, selling, instead of to my particular investment needs. It was time to go and Johnson had another customer waiting. I thanked him for his time and promised him that I would think about what he had said.

Bank One: Investment consultant Kevin Turner met me at a local Bank One branch. Turner was in his mid-thirties, and after a few minutes of small talk I told him that I was in need of some good investment advice. Perhaps he could tell me the difference between a broker, a financial planner, and a representative like himself? At that point Turner got up and shut the door to his office. When he settled back down in his chair, he began to tell me how he differed from his competitors. First, Turner said, brokers would call me all the time, and earned commissions for continually moving people's money around. He said this was not in my best interest, and trading was often contrary to his style of money management. "What about financial planners?" I asked. He said a good friend of his was a financial planner and he charged his customers hundreds of dollars in fees for investment recommendations. But Turner's design of my portfolio would be free. "Aren't there fee-only financial planners that don't charge an up-front fee?" I asked. He shook his head and said he was not aware of any, but later in this chapter we will see that some financial planners charge a fee for their services, but not for making recommendations. Turner's information about financial planners was incorrect, but if I had not known better, it would have discouraged me from seeking out a financial planner. I described my financial situation, and he said that before he could recommend any investments, he needed to do a financial profile. This service would also be free. I thought it might take hours to do, but once I saw the company's questionnaire, my fears were laid to rest. The investor profile consisted of only five multiple-choice questions that took less than one minute for me to answer. There were a few blank spaces for the customer's current asset allocation, income, and investment objectives. After I answered Turner's questions, he was ready with his recommendations, which he had somehow formulated in a matter of minutes. He said that I should pay off my credit-card debt, which I told him I would do. He then suggested that I leave at least $15,000 in cash for emergencies. The remaining $98,000 Turner recommended I invest only in Bank One proprietary (i.e., firm-owned) products, even though he said he could purchase stocks, bonds, other mutual funds, and so on. This is how Turner wanted to see my money invested:

Retirement Account Investments

The One Investor Annuity

Nonretirement Account Investments

One Group Large Company Growth (Class B)
One Group Large Value (Class B)
One Group Growth Opportunities (Class B)
One Group Government Bond Fund (Class B)

Twenty-five thousand dollars would go into the annuity, and $73,000 would be spread evenly over the four mutual funds. An annuity is a hybrid product that generally consists of mutual funds, but the underlying company that markets it is an insurance company. The One Investor Annuity, he explained, would grow tax-deferred as long as I kept the money in the account. He pointed out that there was a deferred sales charge on the product. If I wanted to liquidate my holdings in the first year, it would cost me a whopping 7 percent. After that time I would be allowed to withdraw up to 10 percent of my principal without a penalty. He glossed over the commission he would be paid on the annuity, so after our meeting, I called Bank One and spoke with a variable annuity coordinator I'll call John. I asked, "If I invested $25,000 in the variable annuity, how much commission would your representative get?" John was taken aback by my question and refused to release that information. He told me that I would not pay an up-front load, and since all of my money started working for me on day one, I should not worry about it. I told him I knew that, but I also wanted to know how much commission I was paying. He said that it was a standard industry practice not to release such information, and that the SEC did not require him to disclose it. No matter how hard I tried to convince him, John was not going to give me the information. He claimed that doing so put him at a competitive disadvantage and that was the end of our call.

Turner's mutual fund recommendations also concerned me. He told me he had picked the B shares because they were "less expensive" than A shares. According to Turner, the customer paid nothing for the B shares up front, but then later he said that the expenses were actually greater on the B shares. This was an interesting paradox. In other words, Class B shares are less "expensive," but their overall expenses are higher than those of Class A shares. It can't be both ways though. A fund can't be less expensive and at the same time have more expenses that drain the investor's returns, but novice investors might be persuaded into thinking this. Turner also said he was compensated from the fund's operating expenses. He then flipped to the Large Company Growth Fund prospectus to show me that the operating expenses were 2 percent. He said that he received a percentage of this figure, which he shared with Bank One. Actually, the standard commission on Class B shares is 4 percent. I called Bank One mutual funds after our meeting and a representative confirmed that the broker "payout" on the funds was indeed 4 percent. During the meeting, however, I pointed out to Turner that his compensation seemed low. He explained that he got additional compensation for signing up new customers. This is why it was in his best interests to treat people right—so that they would recommend him to others. I had to restrain myself from laughing, because on the investments Turner recommended, his commission would have been $2,920 on the mutual funds, plus the commission on the variable annuity, which I will estimate to be 5 percent. The grand total would be around $4,170.

My first thought was that Turner had been less than forthcoming about certain fees, but upon further reflection, I came to a different conclusion. Let's say that Turner had disclosed all of his fees and the commissions to a customer, knowing full well that his competitors would not do the same. The customer would leave thinking that his services were more costly than the bank or brokerage down the street, and probably go elsewhere. Turner works in an industry that allows its fees and commissions to be hidden, with the blessing of its regulators.

If mutual fund companies and salespeople were required to state all of their charges, you might be surprised at what your friendly bank salesperson had to say.

FULL-SERVICE BROKERS

Imagine me, a former full-service broker, walking into two full-service brokerage firms to get advice. Brokers move from firm to firm, so it was very possible that I might run into someone I used to work with. I knew that if anyone recognized me, my cover would be blown, so most of the time I hid behind the pages of open magazines and newspapers as I waited in the lobby. I avoided the risk of meeting a former coworker as the broker and I walked toward his office by looking down at the floor or casting my gaze toward the wall. Fortunately, I was never found out.

Edward Jones: My appointment was at nine A.M. sharp, and Tim Robinson, a financial advisor for Edward Jones, was there to greet me with a warm smile and firm handshake. Robinson and his secretary were the only staff and the atmosphere was far removed from the hustle-bustle, take-no-prisoners atmosphere I had been used to as a broker. I asked Robinson to tell me a little about his company and how it compared with other firms on Wall Street. He said that at Edward Jones, unlike other firms, he had no quotas to meet on products and that the firm did not sell commodities, options, or penny stocks. He said the liability and the risk in selling these products was far too great and that the firm was proud of its conservative approach. He also said they did not sell any proprietary products like mutual funds, which he felt was good policy because such products posed a conflict of interest. He revealed what I already knew: brokers at some firms were given extra incentives to sell their firm's funds, and if the customer wanted to transfer his account, he might have a hard time doing so because the new firm might not accept another firm's proprietary products. I found Robinson's honesty refreshing; he was giving me a clear picture as a customer of some of the inherent conflicts of interest that existed in the brokerage industry.

Next, I asked him what differentiated him from the standard bro-ker, bank salesperson, and financial planner. He said he had much in common with financial planners, but that brokers had a bottom-up approach. In other words, they generally pitched the stock of the day to clients without first considering the clients' overall financial picture. His approach was just the opposite; he first looked at a client's overall financial situation and then made his recommendations. Brokers were also transactional in nature, he said, and in their jobs they had to move money constantly in order to make a living. He, on the other hand, had more of a long-term view on investing. In his view, bank sales-people were limited to the number of products they could offer, and then in a hushed tone he said that it was generally known that low-quality brokers who could not make it at more reputable firms landed at banks. He softened this statement a bit by explaining that this was generally the case, but he was also sure that there were some exceptions to this "rule."

After explaining himself in this matter, Robinson went right into his investment philosophy. According to him, there were basically three "buckets" in which a person could invest money. The first was emergency money, which had a three- to six-month time horizon. The second category, net worth, was money that could be invested for up to thirty years. The last category was retirement money, which could be left untouched for thirty-plus years.

His initial focus was on my retirement. When I told him that I did not have a retirement plan, he suggested that I open up a Roth IRA and a Simplified Employment Plan (SEP). The SEP retirement plan, used by many who are self-employed, allows people to contribute up to 15 percent of their income per year. Contributing to the SEP would give me a tax break and he was adamant about me making multiple contributions for 1998 and 1999. Volatility should be a factor in picking investments, but in Robinson's view this should be a con-cern only in the net-worth account, not the retirement money. Since retirement money was thirty-plus-year money, it did not matter whether stocks went up or down; what mattered was the quality of the investments. Robinson was a big believer in such blue-chip companies as Disney, Home Depot, and Merck. By investing in companies like these, the investor could not go wrong. Robinson calculated that my contributions to the retirement accounts would be in total $18,000. Four thousand dollars would go into the IRA, $2,000 per year, and the rest would be allocated for the SEP plan for 1998 and 1999. He suggested that I pay off my credit-card debt and fund my retirement accounts with large-cap stocks, which left $95,000 to invest. He recommended that I put $50,000 of the nonretirement money in Class-A-share mutual funds and the rest of the money in a number of stocks as follows:

Retirement Accounts Investments

IRA	Microsoft, GE, Intel, Merck
SEP	Wal-Mart

Net Worth or Nonretirement Account Investments

Mutual Funds	Stocks
American Mutual Fund Family	Hartford Life Insurance, Fannie Mae, Gillette
Washington Mutual Fund	Walgreens, Merck, Medtronic, Cisco
American Mutual	Systems, Lucent Technology, Applied
Euro Pacific Fund	Materials, Home Depot

It took Robinson only an hour and a half to come up with his recommendations. I didn't feel that he had done any elaborate research on these companies because all of his stock picks had been chosen by his firm. First, he said that I should invest $3,600 in each of the five companies in the two retirement accounts. Next, he suggested that I spread the $50,000 among the four mutual funds and the remaining $45,000 evenly in the ten stocks listed above.

His advice about saving as much as possible for my retirement was sound, but I didn't think having my retirement invested in only five stocks, two of them in the highly volatile high-tech sector, was such a good idea. When I looked at the stock portfolio in the net-worth portion of the portfolio, I had similar concerns. Remember, Robinson said that he believed that volatility was not really a factor in a retirement account, but it should be a factor in terms of any money that I might need in the near future. If this was the case, then why did he recommend that 47 percent of the portfolio be invested in individual stocks that could be subject to a downturn in the market? Why not invest all the money in mutual funds, which would give a greater diversification and less overall volatility to the portfolio? The answer seems clear from my own experience as a broker. If Robinson had invested all of the money in mutual funds, the prime commission opportunity would have been realized in one day, essentially removing the possibility of generating additional commissions. Generally, whenever a broker designs a portfolio, he wants to leave open the possibility of generating more commission from the account. Stocks offer a practical way to achieve this goal. But how can this be, if Robinson said that his investment philosophy was to buy quality companies for the long term? Well, there is a difference between "buying" companies for the long term and "holding" companies for the long term. When investors buy stock for their long-term prospects, that doesn't mean that they won't panic when they see their stock price begin to tumble. The broker will say, "Gee, if you loved Intel at 60, you're really going to love it at 45," and scenarios like this present additional buying and selling opportunities for the broker that result in a steady stream of commissions for the life of the account.

I asked Robinson why he had chosen the American funds, with an up-front load that would compromise my principal, instead of recommending a no-load fund family. He said that he was well acquainted with the American funds, and that while it was true that the load would reduce my principal, long-term no-load funds are more expensive because their annual expense ratios (the expenses that are extracted from the fund) were higher. Here Robinson, unlike Turner, was accurately describing the cost of a fund, because he included the load and the fund's expenses. Once again I appreciated his honesty. He did say that he had suggested $50,000 for the funds because that amount gave me a commission discount from 5.75 percent to 4.50 percent. Commission discounts like these are called "breakpoints" and they are clearly spelled out in the fund's prospectus, and Robinson was ethically bound to inform customers about them.

After Robinson gave me his advice, I had some questions. The first was, couldn't at least three quality no-load funds with low expense ratios be found out of a possible universe of over seven thousand funds? Wouldn't investing in low-cost index funds save me the commission and put more of my money to work? The answer to both questions is, of course, yes, but once again neither option would have paid Robinson up front as much as he would have earned on the Class A shares of 4.5 percent ($2,250). Robinson told me that he was also paid 1 to 2 percent on stock commissions, so with an average of 1.5% he would have earned an additional $945 in one day. The grand total for his initial hour-and-a-half consultation with me would have been $3,195, which is not bad for a day's work; indeed, it's more than many Americans make in a month.

Robinson's recommendations don't make him a villain by any means, but they do show the high cost of running a business. The overhead of an office means that entrepreneurs like Robinson have to be concerned with top-line revenue in order to meet the expectations for the bottom line. Running an office and paying a secretary cost money, and Robinson, like many other financial advisors, is paid on commissions. Moreover, Robinson told me he had a mortgage, and I saw the pictures of his wife and two children. The pressures of providing for a family can come into play when a financial advisor is faced with choosing between investments. In all, I liked Robinson's presentation because he struck some honest chords in talking about the securities industry. He didn't give me a high-pressure pitch, and even though I told him my phone number, I have not heard from him. He also took the time to try to educate me about the basics of investing before he made his recommendations, which gets high marks from me.

American Express Financial Advisors: I had not planned on visiting a local American Express office, but I changed my mind when they sent me a voucher for a $50 Barnes & Noble gift certificate. All I had to do was have a meeting with an American Express advisor. Since their timing was right, and I am an avid reader, I gladly accepted their invitation. The broker, William Wilson, took my call and we scheduled an appointment for the following day.

Wilson was in his early thirties and had been with American Express for about eight years. No more than fifteen minutes into our conversation, he told me how he was compensated. Instead of letting cost be an issue, Wilson's approach was to meet any cost objections head-on and get them out of the way early so that he could focus on investments. He was compensated in four ways:

1) Through any tool of investing like mutual funds and stocks

2) By internal rankings from American Express

3) By nonmonetary referrals to other clients from his existing clients

4) Through fees from financial planning

I knew from my days as a broker that American Express liked to emphasize the importance of financial planning. American Express representatives try to sell their customers first on creating a financial plan, then they make investment recommendations based on the plan. Wilson said a typical plan costs between $300 and $750. Recommending a financial plan gives the broker a varnish of professionalism and positions him more as a financial consultant than a salesperson. A typical financial plan is a wonderful sales tool that allows the broker to better sell her clients on what the firm has to offer and gives her an opportunity to capture all of the client's assets. Once she knows all of her customer's assets and where those assets are, she can better tailor her pitch to capture them. I wondered if Wilson would hold to his firm's financial planning approach if he thought I might go elsewhere. When he told me it would take a few weeks to create a plan, I told him that because of the delay, I would have to take my business to another firm. Suddenly, Wilson retreated from his position on the necessity of a financial plan. He said we could create one at any time, and he could make some recommendations during our first meeting.

American Express is a reputable firm and their brokers have literally thousands of investments to choose from, but Wilson focused on selling me American Express's proprietary products. After I told him my investment goals and how much money I had, it took him about five minutes to come up with the best recommendations for me. Just like Robinson, he first recommended a Roth IRA and a SEP, but unlike Robinson, he concerned himself only with a 1998 contribution. He recommended that I contribute $2,000 to the IRA and he approximated $10,000 for the SEP account. He also advised me to get rid of my credit-card debt, after which $101,000 would be left over to invest in a nonretirement account. These were Wilson's investment recommendations:

Retirement Accounts Investments

IRA	IDS New Dimension Fund Class A
SEP	IDS New Dimension Fund Class A

Nonretirement Account Investments

IDS Growth Fund A
IDS Blue Chip Advantage Fund
IDS Equity Value Fund

Out of over seven thousand mutual funds Wilson picked the New Dimension Fund for my retirement accounts. This fund is an American Express proprietary fund, or an in-house fund. His recommendations for the rest of my money also included funds in the American Express family. Wilson suggested that I put 27 percent of my money in the first fund, 50 percent in the second, and 23 percent in the Equity Value Fund. I asked him if he'd chosen these funds because they were the "best" funds, and he said no. The reason, he said, was that they all had good long-term track records and he was familiar with them. This was the same pitch I used as a broker when someone asked my why I had chosen my firm's funds. I had to smile because he never mentioned that they were his firm's own funds. He explained the difference between Class A and Class B shares and stated correctly that over time Class A shares would be less expensive. Finally, I asked him what the commission on Class A and Class B shares was. He surprised me by disclosing both without hesitation. This was not my experience with several American Express customer representatives I contacted after our meeting.

I give Wilson high marks for being forthright, but recommending house funds with a one-size-fits-all mind-set is not really "full service." Brokers at some firms are under pressure to sell their own firm's funds because it is more profitable for the firm. When Wilson was faced with the prospect of losing my business, he tried to give me exactly what I wanted, and the easiest way for a broker to make a sale is to give the customer what he wants—which is not necessarily what the customer needs. If I had followed Wilson's advice, I would have paid approximately $5,000 in commissions, account fees, and the ongoing expenses of the funds. If I wanted to transfer my account to another broker, I would have to make sure that the new brokerage firm accepted the mutual funds. If they did not, I would have to sell them. The sale of the funds in this scenario would be a taxable event, which could cost me thousands of dollars, plus any of the new broker's fees and commissions. Getting professional advice can sometimes come at a high price when there is more than meets the eye to investment recommendations.

FINANCIAL PLANNERS

The only guide that I had in choosing a financial planner was the phone book. Since hundreds of financial planners were listed, I adhered to a rigid scientific method in my selection process: while the phone book was open, I closed my eyes, then pointed my index finger in a clockwise motion until I hit the page. In the end, however, the planners I chose were not the first ones that I picked. Some of the initial selections wanted to charge me a fee for designing my portfolio or they said that they would charge me an hourly fee for their services. I declined to meet with three planners who described their pricing structures in this way, but learned always to ask the planner about his fees prior to scheduling an appointment. Ultimately, this "scientific" method worked wonderfully, because the two financial planners I went to see each gave me difference advice.

Luke Miller: I made an appointment to see Miller not knowing what his credentials were or what advice he would give. In the waiting area of his office, I noticed a frayed copy of *Worth* magazine. There was a small handwritten note on the cover of the magazine, which said "see page 105." To my astonishment, *Worth* magazine had named Miller one of the nation's top three hundred financial advisors. My appointment was at eleven A.M., but Miller was fifteen minutes late. He apologized, attributing his tardiness to arrangements he had to make for a new home he was having built.

Playing to Miller's ego, I told him I was impressed that *Worth* magazine had selected him as one of the nation's top financial advisors. I told him this was quite an honor and flattered him with a couple more compliments. He took them well, though each seemed to make him rise slightly higher from his seat. I have heard it said that a person's ego can at times cause his body to levitate and I seemed to be witnessing the phenomenon firsthand. Miller gave me a packet of information about him. He had been listed in the *Who's Who in Finance and Industry* and had been quoted in *Money* magazine, *The New York Times,* and *The Wall Street Journal.* He had a master's degree in theology and the brochure said that he was active in his church as a Bible teacher, deacon, and was even chairman of his church's finance committee. I made my eyes open wide. I told Miller that he was just the man I wanted to manage my money. He smiled, rose still higher in his seat, and then we began to talk about how my money should be managed.

I asked him his view of the difference between a financial planner, broker, and bank salesperson. He distinguished himself from a broker by saying that brokers were primarily concerned with investments, not financial planning. He told me that brokers liked to pick the stock of the day and sell it to their clients. He, on the other hand, favored a more client-oriented approach. Bank salespeople were much like brokers, he continued, in that they were paid on commission, which he considered an inherent conflict of interest. Unlike them, he was not paid a commission for his services, but simply a flat annual fee of 1 to 1¼ percent of my portfolio's value, paid quarterly, and as my assets rose in value, he would reap the rewards as I would. A fee structure put the financial advisor and the investor on the same side of the table and in this way the investor's interests were protected, he said. He also told me he generated millions per year in fees, letting me know his record of success and confirming that others had decided that his fee-based system was the way to go.

Next, we chatted briefly about investing in general. He pointed to the same chart that Johnson at NationsBank had used and expressed his deep and abiding faith in the long-term performance of the stock market. I nodded in agreement, so Miller whipped out a one-sheet on the factors that contributed to portfolio performance. It featured a pie chart showing that 91.5 percent of a portfolio's performance was attributed to asset allocation. Market timing accounted for only 1.8 percent, security selection for 4.6 percent, and other factors made up the remaining 2.1 percent. I felt a pitch for mutual funds coming on, and sure enough, within a matter of moments Miller said that most of his clients were in no-load mutual funds. Once he had determined which funds, out of the thousands, were best for me, my only fee would be the annual one of 1¼ percent. The educational part of our conversation lasted only about fifteen minutes.

I asked him what funds he had in mind. He politely excused himself from the table and moments later returned with a Morningstar report—Morningstar is a company that independently ranks mutual funds—for each of twenty different funds. Miller briefly explained to me why he had chosen these funds out of all the possibilities. He told me that after hours of research he had cherry-picked these as the best opportunity for his clients. "What do you recommend for me?" I asked. He could best answer this after he looked at my investor profile. Unfortunately, he had a lunch appointment in fifteen minutes and would not have the results of the questionnaire by then. My answers would be run through his computer and then analyzed before a sound recommendation could be made. I expressed disappointment, and told him that I wanted to make my decision sooner rather than later. This posed a sticky problem for Miller. I was a potential customer, who wanted to hear his recommendations right away. A quick investment recommendation could be a disservice to me, however, because he had only talked with me for about thirty minutes and really did not know that much about me. Miller resolved this dilemma in a matter of moments. His son would run my questionnaire through the computer and I could have his recommendations immediately. The questionnaire took me all of two minutes to fill out, and although I told Miller that I was a moderate investor, his cursory glance at my answers classified me as an aggressive one. He exited the conference room with the questionnaire in hand, and within a few minutes the "computer" results were in, just as Miller had predicted. Sure enough, I was an aggressive investor and here are the funds that he recommended to me:

Retirement Account Investments

None

Nonretirement Account Investments

Vanguard 500 Index Fund
American Century Income and Growth
Janus Twenty
Janus Enterprise
Janus Worldwide

The total amount invested would be $113,000 and Miller had the percentages for each fund marked in red. The total excluded my credit-card debt, which he recommended I pay off. Seventeen percent of the $113,000 would go into Vanguard 500, 16 percent to American Century Income and Growth, 33 percent to Janus Twenty, 13 percent to Janus Enterprise, and finally 20 percent to Janus Worldwide. Miller left 1 percent in cash for his fee; the other quarter percent would be extracted from my assets in the future. Within a mere forty-five minutes my financial future had been set and the best funds had been chosen with the aid of no doubt one of the most sophisticated computer programs known to man. One of the best financial minds in the country (*Worth* magazine had said so) had seen me; it was time for him to go to lunch.

By now I am sure you know what was missing. Miller overlooked my retirement. I guess it never occurred to him that retirement accounts would be important to my financial welfare. I thought the charade with the computer was pretty funny. It worked just as quickly as a broker who had a stock-of-the-day to pitch. I never got a chance to examine his computer, but my suspicions led me to think that it might have been his son, who may have had a computer science degree, but whose true talent lay in quickly calculating percentages. I told Miller that I thought his fee was low and he responded by saying, "I am glad you think so." But notice that he did not agree with me. Actually, his fee was very high and it boggles my mind that someone would pay a financial advisor to choose no-load funds when he can do it himself for free. A 1 percent fee on no-load funds does the investor a tremendous disservice, because over time that little 1 percent fee will erode the investor's return. Advisors who slap a 1 percent fee on a portfolio are thinking more of themselves than of their clients. Not only is their management style harmful to the portfolio's short-term returns, but the fee may also cause the investor to say a long good-bye to healthy long-term results. For example, if the fund is held for twenty years, the 1 percent fee will decrease the value of the portfolio by 17 percent.[2] Let's say that a fund returns 10 percent and the fee is 1 percent. That 1 percent fee should be thought of as 10 percent of the return. In other words, the fee diminishes the annual return by 10 percent, thus making Miller's fee-based pricing system more like buying at Tiffany's than at Wal-Mart.

As you know by now, the quest for money can make financial advisors overlook their clients' best interests. Miller was interested in making a sale more than he was looking out for my well-being. His approach was counter to the framed code of professional ethics displayed in his lobby, which said, "Endeavor as professionals to place the public interest above their own."

Matthew Myers: The first thing I noticed in Myers's office was the chart that both Miller and Johnson had displayed in their offices. By now it was becoming an old friend. As I waited in the vestibule, I looked around to see if I could find out any more information about Myers. On the wall were plaques from Alliance and MFS mutual funds.

Myers had been deemed an Alliance Elite Advisor in 1997, and perhaps at the awards ceremony he was given the regal-looking gold-plated Alliance paperweight that rested securely on the vestibule table. A glass-encased award from MFS was also mounted on the wall, thanking Myers for his support. It wasn't hard to figure out what family of mutual funds this financial planner would try to sell me.

Myers's company brochure also caught my eye. It described his credentials, adding in bold: "Does not charge fees—the Firm is compensated by the Investment Companies." I wondered what kind of investment would compensate Myers that the customer did not have to pay for? The only possible answer was Class-B-share mutual funds, but as we know, in this case the customer winds up paying the salesperson's fees in the form of a reduced return. Was it true that Myers did not charge fees? That his firm was compensated by the investment companies? Once again the answer was yes, but it is untrue to declare that the investor doesn't pay anything. I didn't want to prejudge Myers, so for the time being I cast aside any doubts that he was something less than an honest financial advisor.

After I told Myers a few facts about myself, he talked to me about investment basics. He explained the different types of financial advisors in much the same way as the other financial advisors had done, then we moved on to the subject of investments. He first said that I needed to address my retirement, and then he briefly discussed the tax implications of some mainstream retirement accounts like a SEP, a money purchase plan, and an IRA. A SEP plan and money purchase plan would both reduce my tax burden for 1998 and 1999, and the combination of the two would permit me to put the maximum amount toward my retirement. A Roth IRA and a variable annuity would also help me save for my golden years. Most of these accounts would be long-term money that I could not take out without a penalty until I was fifty-nine and a half. The next category he called tax-favored investing, and the principal investment for this midterm growth category was mutual funds. The last category would be investments for liquidity, and he suggested that I have some cash set aside for emergencies, which I told him I already had.

How much money should go into each category? He felt that I

should pay off my credit cards with the cash I already had in the bank. He suggested that I make the maximum contributions to my retirement accounts for 1998 and 1999, approximately $9,750 times two for the SEP account, $6,500 times two for the money purchase plan, and $2,000 times two for the Roth IRA, making a grand total of $36,500 for the two years in question. Sixty-one thousand five hundred dollars would be invested in mutual funds and $58,000 would go into a variable annuity, leaving $5,500 in my cash account. This is how Myers wanted to see my money invested:

Retirement Account Investments

SEP	MFS Investors' Growth Fund (Class B)
	MFS Large Cap Fund, MFS New Discovery (Class B)
Money Purchase Plan	Putnam Growth Opportunity (Class B)
	Putnam Investors, Putnam Voyager (Class B)
Roth IRA	Alliance Premiere Growth (Class B)
	Alliance Growth Fund (Class B)
	Alliance Technology Fund (Class B)
Variable Annuity	

Nonretirement Account Investments

Alliance Premier Growth (Class C)
Alliance Growth (Class C)
Alliance Technology (Class C)
Alliance Quasar Fund (Class C)

My original suspicions were confirmed when I noticed that his recommendations corresponded to the sales awards in the lobby. Myers was telling customers that when they purchased Class B shares, the companies paid him his fee and that it was a better deal for them because all of their money went to work on day one. He did admit that the expenses on Class B shares were greater than those on Class A shares. Since this was the case, I asked him if it wouldn't be smarter to buy Class A shares for the retirement accounts. In other words, wouldn't it be cheaper for me over time if I bought Class A shares? By now you know the answer was yes, and lowering the costs of the funds would naturally improve the investor's portfolio performance, but if Myers had agreed with me then he would have had to withdraw from his position that the companies compensated him. He would have had to convince me that buying the Class A shares was actually less expensive to me in the long run, but instead he held firm to his recommendation. He said that he had seen a number of studies, none of which gave a conclusive answer to my question.

For the nonretirement account, he recommended Class C shares and the variable annuity. When I asked him why he chose C shares, he said that the holding period was only a year and if I decided to liquidate my holdings, I would be charged only a 1 percent fee. This would give me the flexibility to sell the funds at any time. He told me that the funds had an annual 1 percent fee as long as I held them. Though all of this is true, he neglected to point out how the fee would erode my return. Selling C shares plays into the interests of the salesperson because they provide a lifelong income stream, which makes the salesperson less reliant on commissions and the stock market in general. Irrespective of market conditions, the financial advisor who sells Class C shares is going to get his fee, and this is why many so-called financial advisors like them. Surprisingly, he did disclose his commission on the annuity, 5¼ percent. I have to place a gold star by his name for doing so. If I had invested my money as he recommended, my total commission bill would have been $4,505. This is of course not counting the fund's other expenses and the persistent 1 percent fee that I would have to pay on the C shares. Most of the assets would have been locked in for years because they had hefty back-end loads or surrender charges, giving me few options if I were not happy with Myers in the future.

THE LESSONS I LEARNED

My search for a financial advisor had come to an end. I learned a few lessons along the way that I want to share with you. First, can you see why mutual funds have become such popular products? It's because the commission that salespeople receive for selling them is usually twice what they earn on a stock transaction. Mutual funds are independently managed, so they free up the time of financial advisors to search for new money. Once they find new dollars to invest, they are inclined to invest that money in mutual funds that will pay them a good commission. Less costly alternatives are usually never discussed with the client, because this is not profitable for the financial advisor. As a result, few investors get the best advice.

My second lesson was that many of the salespeople use deceptive sales practices. I visited only six advisors, but multiply my visits by hundreds of thousands of advisors, and it is easy to understand why industry regulators cannot be in all places at all times. Every investor must learn how to keep from being taken advantage of, but unless she knows the basics of investing, this goal presently seems unreachable. Some of the salespeople I visited did comment on the fact that it was unusual for investors like me to take notes, and I strongly recommend that you do so the next time you pay a financial advisor a visit. Having notes on what was said during your meeting is always a good idea, and will persuade some advisors to be more careful about what they say to you.

There are few absolutes when it comes to investing, which is, finally, more of an art than a science. As we have seen, a financial advisor's interests will always play a part in his recommendations. This inherent conflict of interest means that a financial advisor's recommendations are rarely the best that money can buy. They are often the most expensive to purchase and at times can actually be detrimental to your financial well-being. If you learn to manage your money, only one set of interests—your own—will guide you in your investment decisions. Investing does not require any specialized, hard-to-learn knowledge. If the people I visited can manage other people's money, believe me, you can manage your own. There is no one better qualified than you to manage your own money and it is my fondest wish that you take steps to do so as soon as possible.

DO YOUR HOMEWORK WHEN SHOPPING
FOR AN ADVISOR

• Ask your advisor about his professional background, then verify this information with the NASD and state securities regulators. You can get contact information for state regulators at this Web site: http://www.nasaa.org/regulator/us/Default.htm. Don't consider doing business with an advisor until you get to know him and the way he does business.

• Ask your advisor how much money and how many accounts she manages. Next, ask her what she plans to do to make your account a priority.

• Your initial meeting with your advisor should always be held at his office. Let him give you an office tour and have him introduce you to the management. Keep all business cards for later reference.

• Tap into all of your advisor's resources that will help you to manage your own money in the future. Feel free to selectively use a full-service firm's research if you have an account with the firm, but execute your stock trades elsewhere.

CHAPTER 6

DISCOUNT BROKERS AND DAY TRADERS: DIRTY DEEDS DONE OFTEN AND CHEAP

Oh, the wonders of technology. When I take a hard look at discount brokers and day-trading firms, I am convinced that all innovation is not good, and all change is not progress. The doyens of the discount brokerage industry love technology, because according to them, technology empowers the average investor and allows him to manage his own money. They laud advances like the Internet, which gives the individual investor access to volumes of information, timely research, and the ability to buy and sell securities in the blink of an eye. Technology, they say, frees the investor from the clutches of full-service brokers, and allows the individual investor to chart his own financial destiny at a price that is affordable to all. Technology is touted as the great benefactor, but I am not convinced that it serves individual investors as well as some in the discount brokerage industry would have us believe.

When all is said and done, it is training and education, not technology, that empowers investors. Training is everything in making a savvy investor. Who would ever think that a car creates a good driver, or a plane produces a quality pilot, or the latest model of boat gives rise to a sea captain? No one would ever hope to pilot a space shuttle without going through the rigors of NASA's training, yet many investors blast off into investment outer space with little or no investment education or financial knowledge. Technology does not in itself make one smarter or more capable. What troubles me is that discount firms know this, but they still perpetuate that reasoning.

The discount brokerage industry spends millions of dollars on advertising, but hardly anything on investor education. They spend vast sums to invite investors to do business with them, knowing full well that most investors do not have the necessary training to invest wisely on their own. This is like hospitals charging patients to diagnose themselves when they know their patients do not have the means to do so. Discount brokers have a responsibility to educate their customers about investing, but to date not one of them has a full-fledged investor education program.

Imagine an Internet-based, year-round investor education program, in which investors could receive a certificate of accomplishment after completing a course of study. The offerings could include an online, multimedia investment library that addressed the needs of individual investors. Firms could sponsor a series of nationwide seminars and workshops to teach people about financial planning and investing. Each firm could promote its efforts in the press, getting enough positive PR to outweigh the costs. Altruistic motives aside, such a program would not only benefit investors, it would help discount firms garner additional customers. I subscribe to the notion that he who educates investors wins their confidence, and ultimately their business. This idea falls on deaf ears at discount firms, who only believe in advertising.

On a brighter note, National Discount Brokers has taken some steps to better inform their customers. NDB, along with *Money* magazine, formed NDB University, which customers and noncustomers alike can access via NDB's Web site. I decided to check it out.

The Money 101 section was composed of twenty-four lessons filled mainly with bulleted facts rather than in-depth discussions on investing. In the introduction, users are assured that "the essentials of each lesson can be absorbed in just 10 minutes." While I had hoped for a better effort, some of the information I found was very helpful, especially to first-time investors. For example, under the top-ten things to know about stocks, the best advice was saved for last:

> *10) It's smarter to buy and hold good stocks than to engage in rapid-fire trading.* Retail investors pay commissions and fees that total an average of 6 percent for one round trip trade—that is, to buy and sell the same shares of the stock. So if you trade frequently for small gains, the costs of those trades can erode—or even erase—your profit on the transactions.

The section under investment basics also had some helpful advice. Once again, the best advice was saved for the end:

> *10) Index mutual funds often outperform actively managed funds.* In an index fund, the manager sets up his portfolio to mirror a market index—such as Standard & Poor's 500 stocks—rather than actively picking which stocks to purchase. And by the strange math of mutual funds, average is often enough to beat the majority of competitors among actively managed funds. One reason: Few actively managed funds can consistently outperform the market by enough to cover the costs of their generally higher trading fees.

These bulleted factoids may not greatly benefit most investors, but at least NDB has done something in the way of investor education.

Today, an estimated 8 million people trade on-line. Roughly one hundred forty discount firms compete for their business. Some firms spend millions of dollars trying to increase their market share. For example, E*Trade, the third largest discount firm, planned on spending $150 million in a twelve-to-eighteen-month time period to promote its site.[1] Charles Schwab is not far behind with a 1998 budget of $100 million, and Ameritrade, during its first fiscal quarter in 1998, spent $25 million.[2] The money is spent on a variety of media including TV, radio, and of course the Internet. Most of the ads feature a low price like $8, but some are a little more creative, like the banner ad, displayed on Web pages, from the on-line broker Datek. This ad featured a woman in a classic horror-film setting, her face filled with terror. Its caption read, "Afraid of the unknown? Dispel your fears with knowledge. Datek on-line offers all you need to make informed investments." When I clicked on the banner ad, I was taken to Datek's Web site and greeted with this message: "Trade Now $9.99 per on-line trade." This was followed by, "You're here. You're ready. So place your trade." And away we go, I thought, but what about all the information and education that investors need? It was nowhere to be found.

Currently, around 35 percent of retail stock trades are executed on-line, a figure that is expected to grow exponentially in the future. A study by Forrester Research predicts that by the year 2002, on-line accounts will total more than 14 million and hold nearly $700 billion in assets. The problems associated with a lack of investor education are like bombs ready to explode, possibly resulting in a rush of investor lawsuits. Look at the case of Lael Desmond, a twenty-seven-year-old graduate student who says he lost $40,000 by trading primarily Internet stocks via Ameritrade. Michael Anderson, a former toilet-paper salesperson for Procter & Gamble and now president of Ameritrade, said it was Desmond's own fault. He claimed that periodically he hears, "Hey, you should have stopped me from selling myself into a hole." His response? "What do you mean, we should have stopped you? It was a self-managed account."[3] Desmond countered by saying that Ameritrade did not treat him fairly by allowing him as a novice investor to trade wide-swinging Internet stocks in a margin account. He says that he thought a margin loan "was much like a bank loan . . . I never dreamt I had the possibility of losing all of my money."[4] Lael Desmond's $40,000 loss could only be blamed on himself if he had been properly educated, but since the discount industry does not sponsor any investor education programs, the industry must bear some responsibility. Desmond lost his college tuition money; with another investor, maybe it will be her life savings.

It seems clear that investors with self-managed accounts may not have the skills to manage their own money, and brokerage firms do not test their customers' abilities prior to opening an account. Only when firms begin to educate their customers will sound investing principles take the place of fast trading and misunderstandings over basic terms like margin accounts. In the meantime, investors should insist that brokerage firms provide them with more education programs.

HOW GOOD IS THE ON-LINE INVESTOR?

Two kinds of limitations confront the on-line investor today. The first limitation, as we've seen, is technology. The second has to do with the individual investor's ability to manage her own money. Some leaders in the discount industry, like E*Trade's CEO, Christos Cotsakos, believe that it is far wiser for investors to have faith in technology than in institutions. The proponents of technology claim that institutions are made up of people who can be fallible and discriminatory, while technology does not discriminate. "Truth in institutions is fading," Cotsakos explains, "whether it's political, religious, governmental, financial. When the market's moving really fast, technology is non-discriminatory. It's there for you."[5] That doesn't mean that it works all the time, however. A number of the on-line brokers, including E*Trade, periodically suffer outages at critical moments that may cause their customers substantial losses. For example, Waterhouse Securities' system shut down for nearly two hours during a heavy trading day; the company blamed the problem on a failed telecommunications device. Ameritrade attributed its system problems to software upgrades that it was installing. Charles Schwab, the largest on-line broker, is not immune to problems either. During a heavy trading period on Internet stocks, the firm halted trading of the securities via their Web site and instructed customers to make orders via phone instead. Failures like these have caused some of the on-line brokers to be targets of lawsuits by angry investors who could not trade in their accounts due to technical glitches or heavy trading volume. These mishaps show that on-line investors face risks posed by the very technology that they are supposed to have faith in. Because of the fallibility inherent in high technology, the systems are a double-edged sword, a situation I fear will only increase as more investors trade on-line. A mishap could happen at any moment, at any firm, leaving investors with losses due not to their trading decisions, but to faulty technology.

Technical limitations aside, discount firms need to address service issues. My own experience with E*Trade's customer service department was a learning opportunity. Calling with a question about the company's customer service agreement, I first heard the recorded message, "Some confirmations have been delayed this morning due to an issue with one of our vendors. Please be assured that your orders will be executed as appropriate." Next, I heard a message stating the special operating hours for the Thanksgiving holiday, which struck me as kind of odd because I was making my call on the evening of December 1. Finally, after two long and frustrating hours of waiting on the phone, I got a customer service representative to answer my inquiry. If I had had a question during market hours that concerned an actively traded stock, two hours might have cost me dearly.

Customer service representatives receive many questions about using the technology. Dennis Marino, the chairman, president, and chief executive officer of National Discount Brokers, said, "We do get a large number of calls from novices who are trying to feel their way along who don't often take the time to walk themselves through the FAQs."[6] Alex Goor, an executive of Datek Online, had similar thoughts: "Most of the questions we get are Internet related—problems with logins and passwords, error messages that pop up when the wrong button is pushed, that sort of thing."[7] Customers who don't know how to use the technology might wait for a lifetime.

Aside from these technical concerns, how do on-line investors fare overall in terms of making money? A couple of university professors have conducted research in this area. Terrance Odean, a finance professor at the University of California, Davis, called on discount firms asking them to share with him their trading records. Only one firm agreed. Odean examined the performance of sixty thousand households that traded with this discount broker over a six-year period, ending December 1996. He found that those investors who traded the most earned the least. Twenty percent of the households that traded the most earned an annualized geometric mean net return of 10 percent a year, compared with market index earnings of 17.1 percent during the same period. It is easy to conclude that these investors might have made a lot more money with less risk if they had bought an index fund. Odean concluded that trading is hazardous to your wealth! This is not an "ivory tower observation," because even the top people at discount firms concur with Odean's findings. Joe Ricketts, an executive for Ameritrade, says, "Trading often and heavy is not something that makes you a lot of money. That's contrary to my own interests, but it's the truth."[8]

I asked Odean to explain why investors traded so much. He attributed much of the trading to investor overconfidence in their own abilities. "People believe that they have more ability than they really do." In his research, he used psychological studies showing that men are more overconfident than women. His own work supported the studies, showing that men traded 45 percent more than women and earned 1.4 percent less than women. The difference was more pronounced in single men and women; single men traded 67 percent more than single women, but earned 2.3 percent less on their trades. Trading presents a kind of catch-22 for investors, he explained, because the more they paid out in trading costs, the more they had to trade to make money, but the more they traded, statistically speaking, the more money they stood to lose.

Odean also thought people traded because of something he called the "disposition effect." This interesting phenomenon prompts many investors to hang on to their losers and to sell their winners. Most people do not like to admit a mistake, so they don't sell their stocks that decrease in value. "People take credit for their successes," he said, "and blame their failures on outside circumstances. This is especially true in a bull market. People tend to say that it was me instead of the market; then they quit their jobs and become day traders."

Speaking with Odean, I got the impression he thought there was little difference between on-line trading and gambling. Discount firms were nothing more than cyber casinos where people could gamble away their futures. When I asked him about this, he said, "Most people, when they go to Vegas, realize that they are going to come home with less money than they brought. They anticipate that they will have some fun and the trip and money lost will be worth it. People going to Vegas have realistic expectations. I don't think that most active traders think this way. People who trade don't realize that they will lose money and I don't think that most traders say that they really get a kick out of looking at the screen all day." Odean's message to the average investor is: Invest in index mutual funds, but if you are going to trade stocks, do it because you enjoy it, not because it's likely to make you wealthier.

I also spoke with Steven Thorley, a finance professor at Brigham Young University's Marriott School of Management, in Provo, Utah, who has also done research on on-line trading. When I asked him whether he believed Internet technology empowered the average investor, he replied, "It is a misconception that most investors could beat the market and it is a misconception that a shift of power had gone to on-line traders by virtue of the technology." Even though the average investor can trade at will, he is pitted against professional traders with far more experience and a broader knowledge of financial markets. Making the technology readily available to investors so they can instantaneously trade tends to make them overconfident, and an overconfident investor, according to Thorley, is his own worst enemy. "If you are overconfident, then the best-case scenario is that you are making your broker wealthy. The worst-case scenario is that you are making your broker wealthy and picking the wrong stocks." He believes that most people would be better off being passive investors (those who do not actually trade securities), instead of hiring a professional advisor. As more investors become better educated, he believes they will turn more to long-term investing instead of active trading. What's the best investment for the average investor? Thorley agreed with Odean: index funds. They are not alone. Believe it or not, Charles Schwab himself is also a big believer in index funds. In his *Guide to Financial Independence*, Schwab writes, "For what it's worth, when it comes to index funds I put my money where my mouth is. Most of the mutual funds investments I have are index funds, approximately 75 percent."[9]

DOLLARS AND SENSE

When I watch TV ads for discount firms, I often wonder, How low can you go? Some firms will execute a trade for $25, some for $5, and there are some who will even allow certain trades for free. Discount firms make the case in 30 or 60 seconds as to why you should do business with them. The main reason boils down to price or the cost of doing business. The backdrop of these ads is that since it's cheaper to trade stocks with a discount broker, it is better for the investor, or price makes right. But this is nonsense! The lure of the price point is way overdone and most investors who are unschooled in investing ask, "Well, I'm on-line and can get a 50 percent discount—now what?"

When it comes to those advertised discounts, all is not as it appears. Most discount firms could not afford to stay in business if they had to subsist on $8 commissions. The other, more lucrative ways to make money are not visible to the customer's eye. Discount brokers enjoy something called "payment for order flow." This is how it works: Let's say that discount firm A has a customer who wants to buy five hundred shares of Intel. In order to fill the customer's order, the brokerage firm has to send the request to a "market maker" for the stock— in other words, a firm that has shares of the stock. For most stocks, especially those that are widely traded, there are a number of market makers to choose from. How does a broker at discount firm A go about choosing his market maker? He's developed a business relationship with one or more of the market markers, and the market maker pays the broker a part of the spread for sending the customer's order his way. The spread is the difference between the bid (the price the stock can be sold for) and the ask (the price at which the stock can be purchased). For example, if Dell is trading at $93\frac{1}{8}$ by $93\frac{3}{8}$, the market maker would pay the brokerage firm a portion of the spread to send the order his way. This charge is added onto the price, so many times the customer may not get the best price.

Most investors don't appreciate the importance of payment for order flow because they are not aware of the charge or they shrug it off because of the relatively small amount per share. The same mistake occurs when a person thinks that one cigarette a day isn't going to kill him, but multiplied by 365 days a year for twenty years, the cigarettes may have the cumulative effect of giving the person lung cancer. The same is true for these charges. One trade is hardly noticeable, but for investors who actively trade stocks, payment for order flow is a cost that adds up.

* * *

The discount brokerage industry values payment for order flow greatly, and it has been estimated to account for a whopping 20 percent of some firms' revenue.[10] All of the customer service agreements from the discount firms I looked at mentioned that they received this kind of compensation. Charles Schwab's language was the clearest on the subject: "This remuneration, known as 'payment for order flow,' is a common and widespread industry practice, whereby monetary or non-monetary remuneration is received by a brokerage firm in return for routing aggregate order flow for execution to a particular specialist, exchange, market or dealer."

In order to calculate the real costs of doing business, customers of discount firms need to know not only the firm's commission costs, but also how much the market maker pays the firm to fill orders. Firms don't necessarily hide the costs from their customers, but they do not take the initiative to disclose it to them. If you want to find out what your payment for order flow charges are for any particular transaction, simply put your request in writing to the firm. Firms who receive such requests are required by the SEC to divulge these costs, and I am sure that they would be happy to do so.

On-line investors also need to be aware of the comparative costs of doing business on-line as opposed to doing business through a full-service firm. When investors compare $8 a trade to $85 a trade, the difference seems clear. In reality, it's not that simple, as Professor Odean explained to me. Most investors have their eye on the commission, but few are concerned with the costs associated with the difference in the spread. He gave me an example to explain what he meant. Let's say that customer A invests $13,000 at a discount firm and the commission is $8 for the buy and the sell of the stock. Customer B, who uses a full-service broker, pays $85 for the same trade. Customer A thinks that he has definitely gotten the better deal because he thinks his total costs are $16, while customer B is paying $170. Both investors have missed the costs associated with the spread. In his research, Odean found that the average spread was 1 percent, so if customer A and customer B bought the stock and turned right around and sold it, each would have paid $130 plus their respective commissions. Remember, in most stock trades, the customer is paying the brokerage firm, but he is also paying the market maker via the spread.

In addition to these practices, discount firms make money on margin interest. When customers borrow money against their securities, they have to pay interest on the money they borrow. There is a spread in what brokerage firms charge customers to borrow money and what the firms are charged by banks. "We have a four-to-five-point spread," says Joe Ricketts of Ameritrade, "and that's really where we make our money."[11] Ameritrade is not alone, because margin interest is a huge revenue source for discount firms. When an investor begins to calculate the costs that he knows about, and adds them to the ones that he doesn't know about, the difference between full-service and discount brokers narrows. Now that the costs of doing business at discount firms is clearer, I am sure that you can see why discount firms need to do a better job in disclosing all of their costs and fees.

MY SHORT LIFE AS A DAY TRADER

I don't think anyone grows up wanting to become a day trader, and after being one for a day, I can see why. Day traders look for fractional differences in stock prices and trade in and out of stocks all day looking for quick profits. Unlike investors, most day traders sell out of their stock positions every day and begin the following day looking for bargains and stocks that move in price. The phrase "buy and hold" is sacrilege to a day trader, and the word "investor" is held in contempt. If you are going to be a day trader, you have to toss out some time-tested notions about investing, like a person's inability to time the market and make money. Certain words and terms, like "long term" and "low risk," must also be removed from your lexicon, but terms like "master of the universe" must be added. I wanted to see what it would be like to be a day trader myself, so I visited a local All-Tech Investment Group office. All-Tech is the largest day-trading company, and as of this writing, they have twenty-seven offices around the country.

I was introduced to one of the owners of the local office, whom I will call Jim Baker. Baker looked like he was in his early thirties and he explained to me what All-Tech had to offer. On the computer terminal in the vestibule, he showed me the software's basics and the importance of level-two quotes. When you get a stock quote from your broker or on-line, you typically get a level-one quote or the best offer and best bid, but knowing what the level-two quotes are can be very revealing. Level-two quotes show the bids and offers from a number of different market makers, and give the user a lot more information about how the stock is trading than a level-one quote allows. The software also shows in real time how many shares are traded and whether they are buy or sell orders. You may glean from the size of the orders whether institutions or retail customers are buying the stock. Orders in the hundreds of shares generally mean the stock is being bought by individual investors, while stocks that trade in thousands of shares are more than likely being purchased by larger, institutional players. The quotes and share sizes are all color-coded, which makes it easier for the user to appraise the market conditions and figure out how the stock might trade in the short term. There were other bells and whistles as well, like intra- and inter-day chartings of different stocks, and the software allows the user to keep tabs on at least four stocks at a time. Baker had to go back to the main trading area for a while, giving me a chance to talk with some of the traders. I first talked with a man in his late thirties, whom I will call Ted. Ted was signing up to manage his own money, and I asked him why he'd made the move. He said he'd worked with a full-service broker for a number of years and was tired of the lack of service. "I didn't go to four years of college and study finance to be treated like that," he said. A woman in her late forties or early fifties named Carla said that for her, trading was a full-time job. She was trading with her retirement money. She thought that All-Tech's training course had been very helpful, and that it had taught her "how the brokerage firms screw you." All-Tech provided two such training courses. One was a seven-day boot camp for $3,000, and the other was a more comprehensive program of four to six weeks with a price tag of $5,000. The courses were not mandatory for trading, but traders who signed up for the longer program were reimbursed the tuition fee over time with a $2.50 reduction on their buy and sell orders (the standard commission being $25 per trade), until the full $5,000 had been reached. An investor would have to execute one thousand buy orders and one thousand sell orders and pay All-Tech $45,000 in commission before he could ever recoup the $5,000 he invested in the training program. When I mentioned the $45,000 price tag to a representative at All-Tech's corporate headquarters, he said that it "should be the least of my worries" and that I should be more concerned with the money I would make while day-trading. With Odean's study in mind, it is easy to see why many people who paid both the commission and the training fee would, in the end, have nothing to show for their efforts, which makes day trading an expensive endeavor.

When Baker returned to the vestibule, he asked if I had any more questions. He offered to let me paper-trade, or trade without real money, the following day, so that I could get a better feel for what day trading was all about. I arrived the next day just after the opening bell to try my luck.

Baker directed me toward one of the computer terminals, and after a few instructions said I was on my own. I was in a room with about twenty-five other traders, only two of them women. CNBC played on two television sets and it seemed that I was the only one looking at the TV instead of being glued to my monitor. The atmosphere was quiet and there was a sense of tension in the air as the market began to slide. This was not a place to crack a joke to brighten the mood, and unlike Vegas, no one really seemed to be having any fun. I tried to make myself believe that I was trading for real and my first move was to get quotes on a few stocks that I was interested in trading: Microsoft, Amazon.com, and Disney. The machine immediately displayed all of these quotes, the number of trades, and more. I quickly succumbed to a mild case of attention deficit disorder due to the information overload that appeared on my screen. The display was video-gamelike and reminded me of a slot machine, because more money seemed to go in than came out. I bought Microsoft first, picking up a thousand shares at 124⅜. I now had over $124,000 of my money invested in the market and about a half hour later I sold my shares at 124⅞, locking in a $500 profit. This was like taking candy from a baby. On my first day, within a half hour, I had proven myself an expert and the image of myself on the cover of *Forbes* magazine momentarily flashed through my mind.

Most day traders would have advised me to stop while I was ahead, but since I was paper-trading I was deaf to such advice. Some of the people I spoke with said that making $200 or $500 was a good day and that I should be happy with this sum. I had a fortune to make, however, so I prepared my next trade. Amazon was the stock, and I bought a thousand shares at 200$\frac{3}{16}$. The stock traded widely and I got a little nervous, so I decided to lock in a profit, albeit small, at the first opportunity. I sold the stock at 200$\frac{3}{4}$ and made $562. There I was with zero experience, and within less than two hours I had made $1,062. Minus the commission of $100, I was up $962 for the day.

I was ready for more. I knew the gods were with me as I pressed the keys on the terminal. Still, after looking at the screen for a few hours, my mind started to become numb. I found myself thinking about my winnings and gazing at the TV. Still, I decided to make one final trade. If the high-tech and Internet stocks hadn't failed me, then certainly Disney would be my friend as well. I was full of confidence and quickly bought a thousand shares of the stock at 31$\frac{7}{8}$. I looked at the bids from all of the market makers, and it seemed that the tide rapidly changed to a downward spiral just moments from the time that I had bought the stock. None of the bids was greater than what I had paid. I got nervous and sold Disney at a loss. My sudden winning streak had come to an abrupt end when I sold Disney at 30$\frac{5}{8}$, giving me a loss of $1,300 including commission. Now, instead of bragging about my winnings, I could only admit I'd lost $338. The vision of my face on the cover of *Forbes* quickly faded.

My short-lived career as a day trader was a learning experience. I risked $200,000 at one point to make several hundred dollars. In retrospect, this seems like sheer lunacy. I applaud All-Tech for offering a training course, but what many people may find out is that after spending the $3,000 to $5,000 to take the course, day trading still might not be for them. I am not sure whether it was better to spend the money on the training or risk losing it to the market. Furthermore, no short training course can possibly prepare someone to trade against the professionals. After a couple of successful sales, even I became over-confident in my abilities when actually it had been lady luck that was responsible. Even with the best technology around, I didn't feel like I had one up on such professional traders as Merrill Lynch, Salomon Smith Barney, and Goldman Sachs. I also didn't feel like I was really buying Microsoft or Disney. MSFT and DIS, the ticker symbols for these companies, seemed to be merely "things" on the screen. Whether it was Disney or a distributor of mousetraps, the company itself didn't seem to matter to day traders. What mattered was whether the stock traded to their satisfaction. However, my experience was positive over-all even though I lost money. I left knowing something new: day trading was not for me.

GET THE MOST FROM ON-LINE TRADING

• Remember, the buy, sell, and cancel orders you enter are nothing more than glorified E-mails, and like all E-mail they take time to be answered. Your orders take time to fill, and during that time the stock can either decrease or increase in value.

• Many popular financial Web sites like Yahoo Finance and Raging Bull.com have message boards where anyone can post a message about stocks and the market. Consider message boards as mere entertainment, not as credible sources of information.

• Never let price alone dictate which on-line broker you choose. Investigate what the on-line broker has to offer and understand how to execute trades before you log on.

• Periodically, magazines and independent third parties will rank on-line brokers. Use these rankings as a guide, not as gospel. The so-called number-one broker may not be the number one for you.

• Before you spend money on a day-trading course, paper-trade for a few hours to see how you like it. Read a couple of books on the subject and trade only with money that you can afford to lose.

CHAPTER 7

MUTUAL FUND MAYHEM:
HIDDEN TRUTHS AND HIDDEN FEES

The American investing public has had a long-term love affair with mutual funds. Currently, over 66 million Americans in 37.4 million households put over two-thirds of their investment assets into these funds. That's over $5.6 trillion invested. Investors can be found along the full range of the socioeconomic spectrum.[1] Mutual fund companies have steered away from the one-size-fits-all credo and gravitated instead to custom-designed portfolios. There are domestic and international equity funds, and sector funds that invest in a particular industry like high tech or health care. A few firms offer "socially responsible" funds and invest only in companies they believe have a good conscience or solid values. There are bond funds, short-term bond funds, municipal bond funds, and international bond funds. For those who adhere to the age-old principal of the Golden Mean, balanced funds are combinations of stocks, bonds, and cash, and if this isn't enough, some funds allow investors to place their money in mutual funds that invest in other funds. Since its creation in 1924, the mutual fund has adhered to the heavenly command to be fruitful and multiply, and this goal has been easy to reach, especially given all the fees that mutual fund companies charge.

ALL THOSE FEES

Mutual fund fees are not generally discussed at the family dinner table. I can't recall my parents ever complaining about loads or having a heated discussion about the fees they were paying that their mutual funds were charging. On the other hand, the slightest increase in the price of gasoline, bakery goods, or milk often made headlines at the dinner table, and any local store sale was a newsworthy event. Whenever a local merchant inflated his prices, the change was instantly noticed by all. Families in the neighborhood mobilized to shop elsewhere, changed brands, or complained. These small-town heroics held local retailers in check and gave working people a voice that merchants listened to.

But mutual fund companies are too large to be held in check by individual investors, and many companies take advantage of this to exploit their shareholders. Most investors don't complain more about fees because they don't realize the impact that fees have on their returns. It's hard for people to complain when the fees, written in fine print, seem so small to the untrained eye. Most of the fees fall into the following categories:

a) Loads: Up-front and contingent deferred sales charges.

b) 12B-1: Pays for distribution and marketing costs.

c) Redemption Fee: Charged when shares are withdrawn from the fund. Money goes back into the fund, not to the mutual fund company.

d) Service Fee: Compensates brokers and financial planners for customer inquiries about the fund.

e) Administrative Fee: Pays for the fund to be in compliance with the SEC.

f) Management Fee: Pays the manager(s) of the fund.

The Office of the Comptroller of Currency and the SEC found in 1996 that 80 percent of investors did not know about the fees associated with their mutual funds. An Investment Company Institute study in that same year found that performance of the fund was investors' top concern, while fees and expenses ranked a distant fifth.[2] The little 1 percent fee that most investors gloss over can have a tremendous effect on their portfolio over time. For example, let's take two funds that earn 12 percent a year; one fund has a 1 percent expense ratio and the other a 2 percent expense ratio. After thirty years, the fund with the 1 percent fee will earn $229,000, but the more expensive fund will be valued at $174,000, or about a third less.[3] This could be hard news to take, especially for a financially strapped couple faced with retirement.

CONGRESS TAKES A LOOK AT MUTUAL FUND FEES AND DOES NOTHING

The issue of mutual fund fees made its way to Congress. On September 29, 1998, the House Commerce Subcommittee on Finance and Hazardous Materials held a hearing on "Improving Price Competition in Mutual Funds and Bonds." Respected members of the securities industry, including financial planner Harold Evensky, university professor Charles Trzcinka, Managing Director of the Vanguard Group William McNabb, and co-founder of the Internet financial Web site Motley Fool, David Gardner, joined forces to make a case against mutual fund fees and common practices in the industry that were a disservice to investors. Most of their comments were lengthy and their arguments precise, but all of them neglected to mention one fact. Out of all of the members of the subcommittee, only six had not taken PAC (Political Action Committee) money from the Investment Company Institute, the mutual fund industry's trade organization.[4] The chairman of the subcommittee, Michael Oxley (R-Ohio), had received the most money from ICI, and had gotten thousands more from financial services organizations. Companies like the Securities Industry Association, Morgan Stanley, Prudential Securities, Aim Management Group (a mutual fund company), PaineWebber, Lehman Brothers, and American Century (both a brokerage and a mutual fund firm), have made contributions that benefit Oxley.[5] It goes without saying, therefore, that all these firms have a vested interest in upholding the status quo. Moreover, Oxley obtained campaign funding from PACs funded from a number of banks and insurance companies that sell mutual funds and annuities to the investing public.[6] Clearly a congressman who receives such campaign contributions will not be inclined to take the matter of reducing mutual fund fees seriously.

Matthew Fink, ICI's president, defended the mutual fund industry well that day and made a strong case in explaining why mutual fund fees were down overall. He first claimed that most shareholders pay less than the industry average: "The vast majority of shareholders in equity mutual funds are paying less than the expense ratio of the average fund: 77 percent of shareholder accounts are in stock mutual funds that have average expense ratios that are less than the 1.5 percent average."[7]

This sounds good, but just because the majority of shareholder accounts are in funds with less than the average expense ratio does not mean that investors have won the fee battle. Second, the 1.5 percent, even if lowered by half a percent or more, can still be costly to investors. Finally, 23 percent of investors, or close to a quarter of shareholders, are paying more than 1.5 percent. The problem with statistical averages is that they sound abstract but are often anything but. Would anyone be pleased with the news that on average forty thousand people die each year from traffic accidents? No, that number is extraordinary, and measures would be taken to lower it. The same applies to the 1.5 percent average that Mr. Fink refers to.

Next, Fink said that competition, not regulation, is the answer to lowering fees. "Performance is probably the most important competitive aspect of the industry," he said. "And, when a fund computes its performance, it must take out fees. That puts pressure on people in the industry to keep their fees down, because otherwise it would hurt their performance."[8]

This sounds convincing, but let's think it through before we make a hasty judgment. First, Fink is correct in stating that fees hurt performance, but if this was such a concern to investors, why are the majority of mutual fund assets in load funds and why aren't index funds more popular? Moreover, when mutual funds state their performance, they remove their fees. But the real test comes when funds state their gross performance. Investors can then compare the gross and net performance and see the impact of fees. Imagine seeing in writing a fund's twenty-year end value reduced by 17 percent in Morningstar as a result of a 1 percent fee. This would no doubt be interesting reading for many mutual fund shareholders. Since investors cannot see the impact of fees, it is hard for them to pressure mutual fund companies to lower them. Where is the pressure that Fink referred to? He claimed that mutual fund companies themselves are pressured to lower fees based on concerns about performance, but still they don't necessarily lower the fees. Only more regulation can force mutual fund companies to decrease their expenses, which would be in the best interests of their shareholders.

THE ABCS OF MUTUAL FUNDS

Charles Merrill, the founder of Merrill Lynch and a champion of the middle class, hated mutual funds and to this day it's a mystery why.[9] Perhaps if Merrill had seen the tremendous business they would create for brokerage firms, he would have thought differently. Few products are more lucrative for brokerage firms.

Mutual funds further the interests of firms several ways, including asset gathering. Brokers cannot generate commissions without having assets in-house, and mutual funds bring an investor's money to a full-service or discount firm. Once the money has been invested, commissions follow. Investors can also borrow against their funds in non-retirement accounts, which gives the firm margin interest. If there are 12-1 fees (fees that are charged by the fund to pay sales agents), the firm splits these payments on a quarterly basis. And if an investor wants to switch to another fund, the broker can get another commission. Moreover, if the investor liquidates the fund, the money can be placed in a fee-based account that will generate a breadbasket of fees. The proceeds could also be used to purchase individual stocks and bonds, each one carrying a commission that will be periodically refreshed for the life of the account. It's easy to see why the full-service and discount firms have helped popularize mutual funds.

It is not surprising that I was inundated with information about mutual funds during my days as a full-service broker. Choosing which of the thousands of mutual funds to recommend can be a chore, so my firm worked with mutual fund companies to help market their funds. Before selling a customer on a fund, the broker has to be sold on it. Rather than burning the midnight oil in a research marathon, most brokers learn about a mutual fund via its sales kit. For brokers' eyes only, these kits offer highlights and "helpful" suggestions on how a broker can best sell the fund to his customers. I have seen kits with cassette tapes that even walk the broker through the sales process, giving him ready-made responses to questions concerning fees, loads, and so on. Most kits also contain a present of some kind, such as a handheld premium with the company's logo, and aren't meant to offer more than a cursory understanding of the funds. The kits are limited to glossies, factoids, and proof of past fund performance, typically laid out in an eye-catching multicolored chart. The commission that the broker will receive for selling the fund is often written in big, bold type with the contact name of the local wholesaler for further questions.

The sales kits are important, yet customers who buy mutual funds are denied access to them. The best way to find out about a product is to learn how it is sold to the public, which is what the kits reveal. Who knows more about cars, after all, than a used-car salesperson? He knows the secrets of the car's past, and the true story about what is under the hood. In the same way, brokers know a fund's secrets through these sales kits. Because this information is not made available to investors, they do not understand the mechanics of how the product is sold, nor about hidden fees and hidden truths.

In addition to the sales kits, the funds hire wholesalers who try to persuade brokers to sell the fund. I remember bracing myself for their weekly parade of meetings. Attendance was required because the office manager did not want a poor showing. A free lunch was the only reward for attending. Each wholesaler talked for thirty minutes about why his fund was the best, and why it was in the broker's best interests to sell it. Few questions were asked at these meetings and some of the more soft-spoken wholesalers were drowned out by the chomp, chomp sound of seventy-five brokers simultaneously consuming their reward for showing up.

More informal gatherings also took place, usually with another free meal. This was where the real selling took place. I tried to pass on most of the lunches, but I was once desperate to find sponsors for the stockmarket reports I was giving on two local radio stations. I called up two wholesalers I knew and asked them for their help. They each gave me $500, and the stations aired their commercials. I received no money from them, but they both pressured me to sell their funds. I finally agreed, selling a number of my clients shares of both funds, while justifying their purchases as the best that money could buy. Well, I was right in that respect, because I considered myself the best that money could buy, and I could be bought for only $1,000. Soon after the transactions had been made, I saw an article ranking mutual funds based on overall performance in *Smart Money* magazine. To my amazement, one of the funds I had sold as a result of my radio venture was ranked among the ten worst-performing mutual funds for the year. I closed the magazine in haste.

You might be thinking right now that what I did was unusual. But this is actually a common practice, only one of the ways that wholesalers use their marketing dollars to obtain sales. Many customers think that brokers are obligated to recommend the very best fund to them, but the securities industry doesn't require them to do so. Brokers must only meet a standard of "suitability." In other words, if the broker can make a case as to why a particular mutual fund is a suitable investment for her client, then she is free to make the recommendation. This minimal standard is a true disservice to investors, because many times there is a gulf between suitable investments and those that are in the client's best interests.

Brokers are not mandated to divulge the real reasons why they make their recommendations, and don't have to recommend the least costly investment either. If a broker recommends a load fund that carries a 5 percent load over a no-load fund of comparable value, she knows she won't be reprimanded by her management. In fact, she might be congratulated because of the commission she produced.

After the broker decides which fund(s) to sell, he must determine the most acceptable pricing alternative for his client. Pricing alternatives are based on the class of shares, and most fund families have at least a couple of alternatives. The more it offers, the greater the chances it will be successfully sold by the broker. Here are the basic pricing alternatives and some oft-recited pitches that brokers use to sell each class of shares:

CLASS A SHARES

The Class A shares of a mutual fund, which some investors might think are the best that money can buy, carry an up-front load that compromises the investor's principal. Perhaps the shares should be renamed Class F, because they fail to put the interests of investors first. Class A does not mean first-class investment, but some brokers sell the funds this way so they can generate a commission. Even though many customers find it painful to pay an up-front fee, the advisor will convince his customer that the fee is warranted and in his best interests. His standard justifications include:

1) *You get what you pay for in life:* Here the financial consultant paints the load fund as if it were a Cartier watch. The load is a clear sign of quality goods, and a necessary cost of doing business. The standard pitch may offer an analogy that buying cheap stock is like flying a low-cost airline that cuts costs just to make a profit. The broker asks if you would feel safe flying on such an airline. The customer, of course, nods no. The advisor then asks, would you feel comfortable placing your money in an investment vehicle that prides itself on cost-cutting? Can you see why this might not be in your long-term interests? The best services cost money, says the broker, and whips out a long-term performance

chart that clearly supports the load fund he wants to sell. After being dazzled by the chart and the prospect for future riches, many clients overlook the load or consider it a small price to pay for buying the "best" funds. Of course, there is absolutely no quality difference based on a load alone. Perception does not have to meet reality in the sales process, and in more cases than not, investors buy because of their perceptions of the product and don't take the time to investigate the realities of what they purchase.

2) *The load is a positive, not a negative:* The most successful financial consultants are good at turning positives into negatives. Out-of-pocket expenses, like loads, are generally seen by customers as negatives, but skilled advisors can persuade their customers that Class-A-share loads have an inherent positive aspect as well. How is this possible? The supporting pitch claims that investors who don't pay a load are often the first to sell their funds in a panic. Short-term sellers do not fare as well as long-term holders of the fund. The load therefore encourages the investor not to sell in a downward market, therefore safeguarding his long-term capital gains. With this argument in mind, it would seem reasonable to handcuff dieters so that they are restrained from going to the refrigerator, but what sensible person would recommend such an action? Moreover, who would argue that a dieter wants to be handcuffed, and would perceive the handcuffs as a positive? Loads are the investor's handcuffs and they have no inherent positives whatsoever.

3) *A small price to pay for good advice:* The argument is that the load is money well spent because it's the broker's expertise in picking funds that is the key ingredient in making the customer money. The number of mutual funds can be overwhelming, and choosing the best fund for the investor is a time-consuming endeavor that must be taken seriously. The time brokers spend being wined and dined by wholesalers can be taxing and they endure sleepless nights, spent examining the innards of a sales kit. Outside of these superhuman feats that drain human

strength, brokers have to be mindful to recommend funds that will help them win sales contests and assist them in meeting their commission goals. But do all these "strenuous" forces really help brokers pick the best fund? Seriously, there is nothing magical or mysterious about picking a mutual fund, and load funds invite a competing set of interests most investors will not know about. Moreover, brokers generally spend more time filling out a customer's paperwork than they do researching mutual funds. An up-front load seems a hefty price to pay for a broker's advice.

CLASS B SHARES

Class B shares give the investor the false impression that all of his money is going to work for him on day one. This class of shares does not have an up-front load, but it does have a back-end descending load that will compromise the customer's principal if she liquidates any portion of the fund during a certain time period. The time period generally ranges from one to five years, and the load decreases in some funds each year by 1 percent. Back-end loads on Class B shares generally decrease over time from 4 to 1 percent and give the investor an incentive to stay in the fund. Here are some of the tricks that advisors use to convince their clients that Class B shares are right for them:

1) *The fund is a cost saver:* Mutual fund companies and brokers take advantage of hidden costs when they sell Class B shares of mutual funds. Since there is no visible load, the broker may suggest that his customer is saving perhaps thousands of dollars in fees. This is one of the oldest tricks in the financial consultant's manual, and as you might recall, some of the advisors that I went to visit tried to use it on me. The elimination of the commission has disappeared by sleight of hand, however, not by the purchase of Class B shares. Let's say an investor purchases $100,000 of Class B shares in mutual fund X. The customer has a back-end load of 4, 3, 2, 1—i.e., if she liquidates the fund in

the first year, she will have to pay a 4 percent fee; in the second year, a 3 percent fee, and so on. The advisor, on the day of the purchase, gets a 4 percent commission ($4,000), which comes directly from the fund's overall return. The back-end load is in place so the fund can recoup the commission if the customer sells his shares. As we know, the overall expenses on Class B shares are generally greater than on Class A shares, and the advisor makes a healthy commission on the transaction. The contingent deferred sales charge, and the greater expenses of Class B shares, are spelled out in the fund's prospectus. Advisors are required to give a fund's prospectus to each of their customers, prior to their purchase, and it should be required reading. Unfortunately, the prospectus usually finds a permanent home at the bottom of the trash. Too bad, because it shows clearly how Class B shares are more expensive to purchase than Class A shares, and over time will substantially erode the investor's overall returns.

2) *The back-end load is good for you:* Some advisors try to convince you that the virtues of the up-front load are matched only by the gifts bestowed by back-end loads. Once again, the standard pitch says that the load is working in the investor's favor, but in reality it works in the broker's best interests. The financial consultant begins by saying that the relationship between the investor and the mutual fund is similar to a marriage, and just like any marriage, there is a price to pay if the marriage dissolves. Like a marriage there will be good times and bad times, but the load is a constant reminder to stay the course for the long term. The advisor will also point out that since the investor intends to keep the fund for years, the back-end load really won't apply to him. After a holding period, the investor can sell his funds without penalty or remorse, which, the broker concludes, makes the fund a good investment for both him and his customer.

The pitch above sounds great, but there are a few important details missing. First, the argument that Class B shares are better investments for advisors than their clients is old news by now. The second negative associated with back-end loads is that regardless of what investors may think when they initially buy the funds, some unforeseen event may happen that will force them to sell their shares. I remember all too well some of my former customers who bought Class B shares thinking they were a bargain; later, when circumstances forced them to sell, they realized this was not so. In some cases, the fund's share price was below their purchase price, and they incurred a 4 percent load, only adding insult to injury.

CLASS C SHARES

Class C shares seem at first to present the best of both worlds. They do not carry an up-front load and they do not have a descending back-end load either. There is a 1 percent annual fee for as long as the customer holds the fund, however, and a 1 percent penalty if the customer sells the fund within one year of its purchase. Here is the standard pitch that advisors use to convince their clients that Class C shares are the best that money can buy:

1) *Reduction to the ridiculous:* Who could argue with a mere 1 percent yearly fee and with a minimum holding period of only one year? It seems like the mutual fund companies are practically giving their product away. The costs of a 1 percent fee can be deceiving though. For example, if a fund has a total yearly return of 12 percent, the investor might pat himself on the back and proudly say that he only had to pay a 1 percent fee to get this double-digit return. What he may not realize is that the 1 percent fee represents a whopping 8.3 percent of the total return, because 1 percent is 8.3 percent of the total return of 12 percent. This is a high cost for any investor to pay. In addition, the investor must pay this fee regardless of the fund's performance. Over time the fund will probably make more money than its shareholders because of this minuscule, but mighty, 1 percent

fee. Numbers don't lie, but the way mutual fund companies and advisors present them can sometimes be deceptive. C shares, in my book, get an A for concealing the true impact of fees, but their high costs prohibit me from giving them above-average marks overall.

NO LOADS

We have come now to the mutual fund industry's version of the free lunch. As we know, there is no such thing as a free lunch, but that doesn't stop advisors from trying to convince their clients that one exists. It amazes me that investors think that no-load funds are free when no-load mutual fund companies employ thousands of people, house themselves in high-rent districts, and spend millions on advertising. The money that goes to pay these expenses comes from the investor's assets, which over time has a negative effect on his overall return.

For all of their drawbacks, though, selling no-load funds was one of the more savvy moves of full-service firms. For decades, firms sold only load funds because they thought they'd cannibalize their own funds and lose commissions if they sold no-load funds. Then, in the late nineties, firms like Merrill Lynch and Salomon Smith Barney decided to sell no-load funds. These funds are wonderful bait-and-switch products because they give brokers an opportunity to liquidate the funds at a future date, without cost. The assets can then be invested in more commission-worthy investments. Offering no-load funds also prohibits cost-conscious customers from automatically seeking out a discount firm, and may provide excellent cross-selling opportunities for the broker. When customers buy a no-load fund, the broker can introduce a wide range of other services like financial planning, retirement accounts, mortgages, and insurance products, all which could generate thousands of dollars in commission. Though no-load funds may not generate profit for brokers, it would cost full-service firms more money in the long run not to sell them.

Discount firms have enjoyed great success in selling no-load funds.

Some major discount firms allow investors to choose from hundreds of mutual funds via so-called supermarkets, like Charles Schwab's One Source program and Fidelity's Investments' FundNetwork. They have seen remarkable growth since their inception in the early nineties. In fact, industry-wide supermarkets in 1997 accounted for 21 percent of fund sales, up from less than 13 percent in 1993.[10] The convenience of one-stop shopping via supermarkets has been a moneymaker for discount firms because of their asset-gathering ability and the fees the funds must pay to participate in the programs. The fees are like the ones grocery stores charge manufacturers for shelf space, and some mutual fund companies, like Women's Equity Fund and Domini Social Equity Fund, have increased their expense ratios just to pay for the supermarket fees.[11] Shareholders of some funds are forced to pay higher expenses whether or not they buy from supermarkets, leading to increased revenue for the brokerage firms and the mutual fund companies. Perhaps some mutual fund investors would be better off if they did their shopping elsewhere.

THREE CARDINAL SINS

In 1940, Congress passed the Investment Company Act to regulate investment companies and their activities. The act itself is hardly exciting reading, and I don't think many copies would be found at the bedsides of mutual fund managers or investors. Still, it's always helpful to be reminded of good intentions that have been written into law. Section I of the act carries this principle: "The national public interest and the interest of investors are adversely affected when investment companies are managed in the interest of investment advisors rather than the interest of [their] shareholders."

No truer words have ever been spoken. Investors and mutual fund managers alike would be helped by posting this passage on every prospectus and in the lobbies of every brokerage firm as a subtle reminder of what managing someone's money really means. It might help members of the securities industry remember not to take advantage of those who entrust their money to them. Today, when so many fall short of managing money in their shareholders' best interests, the above standard is something mutual fund companies should strive to live up to. There are a few sins associated with mutual funds, and learning about them in the following pages might make you think differently about these investments.

Victims of their own success: When people go shopping, they take great comfort in name brands, especially from large, well-established companies. With so many uncertainties, the brand can act as an insurance policy against tomorrow's troubles, while the size of a company can play a role in lending credibility to the company's goods and services. General Motors and Honda need no introduction to American consumers, but who would feel safe driving a car from a little-known year-old company? The bigger-is-better rationale is also used when investors buy mutual funds. Many know the name brands of the industry like Fidelity, Putnam, Vanguard, and American Funds, and it's easier for financial advisors to sell these funds.

The only problem here is that oftentimes bigger is not better, because the performances of mutual funds that manage the most money and have become household names often lag behind traditional indexes like the S&P 500. These funds lag in performance for shareholders while they rake in billions of dollars for the managers. Put yourself for a moment in the shoes of a mutual fund manager who is in charge of an up-and-coming fund with assets of $100 million. The fund is a load fund with a 1 percent management fee. He invests in twenty to thirty stocks at a time, heavily in those he thinks will be winners. He puts $10 million, or 10 percent, of his fund in Company A, which has a $200 million market capitalization. The stock at the time of his purchase is selling at $10 a share, so the mutual fund manager now owns 5 percent of the company. In a few months it triples in value, going beyond the manager's expectations. He sells the stock at $30, making his shareholders $20 million and increasing the fund's overall value by 20 percent. As years go by, the manager has more successes like this, and within five years he has achieved celebrity status among mutual fund shareholders and is lauded by the financial press. Millions of investors place their hopes in his ability to duplicate his success. The fund grows from $100 million to $8 billion in assets, making its company one of the more successful in the business. A success by any measure for the mutual fund company, because it has increased its fees from $1-million-plus loads to $80-million-plus loads. But the investors will experience a different story.

Eight billion dollars can buy a lot of stock, but now the fund's size will work against its performance. The fund philosophy that made our fund manager successful has now been rendered outmoded by the size of the fund. If the manager wants to buy Company B with a market capitalization of $4 billion, he strives to take a sizable position in stocks that are winners. But if he invests 10 percent of his fund in the company, he will own 20 percent and federal law restricts mutual fund companies from owning more than 10 percent of a company's stock. He is now faced with taking a reduced position, and forced to invest in other companies he may not believe to be equally good performers.

After consulting with the fund's attorneys, he decides to buy 5 percent of the company, or to invest $200 million. The stock moves from $10 to $30, and he makes $400 million in the transaction. When the fund's assets were $100 million, a $20 million capital gain increased the fund's value by 20 percent, but now, since the fund manages $8 billion, a $400 million capital gain yields only a paltry 5 percent return for shareholders. The larger the fund, the harder the manager has to work to find winners, but the more stocks he buys, the more losers he can hope to purchase as well. The more cash that floods into the fund, the more hard-pressed the manager is to buy more securities, and the less time he has to spend on researching individual securities. Case in point: Of the forty-five largest stock funds (those with $2 billion or more in assets) in 1993, only one, Janus Twenty, has outperformed the S&P over a five-year period.[12] And it has beaten the S&P by only two-thirds of a percentage point each year.[13] The larger they are, the harder mutual funds fall. Managers become victims of their own success, but funds reap the rewards of larger fees by virtue of their size.

Taxes and the high cost of portfolio turnover: Most investors don't take the high costs of taxes and portfolio turnover into account when they purchase mutual funds. Mutual fund managers, graded on quarterly and yearly performance, are under extreme pressure to get short-term results. This is a basic irony in the mutual fund industry, because mutual fund managers want short-term results that they can be proud of, but shareholders buy the funds for their long-term performance. Buying quality investments and holding them generally rewards investors with the greatest returns, but this is not a luxury mutual fund managers can afford. Investors with a buy-and-hold philosophy are deceived into thinking they will automatically be rewarded by holding a fund for the long term, when in fact the securities that compose the fund are being bought and sold all the time. The old saw often recited by brokers and financial planners is "It is not timing the market, but time in the market that makes investors money." This might be true, but the saying doesn't really apply to mutual funds, because excessive trading may serve the interests of the fund, but in the end it can be a real disservice to the shareholders.

When securities are sold in a mutual fund, investors might find they have a tax liability at the end of the year, even if their fund suffered a loss in value. This is a distinct disadvantage of buying mutual funds over individual stocks. The combined negative forces of paying capital gains and a reduction of principle can be substantial, but most investors do not realize the impact of portfolio turnover and taxes until it is too late. Thomas Southerly, a practicing CPA in Fairfax, Virginia, for twenty years, says investors need to consider the effects of portfolio turnover and tax implications before they buy a mutual fund. Other investments, like tax-free bonds, take tax implications into account, and the same should be done with mutual funds. Most investors will have to do this for themselves because it is not generally in the best interests of financial advisors to disclose the impact of taxes on the mutual fund they are trying to sell. You can just imagine the advisor's pitch: "Well, Mr. Smith, I love mutual fund A for you, and by the way the manager is an aggressive trader, so expect a huge tax liability at the end of the year that will reduce your returns." By the time the advisor completes the sentence, Mr. Smith will be out the door.

"Most average investors view a mutual fund as a savings account," Southerly says, "and don't understand the tax consequences of the investment." He suggests that investors read the mutual fund prospectus and consider quality funds with lower turnover to maximize growth net of taxes. That way, investors can avoid paying as much tax and keep a larger percentage of their returns.

Quality and performance illusions: When you are managing one of over seven thousand mutual funds, the competition for new dollars can be fierce. Most mutual funds have only quality and performance achievements to sell, and investors are impressed when a fund has a short-term, double-digit return. The past performance of the fund is no guarantee of future results, but still that's what most investors rely on when choosing a mutual fund manager. Many investors check in with the scorekeepers of the industry, like Morningstar, Lipper Analytical, and Value Line. Many investors consider Morningstar a bible of the mutual fund industry because it "objectively" evaluates and ranks mutual funds according to their performance, risk, and other factors. This analysis is distilled into an easy-to-read format ranking mutual funds with one to five stars. This format makes for a wonderful sales tool for financial consultants because it showcases a fund's star ranking, and can distract investors from concerns like fees, loads, and turnover that might hinder a sale.

Many investors use the star ranking to choose mutual funds whether they buy from a broker or not. This is a mistake, because it assumes that all of the dirty work of investigating a mutual fund has been done. Most investors don't realize that there is no bible in the securities industry, and quantifying mutual fund returns does not necessarily lead to an objective performance analysis. I can think of no human endeavor in which a high standard of objectivity has truly been met, because whenever people are involved, subjectivity muddies the waters. Morningstar claims that its analysis is objective, but the star system is more truly analogous to Roger Ebert's two-thumbs-up ranking system. Morningstar can at times be a valuable tool in evaluating funds, but investors should trust their own opinions instead of relying on the recommendations of others, who do not know their financial situation.

The subjectivity of Morningstar's staff can easily be seen in their text overviews. For example, Morningstar researcher Christopher Traulsen said in his favorable opinion of a blue-chip fund, "Despite Kemper Blue Chip Fund's struggles in 1998, it retains a certain charm." A certain charm? Charm is not a quality found in any lab; like beauty, it is in the eyes of the beholder. Hap Bryant said that Vanguard's European Stock Index Fund "may not be exciting, but it has compiled a record that rivals that of any managed peer." In the past three years the fund has produced returns of over 20 percent. If this isn't something to get excited about, what is? Dan Kobussen, another staffer, claimed in a review that "Colonial US Growth and Income Fund's new manager is making a decent start, but he has to be better than decent." Again, opinion, not fact. And in stating her thoughts on the American National Income Fund, Emily Hall wrote, "All but the most risk adverse investors would probably find better opportunities elsewhere." How does she know this, and by what method has this "objective" conclusion been reached? If opinions like these pepper the text, shouldn't they affect the star analysis itself? And if the star analysis is truly objective, then why muddle the findings with opinion-laden fund overviews? Such reviews defeat the objective air of the analysis.

The evaluation of mutual fund performance can also be tricky. The long-term average returns of stock mutual funds can be deceiving because they don't take into account funds that have gone out of business. All of the major mutual fund rating services, whether it be Morningstar, Lipper Analytical, or any other, have a "survivor bias": they exclude out-of-business funds from their historical averages. This bit of editing weights performance averages toward the survival-of-the-fittest funds, but gives a distorted view of performance averages. Mark Carhart, a finance professor at the University of Southern California, researched this problem and drew some startling conclusions. He looked at 2,071 U.S. equity funds from January 1962 to December 1995 and found that during this time 725 funds, or 35 percent, went out of business. His study showed that investors had a one-in-three chance of buying a fund that would go off to the mutual fund graveyard. Second, when he added in the defunct funds with the surviving funds, the long-term average changed remarkably from a respectable 10.7 percent to an anemic 9.5 percent—the S&P 500 during this same time period had a 10.6 percent return. He also found that aggressive growth funds had the greatest tendency toward failure, and when the dead funds were added into this mix, their long-term performance average was only 11.6 percent.[14] Clearly, this less-than-stellar performance does not justify the risks most investors take when they purchase aggressively managed mutual funds.

The message of Carhart's study seems clear. The law of averages allows rating services to get away with excluding funds in order to boost overall performance averages. Investors might invest in an aggressive stock portfolio because this historically produces the greatest returns, but they don't realize that better returns could be found in index funds, with much less risk and cost. Also, buying funds based on broad-brush categories can be deceiving. Categories like "growth and income," "growth," and "aggressive growth" give investors faith in the law of performance averages, but because all funds have not been counted, these averages are less than trustworthy. It's like calculating the average age of World War II soldiers without taking into account the ones who died on the battlefield.

USE THESE STRATEGIES WHEN CONSIDERING MUTUAL FUNDS

• The first question you need to ask yourself is "Do I really need a mutual fund and why?"

• Be skeptical of all mutual fund recommendations from your financial advisor that pay him a commission or fee. Investigate these funds yourself first, then look for more cost-effective quality alternatives.

• Don't be dazzled by marketing ploys from mutual fund companies that tout performance. Regardless of the fund, past performance does not guarantee future performance and today's biggest winner could be tomorrow's biggest loser.

• Never be rushed into making a mutual fund purchase. Mutual funds are long-term investments and making a decision for the long term takes time and effort.

• Always consider the costs of the mutual fund when making your purchase. Read the fund's prospectus thoroughly and inquire about the costs and expenses of the fund and how they will affect your overall returns.

• Avoid buying proprietary funds because they generally better serve the interests of your advisor.

CHAPTER 8

INITIAL PUBLIC OFFERINGS:
A WORLD OF PAYOFFS, PRIVILEGES,
AND PENALTIES

Show me an investor who has never had an interest in an IPO and I'll show you someone with no pulse. IPOs have captured the attention of many, but unfortunately, the chances that any average investor can buy shares in a hot IPO are about as good as getting struck by lightning on a clear day. IPOs are one of the most lucrative short-term investments Wall Street has to offer for wealthy individuals and institutions like investment banks, mutual funds, and insurance companies, but the average investor is generally shut out from participating in them. IPOs epitomize how unfairly average investors are treated by Wall Street, and they help draw the line that separates the rich from the middle class, or the haves from the have-nots. The line is drawn so firmly and boldly that it's clear that even in a so-called free marketplace like Wall Street, certain freedoms and privileges can be denied by the powers that be.

THE MAKING OF AN IPO

When a privately held company wants to raise capital to become a public concern, the IPO process begins. Investment banks with an interest in underwriting the IPO vigorously compete for the company's business, because millions of dollars of underwriting fees are typically at stake. Investment bankers will often wine and dine prospective clients to try to curry favor with them, going so far as to offer very extravagant gifts as well. In addition, bankers sometimes purchase services or goods from the company to engender feelings of goodwill. The investment banker, of course, hopes that her kind gestures will be reciprocated when the company selects her bank to underwrite the IPO.

These wink-and-nod business arrangements may go on for years, but once the underwriting team has been chosen, the next step is an "all-hands" meeting. At this meeting, which takes place about six to eight weeks before a company goes public, the company sets up a firm timetable for launching its public offering. Each member of the underwriting team—typically one lead bank and two other banks—is assigned certain tasks and an overall game plan is discussed. As part of the process, the lead bank assembles a syndicate, or other investment banks, who will help sell the shares. They begin to test the waters about the stock from their institutional customers. This will help determine the initial demand for the company in terms of pricing, offering size, and other matters.

The first step in the selling process is to create the prospectus, which is basically a brochure about the company. Investment bankers and the company's management team spend a lot of time writing this piece, making sure it accurately reflects such things as the nature of the company's business and its financial situation. During the initial stage of an IPO, the company adheres to what the SEC calls a "quiet period," during which it cannot aggressively promote or advertise itself. This period officially begins with the initial filing of the IPO with the SEC and ends twenty-five days after the stock begins to trade. During this time the prospectus and other sales literature become important tools in selling the company to large institutions.

The prospectus is important, but the best way to find out about a company is, so to speak, to pay it a visit. After all, who would argue that you could really know what McDonald's is all about by reading the company's prospectus? If you want to find out about McDonald's, read the prospectus, but then go eat a Big Mac with fries. This same rule applies to an "IPO road show," except the company comes to the investors instead of the investors going to the company. Management travels from city to city, pitching the company, primarily to institutional investors and wealthy individuals. New York, Los Angeles, Chicago, and selected cities in Europe and Asia are favorite destinations. The road show lasts for about a week. Management, all the while, is on the lookout for interested investors and investors are in search of good opportunities. Attendees have a chance to ask management questions, and the company's current financial situation and future prospects are openly discussed. Much information is shared during these discussions and this gives attendees a good sense of the company, including the quality of the management team and their vision. Future investors learn much that is not offered by the prospectus, but as long as this valuable information is presented orally and there is no written record of the discussion, the SEC permits it. Needless to say, average investors are not allowed to attend IPO road shows, and do not have the benefit of meeting the management team or asking questions that could give them additional insights into the company.

Once the indications of interest have been taken, the banks will determine the price of the issue. Pricing an IPO is more art than science and the bankers have two customers to please. First, the company, which wants as high an offering price (the price that the IPO shares will be sold at before they begin to trade) as possible. The more money the IPO raises, the more capital the company receives and the richer the founders of the company become. Second, the institutional buyers, who want a fair price so that they can sell—or "flip"—the issue to make a quick profit. Most new issues have an opening premium of 15 percent so both the company and the institutions can be pleased with the offering. The investment banks make their money primarily on the purchase and selling of the shares before the stock begins to trade. They buy the shares right before the offering at a 7 percent discount, then sell to their customers for 7 percent more than what they paid. This is a heavy price for companies to pay, but the banks justify the fee by the supposed risk they take in underwriting the new issue.

The first trade of the new issue is called the opening price. Once the IPO is on the market, anything can happen to its price. A company could trade below its offering price, or it might skyrocket 300 percent or more. After the stock becomes public, the underwriting firms typically require at least one analyst from each firm to follow it and periodically to issue research reports on it.

It's interesting to note that IPOs may be wonderful short-term investments, but typically don't fare well over the long term. According to Manish Shah, president of Otiva, a new-issue research boutique, 60 percent of IPOs disappoint investors with bad earning reports in the third quarter. Once this news reaches the market, investors often sell the stock.[1] Moreover, another study, by CommScan, a New York investment-banking research firm, showed that IPOs that gained 50 percent on the first day of trading lost 35 percent thereafter.[2] IPOs are faithful to the adage "what goes up must come down." Hopefully, the same will be true someday about the barriers confronting average investors when it comes to IPOs. In the meantime the real world of IPOs is filled with payoffs, privileges, and penalties.

PAYOFFS

I am not sure what would be more difficult: finding ten good men in Sodom and Gomorrah or one honest person on Wall Street. As the biblical story goes, God destroyed the cities of the plain because ten good men could not be found, but no such standard applies to Wall Street. Maybe it should. I did come across at least one honest person, Thomas Brown, who discussed the secret world of IPOs with me. His message should cause every investor concern. Brown has more than fifteen years of experience as a financial services analyst and has worked for some of the most prestigious firms on Wall Street. During eight out of ten years, he was ranked as the number-one analyst of regional banks by the renowned *Institutional Investor* magazine. His other credentials are just as impressive.

Brown's career began at Kemper mutual funds, followed by stints at Smith Barney and PaineWebber. After PaineWebber, he was hired as an analyst for Donaldson, Lufkin & Jenrette, but after seven years of loyal service was let go by the firm. According to Brown, DLJ at the time was looking to make inroads into underwriting financial services companies, but Brown didn't think the acquisitions and mergers in this field would lead to increasing shareholder value, and made his opinions publicly known. The investment bankers threw a fit and successfully petitioned DLJ to fire him from the company. Brown's candor cost him his job. DLJ was not heartless in the matter; they offered him $450,000 with the understanding that he not talk about the firm for five years. Brown turned down DLJ's offer, and when I asked him why, he said, "My thoughts were that it would be totally against my own morals to take money from them and not tell the true story." At the time of our interview, he was managing a bank-stock portfolio for hedge fund Tiger Investment Corporation in Manhattan.

Brown spoke frankly about the myth of Wall Street firms, especially full-service firms, touting their research as an indispensable tool for the savvy investor. To listen to many firms, you would think their analysts to be Moses in pinstripes who have come down from the mountain to tell the masses the truth. The so-called Chinese Wall separating analysts from investment bankers is another myth. According to Brown, "The Chinese Wall has never had more holes in it than it does today." Investment bankers place tremendous amounts of pressure on analysts to form opinions that suit their needs, which may be contrary to the interests of investors. Thus an analyst's opinion about a company may come less from the heart than from pocketbook concerns unknown to investors.

This pressure usually begins early on, when the company reveals its desire to go public. The investment banker visits a start-up company with the analyst in tow, and sees the potential to make a bundle in underwriting fees. The banker begins his pitch to management proving why his firm is the best to underwrite the offering, at the same time pitching and pressuring the analyst to form a positive opinion of the company. With millions of dollars at stake, only an analyst with herculean courage would dare to pen a negative opinion, or utter a negative comment about the company. A negative opinion from the analyst would sever the relationship between the investment bankers and the company, and the former would stand to lose millions in underwriting fees. In a typical scenario, the banker assures management that the analyst will voice a positive opinion about the company regardless of his personal feelings. Brown told me that when bankers try to woo new clients, the analyst is little more than a second salesperson. In his own career, 40 percent of his time was spent on the road pitching new prospects and only a fraction of his time was spent in authoring research reports.

Although the practice is common, Brown thinks it is dangerous for investors to look to analysts for objective opinions about a company: "Wall Street research has become almost worthless and I don't think the average investor can know enough given all of the bias," he says. His best advice about investment research: "Absolutely avoid it." In addition to the pressure on analysts to craft positive opinions, Brown went on to say that "the IPO process is all about greed" and that analysts are kept in check by money. At DLJ, for example, Brown said that he made a seven-figure income, but his official salary was only $150,000. The majority of his income was determined by the research manager, who based his bonus, as well as that of other analysts, on the feedback he got from investment bankers and institutional salespeople. The manager wanted to know how helpful Brown had been to them in generating commissions from institutional clients, and based his bonus on their feedback.

For example, let's say Fidelity's analysts and their mutual fund managers used Brown's research on the banking sector heavily. When Fidelity wanted to buy 100,000 shares of IBM, they could do so at any number of broker/dealers, but the institutional salesperson would use Brown's research as a bargaining chip to persuade Fidelity to execute the trade with DLJ. But this scenario works only if the research is positive. If Brown had authored a negative report on a company Fidelity was holding in their mutual funds, it might increase selling pressure on the stock and ultimately affect the values of Fidelity's mutual funds. This would prompt concern from Fidelity shareholders and the chain reaction might end with Fidelity doing its trading elsewhere, DLJ losing commission, and Brown having his bonus cut.

Brown's message was clear. Investors should be skeptical of any support for a company that comes from an analyst who works for the underwriting firm, and they should be especially cautious when it involves an IPO. He then relayed an all-too-common story to me, one I knew well from being a stockbroker. Let's say a company's stock tumbles in price and the CEO calls the investment banker with his concerns. The banker then calls the analyst and pleads his customer's case, and soon after, a glowing review of the company hits the press. The average investor has no knowledge of these behind-the-scenes maneuvers and goes out and buys some of the stock. The analyst is happy because he gets to keep his multimillion-dollar job; the CEO is happy because his stock price has gone up; and the investment banker is pleased because he may have a chance to do more business with the company. But the story may have a sad ending for the average investor, whose misplaced trust in Wall Street may cost him dearly once the stock begins to slide in price. The likely sellers will be large institutions, and while they take their profits, the average investor is taken to the cleaners.

On Wall Street, according to Brown, "The only way to get business is for analysts to remain bullish all the time." Several studies support his claim. One such study, in 1998, by Zacks Investment Research, showed that at the time only 1.4 percent of all analyst recommendations on some six thousand companies were sells versus 67.5% buys and 31.1% holds.[3] Another study, coauthored by Georgia State University Assistant Professor Silva Nathan, examined 250 companies covered by analysts with investment-banking ties, and an equal number of companies with analysts who had no ties. She found that the investment bankers' analysts had 6 percent higher earnings forecasts and nearly 25 percent more buy recommendations.[4] Investment research on companies, especially from the firms that underwrite them, is, in Brown's view, only what the company wants investors to know. Such research is not far removed from PR releases and in many cases conceals a hidden agenda. "Wall Street has become an amplifier for companies," he said.

PRIVILEGES

What is the difference between an institutional investor, like a mutual fund or brokerage firm, and an average investor? The institutional investor is given special privileges when it comes to IPOs. As we have seen, institutional investors attend the road show, while average investors cannot. It is utterly baffling to me why the SEC excludes average investors from these shows, because average investors may have the most to lose when investing in an IPO. They, too, should have an opportunity to be informed.

In addition to receiving privileged information, institutional investors can sell their IPO shares whenever they please. On the first day of trading, increased demand for a stock can boost its price well above the offering price. At that time institutional investors are free to sell their shares and lock in their double-digit profits, but when it comes to individual investors, this practice of flipping (buying and then immediately selling the shares) is frowned upon by the industry, and usually prohibits the average investor from receiving any shares of a future IPO. Institutional investors sell their shares to help themselves, but individual investors are asked to be charitable, and not sell their shares immediately in order to support the price of the stock.

Becoming one of the privileged few at full-service firms who get IPO shares is determined more by who you are than by what your financial needs are. Firms that are part of the selling syndicate are given X number of shares, which they divvy up to their local offices. The manager in each office gives shares of the new company to the brokers who produce the most commission and who can convince their clients not to flip their shares. The brokers typically call clients who either generate substantial commissions or who have large assets under management. The IPO, an invitation for quick profits, ingratiates the broker with clients he cannot afford to lose. Since most brokers are willing to risk losing the accounts of average investors, they rarely call those clients. Imagine a world where IPOs were given because they would make the customers money, not because the customers had a lot of money in the first place. Giving some IPO shares to average investors would be a positive step toward good financial planning. Many full-service brokers pride themselves on financial planning, but when it comes to deciding who get shares of a hot IPO, they have sadly forsaken their abilities.

This same sort of class distinction carries over to some discount brokerage firms. Charles Schwab has an alliance with investment banks: J. P. Morgan, CS/First Boston, and Hambrecht & Quist. Fidelity works with Lehman Brothers and Friedman Billings Ramsey, and E*Trade has forged an alliance with BancBoston Robertson Stephens. The rules for IPOs are also in play at Schwab, where IPOs are available only to its Signature Gold and Signature Platinum customers. Fidelity makes IPOs available to customers that have $500,000 in assets or make at least thirty-six or seventy-two stock, fixed income, or option trades per year. Discount firms like Schwab and Fidelity give preferential treatment because it helps the firm retain assets that they might lose to a full-service firm. E*Trade, on the other hand, does not restrict participating in IPOs to one segment of their customer base, but they do give preferred IPO allocations to their Platinum customers, or those that make at least 75 trades per quarter.

Special privileges can also accrue to people who work for companies that have recently gone public. Owning IPO shares of a company is a privilege, especially when they are purchased at a deep discount to the offering price. Many start-up companies make IPO shares available to their employees in place of a higher salary. Investors who initially purchase the company's stock without realizing that a large number of shares have gone to employees may have unrealistic notions about the stock's price and purchase their shares in a "rigged" atmosphere. This happens because the employees who have shares of the company are prohibited from selling them for up to 180 days after the first day of trading. Let's say that Company X has 12 million shares outstanding, but the company sells 2 million shares to the public. Those 2 million shares represent only 17 percent of the total shares and are absent the sales pressure that employees might bring to the stock if they could sell. On the 181st day, if the stock is selling at a lofty price, the company's employees will sell their shares and take their profits. Outside investors will be along for the long downward ride.

Locking them out for 180 days is also a disservice to employees, and presents an illusion to investors who initially invest in the company. It artificially preserves the price of the stock, which is not in keeping with the spirit of a free marketplace. It also prohibits employees from taking profits when the company's stock may be at its highest, and may cause them to sell when the stock is at its lowest. Company lockouts do lend support to the stock, however, so that it will not immediately fall below its offering price. Only in this way can institutional investors and underwriters be assured that they can preserve their profits on day one without fearing that employees, the people who built and help run the company, will try to do the same.

PENALTIES

Penalties are meant to discourage bad behavior, but when investors are penalized for selling their IPO shares, it is Wall Street that is behaving poorly. When brokers pitch IPOs to their clients, they often leave the word "sell" out of their presentations because they face penalty bids or the withdrawal of their commission if their customers sell their shares within the first ninety days. Brokers may also be excluded from future IPOs, which could cost them thousands of dollars in commissions. In the world of IPOs, investors are punished for doing what comes naturally—selling to make a profit. Imagine that your financial advisor told you to buy the next Microsoft or Dell, but then says it doesn't merit a sale after the stock rises over 100 percent in its first day of trading. You might conclude that this logic is twisted, and that your financial advisor might be working more for himself than you.

IPO shares are lucrative for brokers, and it is understandable why they don't want their clients to flip their shares. With most IPOs, brokers are paid double what they would make on a regular stock transaction. A full-service broker can expect to make 4 percent on IPO shares, and brokers who persuade their clients to hold their positions stay in the good graces of their management. The SEC does not prohibit penalty bids and SEC spokesperson Chris Ullman has gone on record as saying, "Chairman [Arthur Levitt] . . . doesn't think the SEC should tell brokerage firms how to compensate employees."[5] Perhaps Levitt has long forgotten his days as a broker, because the way brokers are compensated has everything to do with how they treat their clients and determines in large part the advice they give. Once a commission is at stake, a customer's trusted financial advisor may switch to a dialect of brokerspeak instead of using the truth to explain his investment recommendations. Brokerspeak is a language that justifies the broker's recommendations while camouflaging his real intentions. Here are some examples of what transpires when a customer calls the broker wanting to sell his shares of an IPO. Our broker's name is Johnny:

Mr. Smith: Johnny, I bought five hundred shares of Wonderland Inc., and the stock is now up over 45 percent and I want to sell. I know that I have had the shares for only a couple of days, but I want to take my profits early. The money is going to help my grandson pay for his college tuition.

Johnny: Mr. Smith, Wonderland has a marvelous long-term future, and I think it would be a mistake to sell the company right now. The sky's the limit on this stock, and if you sell now, you're going to be leaving a lot of money on the table. I am sure you can see why it would be in your best interests to be a long-term holder of the stock. This way you will have more money overall, and be able to help your grandson even more. Let's give the stock its best chance and take another looking at selling in around sixty days.

Mr. Smith: Do you really think holding the stock is in my best interests?

Johnny: Absolutely! You'll regret selling now. Trust me on this one.

Ms. Robinson: Johnny, I want to sell Gizmo.com today. I am really happy with the stock's performance, but you know how finicky Internet stocks can be. Put in a sale order for all of my shares at the market price and call me later today when you confirm the sale.

Johnny: Ms. Robinson, as you know, you are one of my best clients, and I owe it to you to be as honest with you as possible.

Selling Gizmo.com would cost you dearly, because some are saying that it's the next Intel. You could make a fortune on this stock if you hold it for even just a few more months. Also, if you sell now I can't promise you that I'll be able to include you in any future IPOs. I certainly want to include you, but the powers that be may not allow me to do so. Please don't sell now. It would be the wrong thing to do.

Ms. Robinson: If you really feel that strongly about it, I'll keep the shares for now.

Such scenarios are played out every day at brokerage firms all over the country. Penalty bids represent an inherent conflict, which challenges brokers to be honest and should make investors leery of their broker's recommendations.

It's important to note that the penalties for investors who buy IPOs at discount firms are just as severe. I made calls to Charles Schwab, Fidelity, and E*Trade, and I told them that I was interested in participating in their IPO program. Each representative I spoke to gave me a general overview of how I might do this, but I was told in no uncertain terms that if I flipped my shares, the chances of me ever having another opportunity to buy IPO shares would be remote. Fidelity's standard holding period is fifteen days, while Charles Schwab and E*Trade each had thirty-day holding periods. I asked the representatives from Charles Schwab and Fidelity if they thought it was right that large institutions like themselves could sell their IPO shares at any time they pleased without penalty, but I, as a customer, could not. Not surprisingly, both representatives declined to respond to my question.

WHAT SHOULD BE DONE

Here are my suggestions for making the world of IPOs fairer for average investors:

1. *Make IPO road shows available to all investors.* The best investor is an informed investor. The Internet could be used to broadcast road shows to a worldwide audience, as could a videotape of the show. The days of closed-door sessions on public companies must come to an end. The SEC claims that it asks companies to fully disclose all material information, but at the same time allows average investors to be denied access to forums like an IPO road show. The SEC must revise this policy. In the meantime investors should make use of every resource at their disposal. For example, at the IPO Central Web site (www.ipocentral.com), investors can get information on companies that have filed with the SEC for an initial public offering. At Edgar (Electronic Data Gathering Analysis and Retrieval System), another good on-line resource, you can review S-1 filings (the registration statement) that companies submit to the SEC prior to going public. An S-1 will discuss the company's business and provide important financial information about the company. You can access Edgar for free at www.freeedgar.com.

2. *Erect a barrier between analysts and investment bankers.* In today's marketplace, an analyst's objectivity may succumb to the ring of the cash register. An analyst's reports should not be mixed with the need for underwriting fees. The "Chinese Wall" between bankers and analysts needs to reflect the interests of shareholders, who shouldn't be deceived.

3. *Eliminate penalty bids and all holding periods.* Brokers who are penalized for selling IPOs penalize their clients as well, giving them less-than-honest advice and shutting them out of future IPOs. Investors and employees of publicly held companies should be allowed to sell their shares whenever they please, just as institutional investors can. It is time for all investors, individual and institutional alike, to abide by the same rules, with the same opportunities to buy and to sell.

4. *Distribute IPO shares fairly.* All customers of full-service and discount firms who are eligible to invest in IPOs should be given

an opportunity to purchase them. It goes without saying, though, that all investors will not be able to participate in IPOs because of the limited number of shares; therefore, brokerage firms have good reason to make IPOs available to their customers who would most benefit from them. Average investors, above all, would benefit from the short-term gains in IPOs, yet they are denied access to them at every turn.

Brokers presumably know their customers' financial needs and goals. Full-service and discount firms can therefore, in good faith, make some IPO shares available to their neediest customers. Brokerage firms that wish to be fair-minded about distributing IPOs might do so on a first-come-first-serve basis or via lottery, once they have determined the neediest of their customers. Basing the distribution of IPOs on the needs of customers would be a new standard in the securities business. But it would be one that would be a great deal fairer than giving IPO shares to high-net-worth customers by default. A little fairness would go a long way on Wall Street and perhaps someday this fact will be realized by the industry.

ANALYZE IPOS AND INVESTMENT RESEARCH BEFORE YOU TRADE

• Take stock upgrades with a grain of salt if the investment bank has an underwriting relationship with the company.

• Ignore increased price targets for stocks being issued by investment banks without the supporting fundamentals to justify the new price target.

• Review all investment research with a critical eye and never blindly follow the advice of an analyst. Relying on your own feelings about a stock may turn out to be more reliable and profitable.

• Before participating in an IPO, ask your broker what the holding period is, and whether you will be penalized from participating in future IPOs if you sell the stock prior to the end of the holding period. Write down his responses.

• Ask your broker for a double-digit commission discount on the sale of all IPO shares. If he doesn't give you the discount, consider transferring the stock to a discount firm who will.

• Never be lured into opening an account with a broker on the promise that you will participate in IPOs. If your broker makes such a promise, make sure you get it in writing. The same advice also applies to on-line brokers.

• Before buying new issues, determine what percentage of the outstanding shares are being held by company insiders and when their lockout expires. Knowing these facts will be helpful to you when deciding to sell your shares.

CHAPTER 9

RETIREMENT, SAVINGS, AND YOUR 401(K)

Having to save and plan for the future seems like an absolute bore to most people. Who wants to take on the painstaking task of planning for the distant future when she can live life to the fullest today? To plan for tomorrow is difficult when the pressures of everyday living are so great. Perhaps this is why the notion of living rich and dying broke has become so fashionable. Americans are invited to spend at every turn, inundated with thousands of advertisements asking them to part with their money. We have become a nation of spenders and consumers instead of a nation of savers and investors. Many people love to shop, and many consumers pride themselves on being expert shoppers. I wish those people could see the real value in becoming expert investors instead.

Americans love to consume rather than invest because consuming is fun, with an immediate, tangible result. The national savings rate is at an all-time low, and personal bankruptcies are at an all-time high. The savings rate in 1975 was 9.3 percent, but as of June 1999 it had fallen to below zero. That's right—a negative number! Most Americans are not saving a penny. In 1998, over 1.4 million people filed for personal bankruptcy, the eighth straight year this trend increased. The trend will continue as more Americans build debt on credit cards that charge them 18-percent-plus interest a year for the privilege of doing so.

When young people look thirty years into the future, they see an eternity, with plenty of time to invest, yet when many elderly people look back thirty years, they say that their life went by in a blink. Young people's perception of time seems to give them license to procrastinate and spend wildly without guilt or fear of the future. When I was a broker I formulated numerous financial plans for my customers, and the great majority of them did not have the assets required to give them the lifestyle they were accustomed to after they retired, because they had not saved enough of their money. Inflation steadily eats away at purchasing power, making the need for investing wisely early on all that more apparent.

One day I had a meeting with an elderly couple to discuss their financial plan. I will call them Charlie and Martha. Charlie was seventy-two and Martha was a few years younger. Both were still working, not because they wanted to, but because they had to. Martha was a secretary and Charlie worked as a customer service representative at a local hardware store. At our meeting I told them the discouraging news that they would have to alter their lifestyle, sell their home, or continue working for years into the future. There was absolute silence in the room. None of these alternatives was pleasant, especially the option of selling their family home, which they had enjoyed for the past thirty years.

The silence was broken after a few moments when Martha looked over at me and said, "You know we've lived beyond our means all of our lives. What are we going to do?" I looked at the two of them and gave them the only possible answer. "I'll do the very best that I can." Charlie and Martha were out of luck because they had not planned for their future.

After thinking about the results of their financial plan, Charlie leaned toward me and asked in a quiet voice, "Do you think that we can afford a Winnebago?" Of course I had to tell them that I didn't think it was such a good idea right then given their current financial situation.

A few weeks later Charlie called, sounding in good spirits. He was very excited about the purchase of his new Winnebago. He wanted me to know that he and Martha would be out of town for a few weeks and that they were looking forward to their trip. I wished him the very best on his journey, knowing that all the financial plans and advice in the world could not have stopped him from making this trip. Charlie and Martha were two of the nicest people I ever knew, but they might well wind up having to work in dead-end jobs for the rest of their lives. Unfortunately, it is often people who think like they do who also outlive their money. Such thinking not only affects them, but it jeopardizes the long-term financial health of the country as well. The lack of savings and investment in America is a ticking time bomb whose explosion, when it comes, will be felt by millions of people who live longer, but must learn to live on less.

However you decide to invest your money, you don't want to wind up like Charlie and Martha. They are a fine example of bad financial planning, and even the most skilled financial advisor won't be able to help them.

To give Americans an incentive to save, the federal government created the Individual Retirement Account, but today only approximately 10 percent of the people who are eligible to open one have availed themselves of the opportunity.[1] Corporate America has also tried to come to terms with retirement by offering an investment vehicle, the 401(k). In this chapter, we will discuss some retirement issues and what you need to know about your 401(k). You might be surprised to learn that in some respects, the 401(k) serves the interests of employers more than employees. Volumes of material have been printed about such plans, but who better to give some insights into the product than its inventor, Ted Benna? The story of how he came to create a product that now holds the investment assets of over 30 million people certainly held my interest.

THE FATHER OF THE 401(K)

Before the 401(k), companies had only defined benefit plans, or pensions, which allowed employees to look forward to a set cash sum at retirement. Normally, they had to wait almost a lifetime to receive these funds, making it almost impossible to leave their companies for better opportunities. The 401(k) ushered in a new type of retirement account, one that did not guarantee a defined benefit, but focused on the defined, or set, contributions to the plan. Employees could contribute a percentage of their income, but ran the risk of not having a guaranteed sum at retirement. This risk was outmatched by the opportunity for greater returns. Companies also liked the plan because it was far more cost-effective for them to run than old-style pensions had been.

In the late seventies and early eighties, Ted Benna was an owner of Johnson Companies, a benefit consulting firm in Pennsylvania. At the time many of his customers were wealthy individuals looking for tax loopholes. It was Benna's job to counsel them within the boundaries of the law. Although this might have been lucrative for him, after a while he didn't find the work fulfilling. The there-must-be-more-to-life-than-this question was on his mind and Benna prayed for some guidance. His prayers were answered when Congress passed the Revenue Act of 1978, whose section 401, paragraph k described a little-noticed law that paved the way for employee tax-deferred savings. The law made it possible for companies to have a tax-deferred profit-sharing plan as long as the plan benefited more than just the top one-third of the highest-paid employees. After reading the section thoroughly, Benna immediately realized its real value. He saw paragraph k as an opportunity for millions of Americans to save for their retirement and to ensure their financial futures. The potential of the new law gave him a great deal of satisfaction, and was far removed from the often unrewarding and laborious task of helping wealthy individuals save on their tax bills. But before his vision could become a reality for millions, Benna needed to make it a reality for one client.

Benna contacted one of his clients at Johnson Companies about opening a 401(k). The customer was a bank that wanted to revamp its defined benefit plan to make it more attractive to employees. Armed with the knowledge about section 401(k), Benna thought that a new defined contribution plan would be ideal. He had to convince his customer that this would be a better alternative, then find a way to make the plan enticing to the bank's employees. The trick was how to make the 401(k) serve the interests of the employer while at the same time serving the interests of the employee. Benna thought he had found the answer when he came up with the idea of matching contributions. The bank would contribute twenty-five or fifty cents per dollar, on which it would get a tax break, while providing an incentive to employees to participate in the plan. Next, he set up the plan so employees could easily contribute to it from deductions in their salary.

The 401(k) plan sounded solid, but the bank turned down Benna's pitch. Like most banks, Benna's customer was conservative, and did not want to risk placing its employees' retirement assets into a plan that did not have a successful track record. This setback did not deter Benna from pitching the idea to two large insurance companies, both of which also turned him down. But revolutions often begin with one person or one company, and the 401(k) plan was no exception. On January 1, 1981, the Johnson Companies, Benna's own firm, launched their own 401(k) plan, the first company ever to do so in the United States. The 401(k) was finally born thanks to Ted Benna's vision and persistence, but the 401(k) revolution took some time to gather steam.

Marketing 401(k) plans in the early eighties was a difficult task, but Benna was up for the challenge. Many companies were hesitant to change their current retirement plans and the financial press at first didn't find the little-known 401(k) a newsworthy item. A reporter from the *Philadelphia Inquirer* was the first to write an article on the subject. According to Benna, after the piece appeared, the reporter got hundreds of calls from financial professionals who claimed that Benna was doing something illegal. They were wrong, and the industry's as well as the public's perception began to change after a subsequent article in *The New York Times*. After that piece, 401(k) plans began to receive national attention and companies began to convert their retirement plans to defined contribution programs. Today, $1 trillion is invested in more than 200,000 401(k) plans[2] that hold the assets of more than 30 million employees.[3] In the last twenty years corporate America has come to subscribe to Ted Benna's vision, but he doesn't take all the credit for the accomplishment. He told me that he had a partner in God. I jokingly said that whenever God and good intentions mix to produce a financial services product, it's a miraculous event. After a good laugh, Benna said he agreed.

Benna said he thought 401(k)s were best suited for persons making $25,000 to $85,000 a year. Those that made less than $25,000 probably would not have the discretionary income to participate. The fact that the plan is self-directed, meaning that participants make their own investment choices, concerned me because so few people are well educated about investing. When I mentioned my concern to Benna, he said, "When the heck did they ever have an opportunity to get educated? A great part of our lives concerns finances, but money management is not taught in our education system," and labeled this the number-one disadvantage of 401(k)s. The plan's greatest benefit, on the other hand, is that it gives investors a tax break, thus transforming them from spenders to savers. Do the benefits outweigh the negatives? This question is best answered by those who administer the plans and participate in them. Ted Benna's good intentions were now in the hands of corporate America, and it was up to individual companies to see to it that their employees' financial futures were in good hands. As we shall see, sadly, many employees are hurt more than helped by their retirement plans.

WHEN CORPORATE AMERICA CHEATS ITS EMPLOYEES

According to Ted Benna, companies have 401(k) plans because employees want them. The 401(k) helps recruit skilled employees looking for a long-term future with their employers. Companies hold out the 401(k) as a sign that they will provide for their employees' futures, but no longer take care of their employees' futures via these plans. Some employees call a 401(k) plan a benefit in itself. But this is not really the case. Unless the plan is administered with the highest of

standards and in the best interests of the employees, it is more a det-
riment than a benefit. We need to take an in-depth look at 401(k)s
and discuss how corporate America sins against its employees. The
following practices warrant your attention:

Can Someone Please Help Me? When someone asks for help, the
closer that help is located, the more likely he is to receive it. This rule
applies in many facets of life, but not when it comes to 401(k) plans.
Employees who want help in making their investment choices in their
401(k) plans cannot and should not rely on their companies. Most plans
have a number of investment choices and today around 57 percent of
401(k)s require that the participants choose between a number of mutual funds.[4] It is common knowledge among corporate benefit managers that the majority of 401(k) participants do not have the skills
necessary to make the best investment choices, nor do they know how
to calculate what they will need to save in order to have a secure
retirement. According to Merrill Lynch, more than 70 percent of employees enrolled in a 401(k) plan look for some investment guidance,[5]
but few if any receive it from their companies. Companies provide the
retirement plans, but out of fear of being sued, they do not give their
employees investment advice. This policy is like a company giving each
of its employees a corporate jet and telling her that the jet has the
capability to take her anywhere she wants to go. But the company
won't teach her how to fly the plane nor will it provide an experienced
pilot to fly it for her. Some might say that employees should take it
upon themselves to learn about investing before they participate in
their company's 401(k), but this alternative is unrealistic for the majority of employees. It is ridiculous to think that this option would
somehow relieve companies of the responsibility of helping their employees and making an investment in their financial futures.

I wanted to see if someone who deals with 401(k) investors every
day shared my opinions. I called Lisa Crosby, who has more than twenty
years' experience as a benefits manager. She currently holds this title
at Fujitsu America in San Jose, California, where she is responsible for
attending to the needs of 3,500 employees. In her experience, about
50 percent of people who signed up for a 401(k) program either asked
for advice or needed some hand-holding. Moreover, most people did

not have the wherewithal to sit down and calculate how much they needed to save. How many of those people was she allowed to help? Not a one! "I get a great deal of job satisfaction from helping people," she said. "It's frustrating when you can't help. Employees say you're the expert, you should be able to help me, but I can't."

Most companies provide their employees with "educational" materials. For the most part, these are generic pieces that state general investment principles, but do not address any individual's particular investment needs. Crosby said that collectively, companies spend millions of dollars on educational brochures, but their overall effect is minimal. "You can show people the materials," she said, "but many of them are overwhelmed by them. Either they don't have the time to read them, or they don't understand them." I commented that such brochures were probably written in a dry, stilted manner that would put most readers to sleep soon after the first page. While not directly confirming my suspicion, Crosby did say that "the materials that employees receive need to be more engaging. They need to draw the interest of the employee." What amazes me is how companies can honestly believe that people can learn from generic investment education materials at all. Investing is based on a person's personal goals and objectives, so how can generalities be truly helpful to anyone? For example, while portfolio diversification is theoretically a good concept, and stocks historically return more than bonds, how will these facts help the average employee make the best investment decisions? The answer resides somewhere between "I don't know" and "you got me."

The costs to companies neglecting their employees can be staggering. Crosby told me that when some employees get their 401(k) statements and see that the fund they chose is down a few cents compared with other funds in the plan, they immediately become concerned. They often make the mistake of switching their money to the fund that has done better, thereby making the mistake of buying high and selling low. This practice, among others, is an indication of the fear that comes with being an inexperienced investor, and shows how a lack of knowledge about money management can lead to poor investment decisions. If you multiply investment decisions like this many times over, the result will be devastating to millions of investors, simply because their employers did not help them make the right investment choices. When I asked Lisa what she thought the final result would be, she said, "People will have to work longer and they won't be able to retire. They'll live below their standard of living and maybe someday they'll join hands and sue the companies they worked for."

Finally, I asked Crosby what improvements she'd like to see in the administration of 401(k) programs. She mentioned Fujitsu's interactive Web site, which aided employees with their 401(k) choices, the first such site in existence and a source of great pride to her. So far, 50 percent of Fujitsu's employees have logged onto the site. She also said it was becoming increasingly common for companies to hire a personal investment advisor for their top executives, but not for the rest of the employees. "The people that need it the most have been left to fend for themselves and typically have to rely on a family member for advice," she concluded.

What About My Financial Future? Unemployment in the United States is currently at an all-time low. More than ever before, employees have a variety of choices, and among the thousands of companies in existence, there are some that actually care about the people who work for them. Some companies recognize employees as quality investments that need to be taken care of not only today (via medical and dental insurance and good salaries), but in the future. This is where the 401(k) plays a part in the recruitment process. The human-resources person shows the employee the past returns on the 401(k) and highlights the quality mutual funds that will be working toward providing her a bright financial future while she is hard at work during the day. A fact that is not mentioned in such meetings is that the overall returns of the funds have little to do with each individual's returns in her 401(k). The individual's returns will be determined by the choices she makes and by her trading activity throughout the year. Since this is the case, the 401(k) in itself does not provide for the employees' financial future. The employee's investment decisions will actually seal her fate.

When one compares the general returns of 401(k) plans and those of individual 401(k) participants, two different pictures emerge. For the last several years the stock market has been bullish, producing double-digit returns in the broad array of mutual funds that make up 401(k) plans. This would lead one to expect similar returns for participants in such plans, but when Brooks Hamilton, president of Brooks Hamilton & Associates, a Dallas-based benefits consulting firm and 401(k) administrator, investigated the real returns of individual 401(k) participants, the results were disturbing. Hamilton discovered a pattern in several large 401(k) plans that clearly showed a positive correlation between individual returns and income. The greater the income of participants, the greater their return in their company's 401(k) plan. One company that exemplifies this trend was a medical manufacturing company with sixteen hundred employees. Hamilton divided the participants into five equal groups based on 1997 returns and this is what he found:

Group	Average Salary	1997 Return[6]
1 (top 20%)	$52,123	28.7%
2	$43,188	24.1%
3 (middle 20%)	$39,079	19.9%
4	$34,254	15.3%
5 (bottom 20%)	$30,883	6.5%

Hamilton was surprised at the study's findings. He believed that the discrepancy in the income and investment performance was due to nonprofessional workers lacking the skills to make the best investment decisions. "If you ask nonprofessional people to exercise a professional skill, you get a dismal result," he said. Professional workers got better returns because they had the resources and skills to make better investment decisions. In one year alone, the effects of poor investing can be tremendous, but the long-term effects can be even greater for an employee's financial future. For example, let's say that an employee invests $2,000 a year in his 401(k) plan for thirty years. During this time, he increases his contribution by 10 percent a year to the maximum allowed and his employer contributes a 50 percent match. Those who make a 6 percent annual return end up with substantially less than those making the double-digit return. The results are as follows:

Annual Return	Value After 30 Years[7]
6%	$657,737
9%	$1,046,356
12%	$1,680,360
15%	$2,781,860

Imagine the lifestyle allowed by $657,737 for the rest of your life versus $2,781,860 or more. At 6 percent, the cost of living, taxes, and other expenses could make you dependent on your children, or force you to take a job. A better return could give you the freedom and quality leisure time you deserve in retirement. Hamilton knows of one company in which eight hundred out of three thousand employees have left their money in a money market for years. The company has known about this, yet has done nothing about it. These employees have missed out on one of the best bull markets of the century, he said, adding that they "are going to be impoverished when they get old." Since 401(k)s are self-directed, companies are not responsible for how their employees' financial futures turn out, but Hamilton thinks they should be: "We have transferred investment responsibility under the illusion that we will not be responsible for the consequences. What is going to happen when a great number of people reach old age and they are poor?" Hamilton believes that companies will eventually be held responsible for their negligence in helping employees manage their 401(k) assets, and he predicts that the legal ramifications will dwarf the settlements that have been made with tobacco companies.

I asked him if he thought investor education was the answer to this problem and he said no. He thinks the line between education and advice is blurry, and for this reason, it is unlikely that companies will marshal an effort to educate their employees. Time constraints also stand in the way of a full-fledged company-sponsored investor education program. Hamilton believes that companies don't have enough time to train their employees to do their jobs, much less turn them into professional money managers. Moreover, employees with leisure time will not spend it on learning how to be better investors. Given the often bland and unengaging investment material that most companies have to offer, Hamilton is probably right, but that doesn't mean that companies should not make an effort to educate their employees. Hamilton feels that "caring about the welfare of the employees is a smart business investment," and what could be better than some quality investment training to show employees that their companies do indeed care about them?

The solution, in Hamilton's opinion, is professionally managed money. He thinks that employees should ask their companies for a professionally managed alternative to relieve them of the responsibility of managing their own money. He was quick to point out that professionally managed pension funds typically grow 2 to 3 percent above the rate that 401(k) assets grow. His message to investors is to double what they save, and while this goal is difficult to achieve, it is worth striving for.

Do My Interests Count? One of the most appealing aspects to employees in participating in their company's 401(k) program is the company match. This typically takes the form of cash or company stock. Unlike pension fund managers, who by federal law are prohibited from investing 10 percent of their assets in company stock, no such rule applies to 401(k)s. Many participants are glad to receive shares of their company, but in the long term, having a large stake of company stock in a 401(k) plan can be dangerous. This will be especially true if there is a downturn in the market. Hardest hit will be those faithful employees closest to retirement who will see their financial futures sold off in the stock market. Diversification of assets is often cast to the wind as employees hinge their retirement on their company's stock alone. Of course, when employees are required to invest in company stock, this supports the stock price, and in this regard 401(k) plans can be said to serve the interest of the company more than the interests of their employees. How widespread is the purchase of large amounts of company stock in 401(k) plans? A study by the Institute of Management and Administration (IOMA) found that in plans with five thousand participants or more, company stock constituted 48.6 percent of the assets invested. In plans with 4,999 or fewer participants, however, only 10.3 percent of assets were invested in corporate stock. Not only is there a tremendous risk in heavily investing

401(k)s in the company's stock, but according to the study, the overall performance of company stock as an asset group underperformed the more diversified S&P 500. As you can see here, IOMA's study showed that the S&P 500 one- and three-year performance beat the corporate-stock-asset class:

RETURNS ANNUALIZED AS OF SEPTEMBER 30, 1998

Asset Class/Index	1-Year Return	3-Year Return
Company Stock	4.7%	15.7%
S&P 500	9.01%	22.57%

IOMA's study focused on well-known companies with thousands of employees who held 401(k) plans weighted with corporate stock, plans whose overall performance was less than the S&P 500. The study also highlighted the 401(k) plans of select companies in which corporate stock was not a large factor but which outperformed the S&P 500. For example:

BELOW THE S&P 500

Company	Total Return from 8/30/95–9/30/98	% of Corporate Stock in Plan
Coca-Cola	19.8%	92.3%
Apple Computer	.09%	31.0%
Gillette	18.3%	73.2%
PepsiCo	6.5%	60.8%
International Paper	5.9%	59.0%

ABOVE THE S&P 500

Company	Total Return from 8/30/95–9/30/98	% of Corporate Stock in Plan
Hershey Foods	30.7%	1.2%
Coors Adolph	39.2%	2.0%
General Dynamics	25.2%	11.0%

The message seems clear. Company matches of corporate stock may not be in the best interests of the plan's participants. There were a few examples in the study that showed good performance in plans with a preponderance of corporate stock, but these plans were more the exception than the rule. Loading up a 401(k) plan with company stock poses an additional risk that employers need not take. It is interesting to note that companies that invest their assets in financial markets diversify their interests in stocks and bonds. By doing so, they lower their overall risk and increase the chances of getting a good return. Imagine a company's CEO telling his board of directors that 50 percent of the company's profits has been invested in one stock. After the board members regain consciousness, they will diversify the company's investments to protect its interests. But when it comes to their employees' money, some companies have forsaken diversification and support a put-all-of-your-eggs-in-one-basket philosophy. What is good for the company is not good for its employees?

How Much Is It Going to Cost Me? The costs of contributing to a 401(k) plan never enter most participants' minds. Of course it is hard to think about these costs when so many of them are hidden from plain view. As we know, the majority of 401(k) plans contain mutual funds, which are some of the most expensive investments around today and over time can compromise the participant's returns. We have also learned that the most costly investment product does not generally give shareholders the greatest return for the cost, but the real cost of having mutual funds in a 401(k) plan won't be realized until most are ready to retire. For example, management fee expenses for a two-thousand-person plan can run from 98 basis points (a basis point is one-hundredth of a percentage point) to 280 basis points. Let's take two people, John and Mary, both thirty-five years old. Each makes $70,000 a year and they are good employees. Let's give them 5.5 percent annual raises. Both are big believers in their company's 401(k) plan and each contributes 5 percent of his or her gross pay to the plan. Both plans do pretty well over time, giving each of them a consistent 10 percent gross annual return. Mary works for the company whose 401(k) has expenses of 98 basis points, and after thirty years her 401(k) will be worth $868,000. John, on the other hand, has paid expenses of 280 basis points during his tenure with his company, and after thirty years of loyal service his retirement nest egg will be only $654,000—a $214,000 difference.[8] Hopefully, Mary and John were friends, because when John retires, he may need to hit her up for a loan.

Plan participants need to be mindful of the negative impact of fees over time. The success of a 401(k) program in most companies' eyes is measured by the number of employees who participate—not the plan's cost-effectiveness or performance. The participation rate is the standard measure of employee satisfaction, but I wonder how many employees will be satisfied when they learn that the costs of their plan, its excessive fees and lackluster performance, is reducing the amount of money they will have to live on in the future. Investing in a 401(k) is a tragedy in the making for some, a tragedy that, ironically, is currently being funded by the participants themselves.

A BRIGHTER TOMORROW

I wish 401(k) s would better serve the employees who are counting on them to provide for their retirement. I wish that every company would institute an investment education program. The fear of getting sued explains why some companies don't offer such programs, but it should not excuse them from exploring constructive ways that would help their staffs invest their money prudently. In addition, the laws that currently restrict such programs should be rewritten; rather than helping people, these laws help perpetuate their financial illiteracy. I would also give employees a hand in deciding what investments compose their plan. And they should be privy to all of the plan's expenses.

Moreover, the amount and form of the company match should be determined in part by the employees so that they could be assured that they are not taking additional risks with their financial futures. American companies are good at making money and increasing the overall value of their companies. Whether it is by the products they make or the services they provide, corporate America wants to make sure that their businesses are prosperous now and in the future. If corporate America began to think the same way about its greatest asset, the workers, everyone would be far better off.

GET A GRIP ON YOUR GOLDEN YEARS

• Replace the spend, spend, spend mantra with this one: save, save, save, and invest!

• Dispense with luxury items that you cannot afford and think of the "keeping up with the Joneses" mind-set as just plain nuts.

• Learn as much as you can about your company's 401(k) plan before you invest in it. The most important concern for you is not whether there is a company match, but whether or not the plan is a good match for you.

• Base your choice of investments for your 401(k) on their long-term prospects, not on their short-term performance. Minor fluctuations in value should not concern you and sometimes the best investment philosophy can be summed up by the title of the Beatles song "Let It Be."

• If you are a young person, learn all you can from elderly people. They can be great teachers and you will learn from their mistakes.

Part Three

GETTING SMART ABOUT WALL STREET

CHAPTER 10

ASLEEP ON THE JOB: REGULATORY AGENCIES AND OTHER INDUSTRY WATCHDOGS

If investors could buy peace of mind, they'd do so in a minute. Unfortunately, the world of investing doesn't offer many assurances. The stock market has been referred to as a wall of worry, made even more uncertain because government organizations like the Securities and Exchange Commission (SEC), funded with taxpayers' dollars, are not in the business of solely protecting investors' rights. I never like to hear about a person losing sleep over her investments, but if insomnia plagues your nights, this chapter will do little to relieve your problem. Indeed, it shows that while you lie awake with worry, the SEC and your elected officials in Washington are often asleep on the job.

FIGHTING IT OUT ON THE AIRWAVES WITH THE SEC

I never thought I would have an opportunity to publicly confront the SEC about some of my concerns, until Boston's WBZ radio talk-show host Ken Witham asked me to appear on a special broadcast on investment literacy. My first book, *Tricks of the Trade,* had recently come out, and Witham thought I would be a nice complement to his other guests, including two SEC representatives. Juan Marcelino, the Boston district administrator, and Jim Alderman, an associate administrator, joined me on the show that night. I told Witham that I had reservations about the SEC and that I was reluctant to confront its representatives with my honest opinions. He convinced me that this would be a perfect opportunity for the SEC to answer my questions.

The show was a learning experience and a sort of catharsis, whose therapeutic value has been long-lasting. During its course I became frustrated at how the SEC representatives sidestepped my questions, and I am sure they didn't like having to address my concerns during a live broadcast. For two straight hours, the SEC representatives and I battled it out. Our discussion centered on two topics.

First, I inquired why the SEC didn't mandate brokerage firms to include commissions and fees paid on investors' statements. I never got a concrete answer to my question, even though I asked it four separate times. If the SEC would mandate brokerage firms to note all of a customer's expenses on their statements, investors could easily compare the costs of investing with the rewards. This is only one example that leads me to believe that the SEC is not an advocate for investors. A true advocate represents only one set of interests, and not having the commissions noted on the brokerage statement plays to the interests of brokerage firms—not of individual investors.

Second, I wanted to know why the SEC allowed sales contests to continue when such firm-sponsored competitions were of absolutely no benefit to investors. Once again, I got more of a "bureaucratic" than a solid answer to my question. During our conversation, I recommended that the SEC require firms to note the costs of investing on all brokerage statements and to eliminate sales contests completely from the brokerage industry. These reforms would protect the interests of investors in the short and long term. Marcelino responded by saying that if the SEC would impose the regulations I had suggested, there would be an outcry, and it was obvious to me where the outcry would come from. It would arise from the brokerage community—not from individual investors. I felt that any listener would have realized then, as hopefully you the reader do now, that at times the SEC supports the practices of brokerage firms that are injurious to investors, and this is wrong!

WALL STREET AND WASHINGTON: A COZY RELATIONSHIP

When Wall Street looks in its pocket, it not only finds billions of dollars, but senators and congressmen as well. A politician's best friend on the campaign trail is money and Wall Street is happy to oblige with hefty campaign contributions that curry favor with elected officials. After a congressman receives a six-figure contribution from a political action committee (PAC) that represents the interests of a group of major brokerage firms, banks, or insurance companies, how aggressive an effort do you think he will make to stop the sales contests held by these brokerage firms? Do you think he'd be likely to introduce legislation requiring brokerage firms to note on statements the commissions investors pay?

First, let's take a look at some of the top congressional donors in the securities, investment, and finance category in the 1996 national election. The following contributions were made between January 1, 1995, and December 31, 1996:

Contributor	Total [1]
American Bankers Assn.	$1,514,328
Merrill Lynch	$855,105
Goldman Sachs	$657,785
J. P. Morgan	$596,820
Morgan Stanley	$569,025
NationsBank	$563,929
Bank One	$505,976
Investment Company Institute	$444,014
PaineWebber	$439,402

Bear, Stearns	$434,650
Smith Barney	$411,533
Chicago Mercantile Exchange	$410,450
Dean Witter	$383,252
Chicago Board of Trade	$372,744

How can the average investor's interests be protected when large financial concerns are funding the campaigns of congressmen who protect those interests? Big-money interests line the pockets of congressmen, who then support securities industry practices that pick the pockets of individual investors. I have always believed that the securities industry as a whole—not the individual brokers—is unkind to average investors. When you see an example of where the money trail begins and ends, it easy to see why.

The Senate Committee on Banking, Housing and Urban Affairs oversees the SEC. The chairman of the committee, Phil Gramm (R-Texas), is a staunch believer in a free-market economy, and espouses an antiregulatory view. Having more regulations to protect investors' interests might not seem such a wise idea to him, especially because his campaigns are financed by some of Wall Street's largest concerns. For example, between 1993 and 1998, Gramm received $759,404 from PACs that support securities and investment interests. Broken down, he received contributions from: Morgan Stanley Dean Witter ($64,150), Bank of America ($39,450), Merrill Lynch ($24,700), Goldman Sachs ($21,500), Equitable Companies ($28,150), MBNA America Bank ($24,050), and Citicorp ($60,450), among others.[2] I don't think that Wall Street fears that Gramm will become an investor's advocate anytime soon. Other members of the committee won't spread the message of securities reform either, because many of them have received money from similar sources. When you come face-to-face with these contributions, it is difficult to know who Gramm and the committee really work for. Are they representatives of the people, for the people, or merely spokespersons for the interests of the Wall Street firms that help reelect them?

When you look at campaign contributions, it's clear why the SEC is not an advocate for the individual investor. Perhaps Wall Street's numerous campaign contributions motivated Congress to nix the SEC's request for an additional $7 million in its fiscal 1999 budget. The SEC had requested the money to increase salaries in order to reduce the agency's high employee turnover.[3] Seven million dollars is a rather paltry sum compared with the funding of other federal programs, but Congress still declined to give it to the SEC. The House of Representatives did not seek to redress this wrong the following year because it passed a bill that decreased the SEC's funding by 7.6 percent for its year 2000 budget. The cuts will require the SEC to cut its staff by 10 percent. The average-investor victims of securities fraud pay the true costs of Wall Street's relationship with Washington, as you will see in the following story.

THE DEVIL IN DISGUISE: THE STORY OF ROGER TURNER

When you read about investors who have lost money to a financial advisor, your first reaction might be, "Oh, this could never happen to me." Stories like this, in magazines and newspapers across the country, are like highway accidents; they pique a passerby's interest but are soon forgotten. Imagine that you have worked hard all your life, and then wake up one day to find that you have no money or investments. Your plans for the future are in ruin, your retirement a shambles, your greatest fears are realized, and there is not one person in the world who wants to help you. You don't know whom to turn to, whom to trust, and all the while the clock is ticking. The rent is due, the electric bill has to be paid, the pantry is practically empty, and the prospect of moving in with one of your children or getting at least a part-time job crosses your mind with increasing frequency. You haven't worked in years, but you are hopeful someone will hire you—that anyone will hire you. The harsh reality of Wall Street's sins is best realized when you hear the stories of investors who have suffered at the hands of people who have taken advantage of them. People like former stockbroker Roger Turner.

The investment bug hit Turner in the 1970s when he was a teenager living in Germany, where his father was in the air force. One day, in a class on investing, Turner's teacher proposed that the students invest in the market. Turner chose McDonald's to invest in, saying, "I guess from there, I just had a fascination about how businesses work and how people can own businesses."[4] Turner knew where his talent lay, so after graduating from high school, he skipped college and began practicing his craft: selling. In 1983, at the age of twenty-two, he became a stockbroker for E. F. Hutton, now Lehman Brothers.[5]

The job was perfect, marrying Roger's love of investing with his sales abilities. He started his business, like many brokers, by calling on friends and acquaintances. After a successful four-year stint, however, his career at Hutton came to an end when he was fired for pocketing a $1,218 commission for the sale of a security not approved by the firm. He was reprimanded by the NASD, then bounced around a number of regional brokerage houses before starting his own financial services company called Annable Turner and Company.[6]

Annable Turner, registered with the SEC, specialized in fee-based investment advice to individuals and corporations. Turner used a number of methods to drum up business. He gave seminars at a number of corporations like General Dynamics, which hired him to present "Financial Strategies for Successful Retirement." He headed an investment club called ATCO, at which he advised participants on investing. He had an arrangement with a company called Royal Alliance, owned by Sun America, that let him participate in the company's Royal Advisory Service. In this capacity, he referred his customers to other broker/dealers and asset management firms that would share transaction and advisory fees with him. Turner would move his clients' assets into these companies, one of which was Charles Schwab, and then, in some cases, liquidate their portfolios and split the commission with the firm. Surprisingly, Schwab and Turner's clients did not know that during most of his dealings with Schwab, he was not a licensed investment advisor.

Another fact Turner failed to mention was that in addition to Annable Turner, he had financial interests in a number of other companies, including Carl A. Johnson & Sons, Health Teamm Management, and Manufacturers Acceptance Corporation (MAC). All of these companies needed cash, so Turner convinced his elderly clients to give him money which he used to fund his own companies without their knowing it. His tricks involved the naming of securities and sleight-of-hand maneuvers that glossed over his real intentions. For example, he convinced some of his clients to invest in MAC, claiming it was a well-respected municipal bond issued by the city of New York when in fact it was his own company, Manufacturers Acceptance Corporation. Other clients fell for the Towers Financial Corporation scam, whereby their money went to fund Turner's other companies instead of what they thought was the traded security Towers Financial. To further the subterfuge, he came up with elaborate, phony statements that showed his clients' investments and their stellar returns all while their money was being used to fund his own companies. Turner continued this practice for a decade, and before he finally came to justice, twenty-two of his clients claimed he had defrauded them out of $2.3 million.

Turner's clients thought at first that he was their friend and trusted financial advisor. Bonnie Bennet, for example, a retired schoolteacher in her eighties, described him as a "handsome fellow with a golden tongue" who had a "beautiful personality."[7] She never doubted his credentials as a financial consultant and his ability to make money for her. "I thought, well, if he passed the test with E. F. Hutton, surely he's all right, because that is a well-respected company."[8] She happily handed Turner $340,000, her entire savings. It didn't take him long to swindle her out of almost every penny.[9]

Tommy and Margie Smith also initially thought highly of Roger Turner. He came highly recommended by some of their friends, who claimed that they were getting first-class returns. The Smiths had accumulated more than a half-million dollars from the oil business. Tommy had taken an early retirement, after forty years, assuming that their retirement would be pretty much worry-free. They told Turner that "they did not know the first thing about investing"[10] and he assured them that he would take good care of their money. Margie recalls Turner as "so pleasant and nice and handsome."[11] He had a boy-next-door charm, could talk about just about anything, she said, and his pleasant demeanor was matched only by his Christian values, which he made readily known to most of his customers. Margie recalls one prayer Turner intoned, kneeling beside them to reassure them that his investment recommendations were in their best interests. "It was the most beautiful prayer you'd ever want to hear," recalled Margie.[12]

Everything changed when Tommy was diagnosed with terminal cancer. He was bedridden and suffered for months before he died. Soon after her husband passed away, Margie called Turner for an update on their investments. She needed the money to pay for expenses the couple had incurred during Tommy's illness. That's when she learned she was broke. All of her and Tommy's money had vanished. Still grieving over the loss of her husband, she had to face the terrible prospect of losing her home. Her life was ruined, all because of Roger Turner.[13]

The cost of Turner's misdeeds is seen not only in the money he lost, but in the lives he damaged. Robert and Maureen Garbarino told their story this way: "Due to Roger Turner's lies and misappropriation of our IRA rollovers, we lost in just principal alone $85,000. This did not include the interest and capital gains that our IRA money should have been earning while under his care. It was an *emotional shock* [emphasis added] to us when we learned of our loss because we trusted this person as our financial advisor. We had hoped to have an early retirement, but because of our losses due to Roger E. Turner, we will now have to work past the age of sixty-five."[14]

Many other victims as well had placed their faith in Roger's ability to manage their money honestly. Investors like Dr. Ernest H. Byers Jr., a disabled medical doctor suffering from Lou Gehrig's disease; Joe and Cathy Cook, a fifty-nine-year-old couple who lost over $80,000 of retirement funds; Beulah Dickerson, a ninety-year-old-widow who lost her savings; Inez Sweet, a widow over seventy who thought that she was investing in a CD; Joseph Dauper, a fifty-two-year-old man who entrusted his lump-sum distribution of $341,000 in retirement funds and lost $315,000; and Franklin Engle, who handed over his retirement funds of $100,000 only to have it all lost.[15]

After the misery that Turner put his clients through over a ten-year period, you'd think the SEC would have shut down his business and thrown him behind bars. Turner's own secretary made an anonymous call to the SEC in 1990, only two years after he started Annable Turner. She informed the agency that Roger was stealing money from his clients. The SEC never responded to her call. On May 22, 1995, one of Turner's clients, Kenneth Ingle, wrote to the SEC asking them to investigate Turner, but a year later Turner was still in business. In a July 1996 letter to Royal Alliance, the company that executed Turner's trades and helped establish him as an investment advisor, Ingle laments his situation: "I did request the SEC to investigate. And what I got was nothing but a bureaucratic response. Plus, they told me if I wanted to learn what they had discovered, I would have to file a freedom of information claim and should expect it to take three years to be processed. A copy of their letter is enclosed. (Our tax dollars at work for us)."

The SEC didn't tell Ingle that they had reason to suspect Roger Turner of impropriety back in July of 1995, two months after Ingle had written his initial letter. In a letter to Turner dated July 28, 1995, the SEC makes it clear they knew he had not divulged his outside business interests and not updated his records with the proper regulatory authorities. On page two of the letter, they state the following:

- "In general, discussion of ATCO's and your other personal business interests needs to be updated." In other words, the SEC was faulting Turner for not fully disclosing that he had outside business interests and requesting that he update his business records to reflect such interests.

- "You were censured and fined $2,500 in 1988 for violating the NASD's Rules of Fair Practice. This fact is currently not disclosed. Item 11 should be marked affirmatively and an explanation should be made on your Schedule D."

- "You claim not to manage money on a discretionary basis. However, it was discovered during the examination that several clients have given ATCO discretionary authority over their Charles Schwab and other brokerage accounts. The Schwab brokerage account application forms give you the authority to transact on your clients' behalf. This is, by definition, discretionary authority."

In addition to these charges, the SEC's letter contains two pages listing repeat violations. These were the violations that they had noted since their last examination of Turner in 1990. Why didn't the SEC investigate Annable Turner when their own findings showed that Roger Turner had repeatedly violated SEC regulations? Why didn't the SEC respond to the call Roger's assistant made back in 1990 and why did they keep Ingle in the dark for over a year about their knowledge of Turner's activities? I wanted some answers, so I asked Jeanne Crandall, the defense attorney for a number of Turner's victims and the person who finally brought him to justice.

Crandall has spent a good part of her legal career fighting fraud or defending those accused of committing it. She welcomed me in her office's vestibule and escorted me back to the conference room, which had a picture-perfect view of the Dallas skyline. She told me that the Roger Turner case had consumed her for two years. Nothing in her career had prepared her for the frustration of dealing with the SEC and the U.S. attorney's office. At times she, as well as her clients, were convinced that they were the only ones who cared about seeing Roger Turner pay for his crimes.

Crandall was upset with the SEC for ignoring Turner's assistant's 1990 phone call and displeased that the SEC had not acted upon Ingle's 1995 letter to the SEC. What infuriated her most was that between the time of Ingle's letter to the SEC (May 1995) and his letter to Royal Alliance (July 1996), a whopping $600,000 of her clients' money had been misappropriated. When I asked her to explain the SEC's negligence in investigating Turner's business practices, she said, "The SEC uses the excuse that they don't have the budget to clean it up. They have the legislative authority to do more than they're doing, but they're just too lazy." Surely, I said, the SEC's knowledge that Turner had outside business interests that could pose conflicts with his clients would have been enough to prompt a serious investigation. She smiled and said, "Even the pillars of the brokerage industry don't regulate conflicts of interest. The SEC relies on the NASD to do that, and the NASD, ironically, is a self-governing organization run by brokers."

Crandall is correct, and I thought her response explained not only why the SEC had not involved itself in the Roger Turner affair, but why it hasn't proactively addressed the other conflicts of interests inherent in the industry as well. "Don't rely on regulators to keep the business clean," Crandall emphasized. "You have to assume this responsibility for yourself." Her message to criminals who commit fraud was equally sound: "Crime does pay when regulators who are charged with catching you do not catch you for a long time."

The courtroom was packed on May 12, 1998, when Judge Joe Fish sentenced Roger Turner. Jeanne Crandall's hard work had paid off, but the verdict, at least to some of the victims, seemed like a hollow victory. Judge Fish had asked that the victims write him letters describing the damage they had suffered at Turner's hands. He acknowledged that many of the victims were elderly, but said in open court that this would not make a difference, and sentenced Turner to only thirty-four months in prison. Once he was released from prison, Turner would have to pay his twenty-two victims a mere $200 a month, to be split equally among them, until he paid a total of $892,000. In other words, each victim would have to wait close to three years before he or she would begin to be repaid by Turner and at that point would receive a paltry $9 a month. It would take Turner, who was in his mid-thirties at the time, a little over 371 years to pay back the money that he stole. This made the verdict laughable and Judge Fish the object of some scorn. The only real monetary reward for the victims came as a result of Jeanne Crandall's out-of-court settlements with Charles Schwab and Royal Alliance, but even these sums paid only a fraction of what the victims lost.

One of Turner's victims, Vivian Palfi, told me, "The judge lived up to his last name—he was the coldest fish I've ever seen. He never looked at us [the victims] once. He kept calling us victims, but he never acknowledged us as victims." Palfi, who had recently undergone chemotherapy, said that if she had been stronger at the time, she would have liked to express her outrage about the verdict to Judge Fish, who, amazingly, refused to allow the victims to speak in court. She would have told him that taking advantage of elderly people should have made all the difference in the world in sentencing Turner. "Where do people our age start over?" she asked.

When I asked her why she thought Judge Fish had been so un-sympathetic, Palfi said, "I think that sometimes they just don't care. I mean they got a case in front of them, okay, let's hurry up and get this off the docket and go about our business. Let's not get involved in the personal side of things. Let's not get involved with the people." Dallas attorney Mike O'Neil, who primarily represents investors who have been on the receiving end of such scams, thought such feelings were common and valid: "The U.S. attorney and the others are not on the cutting edge of consumer protection," he said. "The feds are heavily loaded and understaffed and somewhat cynical about whether the customer really got hurt."[16] Todd Moore, who represented one of Turner's victims, agreed: "The garden variety of securities fraud starts out with a handful of individuals who get bilked. But the dollar amounts aren't large enough to warrant the attention of regulators, whose limited resources are earmarked for the bigger players."[17]

I suppose Turner's victims took some comfort in seeing him go to prison, and hopefully it taught him something as well. He never apologized to his former clients in court, but he did send Vivian Palfi and Bonnie Bennet a letter voicing his remorse. "I am very embarrassed and ashamed about the situation I have put you in, as well as my wife and family," he wrote. "I am very, very sorry." The letter was written before he went to jail; his offer to work off his debt instead of going to prison was rejected by both Bennet and Palfi.

LOOK OUT FOR NUMBER ONE

- Don't count on industry regulators to protect your interests. Be mindful that the Securities and Exchange Commission (SEC) does not have the necessary resources to effectively police the securities industry.

- "An honest man cannot be cheated." Keep this maxim in mind when the next too-good-to-be-true investment comes your way.

- Con artists are generally pressed for time and will try to convince you about the urgency of the sale. When time is of greater importance than the investment itself, you should know that interests other than your own are at issue.

CHAPTER 11

SETTLING DISPUTES WALL STREET'S WAY: HIGH-POWERED LAWYERS AND SLEEPING SOLOMONS VS. THE INVESTOR

When an investor buys stock from a broker, and the stock increases in value, the investor often pats himself on the back. When he loses money, he generally wants to blame someone else. More often than not, that person is his financial advisor.

One of the hardest lessons to learn, especially for first-time investors, is that a decrease in the value of an investment doesn't necessarily show that the the broker or financial planner who advised its purchase was incompetent. Who is to blame for bad judgment calls and inappropriate advice is a matter of dispute, which should be settled in an appropriate forum, usually an arbitration hearing. Most account-opening documents contain an arbitration clause, which requires investors to sign away their right to settle disputes with the firm or their broker in a court of law. I spoke with several attorneys who defend investors, as well as an arbitrator, an expert witness, and even a defense attorney who defends brokerage firms against customer complaints. All were candid about the arbitration process. Their views were wide-ranging and they all agreed on only a few points, some of which may be as surprising to you as they were to me.

HOW ARBITRATION WORKS

The National Association of Securities Directors (NASD) is the organization primarily responsible for conducting arbitrations. There are roughly seven thousand securities arbitrators, and the NASD conducts thousands of arbitration cases every year. That the arbitration process is run by the NASD might lead some investors to question whether they can get a fair hearing. Since the claim is against the members of the securities industry, one might well wonder about the objectivity of a hearing supervised by a body that represents this industry. This concern was shared by most of the attorneys that I interviewed, yet none of them thought that going to court would be a better alternative. The investor starts the process by filing a complaint, or a "statement of claim," in which he details his case against the firm and/or the broker. He first states the damages he has suffered and the amount of money he thinks that he is entitled to in reparation. He does not have to justify his calculation of the damages, and in many cases plaintiff's attorneys knowingly inflate them in hopes of maximizing their settlement. Twenty days after filing the statement of claim, the broker and/or the firm has to file a statement telling their side of the story.

If the damages are less than $50,000, one arbitrator hears the case. If the amount exceeds $50,000, a panel of three decides the investor's fate. The panel is generally composed of one member from the securities industry and two members—typically a lawyer or a full-time arbitrator—not in the industry. During the panel selection, each side gets a brief biography of the arbitrators and has an opportunity to request that randomly selected arbitrators not sit on the panel. During the proceeding each side can call and cross-examine witnesses, but the rules of evidence are more relaxed than they are in a court of law. Most anything can be deemed evidence. A few days after the proceeding, each side will be informed of the panel's decision, but unlike court, neither side can appeal the decision. Moreover, the arbitrators are not obliged to divulge the reasoning they used in reaching their verdict, which adds a level of mystery and secrecy, if not arbitrariness, to the proceeding that many investors find unsettling. Most plaintiffs opt to settle rather than go through the entire process. For example, in 1997, out of the 6,500 securities arbitration cases that were filed, only 1,653 cases made it to an arbitration hearing. A full 76 percent of the cases were either settled or dropped.[1]

THE PLAINTIFF'S ATTORNEY

Jeff Ferentz of Greenbaum & Ferentz, a firm located in Newport Beach, California, has a little over twenty years' experience in securities litigation. He agreed to be interviewed, promising to give me "an earful" about the arbitration process.

He told me in no uncertain terms that he firmly believes that the arbitration process is stacked in favor of the brokerage firms. "The brokerage industry has unlimited finances and resources to develop a case, but plaintiffs rarely have this sort of finances or the mental energy," he said. He also mentioned a problem with "delayed justice" that is inherent in the system and runs counter to the interests of the clients he represents. Plaintiff's attorneys work on a contingency basis, receiving 30 to 40 percent of the reward, but the defense attorneys who handle cases for the brokerage firms are paid hourly; hence it is in their best financial interests to bill for as many hours as possible. This sometimes causes unnecessary delays of months or even years. Such delays make the system especially taxing to elderly clients.

Ferentz goes so far as to question the fundamental fairness of the entire proceeding. Like many of his clients, many arbitrators are elderly and, in Ferentz's view, dependent on the income—$400 a day, paid by the NASD—they receive from being arbitrators. Since an arbitrator can be tossed from a proceeding by either side, a brokerage firm that knows that an arbitrator has rendered large judgments against firms before is not likely to wish to see him on any future panels. As a result, arbitrators who might reward a plaintiff a substantial judgment face the possibility that they may not be asked to arbitrate again if they do so. "Many of these people live on the income, so instead of being unbiased, they are slightly prejudiced for their own protection," Ferentz says. In his view, arbitrators, in many cases, grant investors less than what they are entitled to; instead of being objective judges, arbitrators sometimes act like modern-day Solomons, splitting the baby in hopes of appeasing both sides . . . while ensuring their own incomes as well.

Ferentz went on to express some concerns about the professional conduct of some arbitrators. In 1996, he contacted the local Los Angeles NASD office and requested that they not be allowed to drink alcoholic beverages during lunchtime. "We frequently saw arbitrators having drinks at lunch and then falling asleep in the afternoon," he said. He claims that arbitrators still often doze off during the proceedings, and described one who regularly takes calls on his cellular phone while hearings are in progress. As I listened to his words, arbitration was beginning to seem less a viable resource for injured investors than a travesty of justice.

Ferentz also expressed some concern about the lack of education and expertise he often noticed among arbitrators. The NASD requires that arbitrators take only a one-day training course, of which 75 percent consists of procedural matters and 25 percent of "product knowledge"—information about mutual funds and stocks. "I think that the NASD does its very best, but the training is insufficient," Ferentz says. "If I were in charge of the panel, they would have to sit in on some live arbitrations first to see how they worked. Furthermore, arbitrators have insufficient product knowledge." After listening to his comments, I wondered how serious the NASD could be about resolving investor disputes if they required arbitrators to take only one day of training.

Ferentz's biggest frustration in his job, however, was about getting paid. Most lawyers like Ferentz work on a contingency basis, so they not only have to worry about whether their clients will be granted an award, but also whether the firm that has been ruled against has the ability to pay. This is not a concern among large firms like Paine-Webber or Morgan Stanley DeanWitter, but it is among small firms. A small firm can quickly declare bankruptcy, and regardless of the skills of the representing attorney, there is little hope that the investors who have been wronged will recover a cent. For example, in Ferentz's case against the firm Blinder Robinson, which he jokingly referred to as "Blind 'em and then Rob 'em," he represented fourteen thousand people in a class action suit and was awarded a judgment of $70.5 million. His victory turned out to be hollow, however, because Blinder Robinson declared bankruptcy. His clients ended up collecting peanuts. While it's true that an arbitration award is binding, investors still might not get a penny if the firm they are dealing with runs into financial difficulty.

I also interviewed attorney Robert Uhl, who has practiced securities law for close to twenty years, and who also criticized the arbitration process. His firm, Aidikoff and Uhl, is located in Beverly Hills, so I just had to ask him if most of his clients were wealthy people or celebrity types. He told me that most of his clients were average investors or working-class people who had been taken in by brokers. It was his job to make sure that they got the most out of an arbitration hearing. I soon discovered that Uhl's view of the arbitration process was similar to Ferentz's.

As with Ferentz, I asked Uhl if he thought that the arbitration process favored the brokerage industry. "Of course there can be no good faith dispute on this, because it is impossible for that forum to be fair," he answered. As I said, arbitration panels are composed of three members, one of whom must come from the securities industry. In Uhl's view, these odds do not work in the plaintiff's attorney's favor. He thinks that his clients should be judged by their peers, as they would be in court, instead of by a representative from the securities industry. He offered the example of a medical malpractice case in which a doctor accused of wrongdoing is judged not by other doctors, but by average citizens who have no particular stake in the medical industry or the subject of malpractice. He felt that the same rule should apply to the arbitration process.

Uhl also has some concerns about the way arbitration judges render their decisions. Since arbitrators are not required to justify their decisions, "the only way to cleanse and sanitize the system is to cast some sunlight on the arbitrators' decision-making process." The fact that decisions cannot be appealed also causes him some concern, but in the end, what matters most to Uhl is the arbitrator himself. He seemed to say that an arbitrator's mood and temperament counts for far more than any objective rules of law. He quoted a line from the infamous attorney Roy Cohn to support his view: "Don't tell me what the law is, just tell me who the judge is." According to Uhl, if he knows who the arbitrator is in a given case, he can determine the outcome of most hearings ahead of time.

Both Ferentz and Uhl made some interesting comments about investors in general and the brokers they charged with wrongdoing. Each agreed that a good portion of the investors who called them did not have legitimate claims. Ferentz said that about 40 percent of the people he interviewed had legitimate cases, while Uhl said only one out of four investor complaints he reviewed had merit. Both of them said that investors often called them after they had lost money in the market, hoping to sue to recover their losses. While both Ferentz and Uhl lent an understanding ear to these investors, they usually had to decline these cases because no wrongdoing had taken place. Both felt that brokers are not entirely responsible for their actions when the industry supports sales contests, recognition clubs, and the like. They believe that the full-service brokerage industry has an inherent conflict of interest, which compromises the customer's interests and tarnishes the broker's career.

THE ARBITRATOR

Dallas attorney Bill Lamoreaux has been an arbitrator since 1987, specializing in employment and labor law. He's worked for the New York Stock Exchange and American Stock Exchange as well as the NASD. By industry standards, he is a mere youngster, being only in his early fifties. I first met Lamoreaux in his capacity as an attorney, not an arbitrator, when I was a broker battling my firm in a salary dispute. I had seen three Dallas attorneys before going to Lamoreaux; one wanted to charge $8,000 to represent me, and another said that his services would range anywhere from $1,500 to $3,000. After hearing my case, Lamoreaux said that he would not charge me anything, and advised me to take my case up with the state of Texas employment board. I followed his advice and the matter was finally resolved in my favor. Bill Lamoreaux is an honest soul, so I was confident he would be just as sincere with me when I asked him about the role of an arbitrator and the arbitration process in general.

He first shared the "pros" of arbitration. He thought that it was less expensive and faster than a typical court proceeding. On the "con" side, he said he had witnessed a number of attorneys who did not represent their clients well and seemed to know little about securities matters in general. His best advice to investors is to be sure their attorney specializes in securities law. The chances of an unskilled attorney winning against a brokerage firm are next to nil.

Lamoreaux felt that overall, the arbitration process is fair to investors. When I mentioned that the plaintiff's attorneys I spoke with thought that the system was biased toward the securities industry, he said he didn't wish to comment on that. I pressed him several times for an answer, but he politely refused each time. Next, I asked him if he thought arbitrators received sufficient training. He replied that he had not learned much from the one-day session arbitrators are obliged to attend, but was quick to add that "for most people one day of training is not going to make a difference, but it's one day more than is given to a juror." I also wanted to know if he believed that arbitrators should be compelled to justify their decisions. He pondered his answer before saying yes, but defended the current practice by claiming that such a policy would result in a clerical nightmare and slower processing of the cases overall.

Finally, I asked him why the securities industry forced investors to go through arbitration instead of settling their disputes in a court of law. He gave me a number of reasons for this. First, the industry perceives arbitration as less expensive, and perceives arbitration panels as more industry-oriented than individual-oriented. In a court of law, on the other hand, jurors are inclined to side with individuals instead of organizations. Second, in cases in which there is a question of liability, the panel is more inclined to find in favor of the firm than of the individual. Finally, he said there was a perception within the securities industry that arbitration panels are less inclined to award punitive damages to individuals, which could total in some cases thousands if not millions of dollars.

I left Lamoreaux's office thinking about a gambler who goes to Vegas to play his favorite game of blackjack. While it's quite true that he can expect a "fair" game (i.e., a game in which the house does not cheat), it is also true that he is at a distinct disadvantage compared with the house. He is playing by the house's rules, and as any gambler knows, the odds are always with the house. In the same way, investors who try their hand at arbitration may get a fair hearing, but they are playing by the industry's rules. This doesn't necessarily mean that they will go home as losers, but it does mean that they have few chances of beating the industry.

THE DEFENSE

Tom Fehn has been a lawyer for thirty years; based in Los Angeles, he is a partner in the firm of Fields, Fehn and Sherwin. Fehn defends brokers in arbitration cases, but has also sued brokerage firms on behalf of individual investors.

I first asked him what he thought about the arbitration process and he answered that it was similar to a court of law in some respects, but it often seemed like "the arbitrators and the evidence were not in the same room," since unlike a court of law, arbitration decisions do not have to be supported by case law and facts. The training arbitrators receive also concerned him. "I find the training positively frightening," he said. Fehn thought the problem of arbitrators who are poorly versed in securities matters was "widespread in the industry." In such cases, he said, investors "come to the party unarmed." Then he assured me that if he, as a defense attorney, were pitted against a less-than-competent lawyer at an arbitration hearing, every advantage would be his. "I will not lose," he said. Fehn warns investors to make sure that their attorney can give them the best counsel. The defense attorneys will show no mercy in trying to win their case for the brokerage firm.

The first job of the defense attorney, according to Fehn, is to establish the investor's competence. Many investors who seek redress through an arbitration claim they did not understand what they were doing at the time, and had totally relied on their broker's advice. Fehn believes this is simply not true in most cases, and that most investors do know what they are buying, especially when they have been receiving their brokerage statements for months, if not years, and never complained. "The higher the stack of paper gets, the more unreasonable it gets for the investor not to look at it," he said. Brokers, in his view, do not have a legal or moral obligation to be right all the time, but individuals need to take responsibility for their actions, regardless of their financial advisor's advice.

In an arbitration hearing, once Fehn has established the investor's competence, he tries to prove that the investor is responsible for her actions. Rather than taking a hostile stance toward the investor/plaintiff, he says, "By the time I get finished, I will be their friend." He tries to show that the investor is "competent at the business of living," that she exercises her common sense in situations outside of investing. Once he has established this, he will typically comment to the panel that the plaintiff has common sense, but unfortunately she abandoned it when she talked with her broker. Since this is the case, she has no one to blame but herself for her investment decisions.

When I mentioned this standard defense-attorney maneuver to Jeff Ferentz, he called it "bullshit." He said that brokers lull their clients into feeling a false sense of security, into depending on them for advice that will compromise their—the clients'—interests. Also, he pointed out that many investors don't know the right questions to ask, so how can they possibly be responsible for their investment decisions? Furthermore, he feels that most brokers really don't know their customers' investment objectives when they make their recommendations. He generally finds that 95 percent of his clients' account-opening documents have been filled out incorrectly, including the customer's net worth and risk level. If this is the case, and the broker makes unsuitable recommendations, then how can the broker not be held liable? As a defense attorney, however, it is his job to show that the investor bears the ultimate responsibility for his investment decisions, just as it is the plaintiff's attorney's job to show that the broker is accountable. The truth usually lies somewhere in between these positions.

If you are a plaintiff in an arbitration case, expect that your tax records will be subpoenaed. Fehn explained that this was standard procedure, its purpose being to reveal the overall trading activity of the investor. Let us suppose that an investor claims that a broker has wronged him, because due to his inexperience, he took the broker's advice at face value. The investor's tax records may show quite a different story, proving, for example, that the investor has dabbled in risky securities for some time at other firms or had in the past traded securities similar to the ones in question. Still, Ferentz characterizes requests for tax records as a bullying tactic and a strategy meant to intimidate investors.

Although Fehn is a respected defense attorney, representing the securities industry, what he likes to do best is to sue brokerage firms on behalf of investors. As a plaintiff's lawyer, he says that he can really make a difference to an investor, but as a defense attorney, the best he can do is walk away from the case once it's over.

THE BROKER

An arbitration hearing can jeopardize a broker's career, because in most cases, it is the broker who will bear the most responsibility for his investment recommendations and not his employer. This seems unfair to me, given the way the industry encourages brokers to sell certain products and thirst after commissions.

In most cases, the broker and his firm are named as codefendants. If the broker is still employed by the firm at the time of the hearing, the firm generally pays for the costs of the defense, but if the broker has left the firm, she will more than likely have to fund her own legal representation. In addition, no matter how innocent she may be, the complaint is listed on her permanent record. A customer complaint blemishes the broker's record and waves a red flag to the broker's other customers and prospective customers. The NASD makes all registered brokers' records available to the public either through their toll-free number (800-289-9999) or their Web site (www.nasd.com), even though they don't provide enough information to evaluate a broker fairly.

As in any dispute, all complaints that go to arbitration are not valid, and all brokers are not guilty as charged. Some of the complaints are crafted by attorneys who think that by suing a major brokerage firm, they are going to retire to the Bahamas, while others are lodged by customers who have simply lost money and want to recoup their losses. Other customers, as well as their attorneys, may launch an arbitration case out of ignorance about securities matters, and in these cases the blind leads the blind.

Mistakes, especially by elderly customers, also lead to pointless hearings. For example, investors sometimes claim to have lost thousands of dollars at the hands of their broker, but an analysis of the statements shows that their loss was due to their own withdrawals. Another difficulty concerns fees and commissions that investors have agreed to pay, but fail to remember, leading to the nasty allegation that they were never told about the fees and they want their money returned to them.

THE EXPERT WITNESS

Of the thirty or so securities industry experts around, Ed Horwitz is one of the best. He spent twenty-two years in the brokerage business as a broker and a manager. He has been involved in over 1,500 arbitration cases, testified in over 370 of them, and has worked as a full-time expert since 1988.

Horwitz's schedule is hectic, since he spends a great deal of his time flying from coast to coast representing brokerage firms and plaintiff's attorneys alike. On a typical Monday he might be defending a case for PaineWebber, and then on Tuesday be siding with a plaintiff's attorney in a case against PaineWebber. What impressed me about Horwitz was that he seemed to have no loyalty except to the investor who had been wronged, the situation in 90 percent of his cases. Usually, his clients were elderly and/or a recent recipient of a large sum of money, from a death in the family, a divorce, or an insurance settlement.

Horwitz blamed the broker in most of these cases. He said, "In the quest for commissions, most brokers who are accused of wrongdoing create excessive commissions and churn accounts." He had some choice words for the industry as well. He talked about how compliance managers are "stomped and put down" by upper management because they do not produce any commission for their firms. The commission-producing broker, on the other hand, helps pay the office manager's and regional manager's bonus, so when it comes time to choose between the broker and the warnings of a compliance manager, the broker generally wins. Horwitz then told me a disturbing story that supported his point of view. A broker at a major firm (he would not disclose the firm's name) was producing an excessive amount of commission. His office manager became concerned about the broker's trading and confronted him about it. The broker dismissed his concerns, so the manager took them directly to the firm's corporate office. Senior management reviewed the broker's trading activities . . . then fired the manager and promoted the broker in his place. I knew, from my own experience as a broker, that this was not an isolated example. Brokers are often promoted to a managerial position because of their commission production, not because of their concern for clients who are taken advantage of by brokers.

Horwitz determines whether a customer has been abused or not by first reviewing all of the customer's statements, which takes anywhere from ten to two hundred hours. Once the statistics have been gathered, it takes him about two hours to make a determination. He doesn't want to know about the customer's age, investment goals, and other personal information until he has reviewed the statements. He looks for trading patterns, positions in various securities, the largest winners and losers among stocks, and he told me that just because an account makes money does not mean that it was handled properly. Just as investing is an art form, so is examining brokerage statements to see whether a customer has been cheated. First, there are no formal industry guidelines to train experts, and second, there are few standards that experts can draw on to show objectively if a broker has taken advantage of a customer. Of the few industry standards that do exist, Horwitz mentioned turnover ratio (how much of the portfolio is bought, then sold) and equity/commission ratio (the amount of commission produced compared with returns). The paucity of such standards leaves

Horwitz and others in his field wide open to attacks from opposing counsel, as well as other experts.

Industry standards, though, are not a paramount concern for Horwitz, because he has faith in his ability to make a proper judgment. His biggest concern is that the brokerage firms he represents do not fully disclose the information about a case before he decides to represent it. He said he couldn't count the number of times a brokerage firm's attorney said that the broker's trades for a customer were unsolicited, and then the broker admitted under oath that he recommended most of the trades. Speaking to Ed Horwitz was a pleasure. I can see where he would be a valuable asset to either the defense or the plaintiff.

THE NASD

It took several weeks before Steve Watson agreed to an interview, but it was well worth the wait. Between 1992 and 1996, Watson worked for the NASD as an attorney prosecuting member firms and brokers. He had the responsibility of helping to make firms and their brokers accountable for their misdeeds and he was all too familiar with the arbitration process. Prior to working for the NASD, he was an assistant regional administrator for the SEC in Fort Worth, and held VP positions at two regional banks, one in Florida and the other in Arkansas. He now lives in Dallas and is an attorney in private practice.

Watson said that at first he had been impressed with the NASD. He felt they did a good job in cracking down on rogue brokers and penny-stock firms that took advantage of investors. After two years with the organization, however, he came to the conclusion that the NASD was a pawn in the hands of the major brokerage firms. To support his claim, he pointed out that the NASD's board of governors is composed of representatives from a number of major brokerage firms. As a result, the NASD may not be as aggressive as it should be in taking actions against member firms, especially if the firm is a major player within the industry. This view is supported by the fact that only 18 percent of awards to investors came from judgments against the top five brokerage firms.[2] "The American public was sold a bill of goods that self-regulation of the securities industry would work," he said. "Perhaps it did work in 1938, but not today."

I wondered if this inherent conflict of interest at the high levels of the NASD trickled down to the arbitration hearings. Watson told me without hesitation that he thought it did. "If the industry did not think that arbitration was beneficial to the industry, they would never have pushed it," he said. Furthermore, as I said earlier, an industry representative is required to sit on an arbitration panel in cases that involved $50,000 or more. Watson claims that "investors suffer by having a member from the industry on the panel. When an industry member is injected into the panel, it's just like putting a defendant into the jury. The major firms have all decided it makes sense to look after each other, and if an arbitrator who worked for a major firm decided in favor of the customer, he could face some tough questions from his boss when he got back to his office." Watson suggests that average investors find some forum other than NASD arbitration (some firms do offer this option) to settle their disputes. He believes that this alternative is worth the extra costs.

A VIEW FROM THE OUTSIDE

After listening to these various views, I wanted to hear from someone who could help me put them all in perspective, so I called on Lynn Stout, a securities law professor at Georgetown University. There are hundreds of securities law professors around the country, but after spending five minutes with Stout, I knew that I had called the right one. She had strong opinions about arbitration and was genuinely concerned about the way the securities industry treated investors.

She questioned the arbitration agreement itself, saying that investors tended not to read brokerage firm contracts prior to signing them. From my own experience, I know she is correct in this assessment. Most clients blindly sign their customer agreements, and for a broker to even bring up the subject of arbitration would mean certain death to the sale. Stout feels it would be fairer to give customers a choice of either court or arbitration instead of forcing them to go to an arbitration hearing to settle their disputes. She thinks brokerage firms push for arbitration for two reasons: one, because it is less expensive and time-consuming than court, and two, because investors generally don't know about the conditions under which they can demand an arbitration hearing, so they are less inclined to do so. This can be easily remedied by a visit to a lawyer, of course, but if investors have no idea what constitutes right and wrong behavior in this situation to begin with, why would they bother talking to an attorney?

Stout agreed that the arbitration process favors the securities industry and places investors at a disadvantage. Arbitrators, she felt, judge a broker's conduct by the standards of the industry, but never question the validity of this standard itself. She claimed that if a broker committed a misdeed that was common to the industry, arbitrators might accept this much as the industry did. This would not be the case in court, she said, where a judge must determine if the plaintiff has been wronged, irrespective of the norms of any particular industry practice. Keeping Stout's view in mind, I must pose this question: If the norms of the industry are contrary to the investor's interests (sales contests, recognition clubs, etc.), then how can arbitrators who accept these norms ever hope to render truly just decisions?

The fact that arbitrators do not have to account for their decisions and that proceedings are held in private also concerned Professor Stout. The secretive nature of the arbitrators' decisions makes it impossible for brokers to learn from the misdeeds of other brokers and leaves investors without any acceptable standards of practice. In arbitration, she said, "The goal is not to provide the best in investor protection. The goal is provide the 'appearance' of investor protection, and as long as they can keep their decisions secret, they can keep up the appearance."

Even though I thought Stout's view had merit, I had to play devil's advocate. I told her that the NASD did provide a public record of all registered representatives, and since this was the case, why did she think that investors were kept in the dark? She said that investors could access only the holdings of the panel, and not their opinions. Holdings without the accompanying explanatory language of an opinion would have little or no educational value to brokers or investors. Moreover, "the notion that investors are going to research their broker ignores reality," she said. Stout explained that when a person goes to the doctor, he doesn't look into the doctor's background or check his credentials; he depends on the medical profession to do that. The same is true for brokers. Most people believe that because a broker is employed by a brokerage firm he must be okay. Often, though, this is too great a leap of faith.

Lynn Stout believes that the securities industry needs to do a better job in teaching brokers and investors the difference between right and wrong. She predicts that the current arbitration system will ultimately collapse. As long as the brokerage industry has something to do with how investors settle disputes, however, investors will be going to arbitration hearings for a long time to come.

SAFEGUARD YOUR INTERESTS AT AN ARBITRATION

• Before you make your claim be sure that you have been wronged as a result of someone else's misdeeds. Try to substantiate your losses and any impropriety in your account before choosing the lawyer who will represent you.

• Have an independent third party who has no interest in your claim detail your losses, if any, prior to lodging your statement of claim. Be leery if your current financial advisor helps you make your claim or volunteers to be a codefendant in your case. This could pose a conflict of interest.

• Choose competent counsel to represent you at the hearing. Investigate the attorney's credentials thoroughly before making your choice.

• Sue only for the right reasons. Make your claim in good faith, not because the brokerage firm has a lot of money or your attorney wants to "stick it to 'em" so that he can pay his mortgage.

• Keep important paperwork (statements, confirmation slips, written correspondence) associated with your account in a safe place. Also, periodically make notes of conversations that you had with your broker and trades that you have made in your account. Finally, keep track of all fees and commissions that you have paid for the life of your account.

CHAPTER 12

JOURNALISTS: THE OFT-MISINFORMED ORACLES OF DELPHI

Vivian Palfi, one of Roger Turner's victims, gave me some good advice. She said that her experience being swindled reminded her of a saying that her grandfather once told her as a child. He said, "Believe only a quarter of what you see and half of what you read." This is advice investors should heed. When they place their absolute faith in journalists instead of themselves, they do themselves a true disservice, because the people in the business of informing others are often misinformed themselves. It is easy to take for granted the unassailable accuracy of words one reads in *The Wall Street Journal, The New York Times, Money* magazine—or, for that matter, this book. My advice, though, is to think through any claims, dissect any statements, and challenge any opinion you see in print, my own included.

In this chapter I will share with you some of the problems I have with the financial press. You should not interpret my criticisms as my way of suggesting that you not read newspapers and financial magazines. I regularly read *The New York Times, The Wall Street Journal,* and a host of Web sites to keep up to date on the latest financial news. I recommend you do the same.

WRENCHES IN THE MEDIA MACHINE

Most media companies are dependent on advertising dollars for their livelihood, especially in the crowded field of personal finance, where many competitors vie for a limited number of advertising dollars. Journalists would probably be discouraged from doing an exposé of one of their company's major advertisers. The loss in advertising revenue would be too great. This helps explain why controversial issues aren't mentioned in any number of financial publications. Most mainstream media organizations are not going to allow a journalist to do a hard-hitting story on industry-wide sales contests, recognition clubs, or internal sales training practices, when full-service brokerage firms spend millions of ad revenue that brighten the media company's bottom line. Moreover, when was the last time that you saw a journalist ask the president of a major brokerage firm why commissions do not appear on monthly or quarterly statements or why average investors don't have access to the many programs designed for wealthy investors? I can't point to one example of a major media organization tackling these issues in the mainstream press, yet these industry practices have been going on for decades.

Advertising pays the bills, but reputable media organizations insist that there is a wall between their journalists and the advertisers who make their cash registers ring. They sing the praises of keeping their editorial and ad sales departments separate. Some people in the media might consider it heresy even to suggest that the need for the public to know can be and often is subordinated to the need of their advertisers to get the public to buy. After all, this would be unsavory, unethical, and erode the trust the public has in journalistic fairness.

It's difficult, however, to imagine that this wall is as high and impenetrable as the industry would have us believe. The financial press, whether it be print or electronic, serves simultaneously as a bearer of information and an effective advertising medium. Ad salespeople increase a magazine's circulation or a television network's audience, and charge according to the number of people their medium can reach. The relationship between editorial content and advertisements becomes sharper when you thumb through a financial magazine and see the number of ads that compete for your attention. The conclusion seems obvious. Many mainstream media companies are servants stuck with serving two masters. The first master is their advertisers, and the second is their readers or viewers. But one cannot serve two masters, and it saddens me to think that in some cases readers may take a backseat to the interests of those who pay the bills. This is, of course, only my opinion, but it is one that a career in media sales brought me to formulate. Prior to becoming a broker, I sold advertising for a number of media organizations in three different major markets, and I have witnessed the battle between advertisers and good-intentioned journalists firsthand.

I am not alone in the belief that advertisers influence what is published. Frank Lalli, a former senior editor at Time Inc., understands the pressures of modern-day journalism when he says, "The public doesn't want censorship. But there is more business-side pressure on editors now than ever before. You're in conversations all the time with advertising and marketing people."[1] Kurt Anderson, former editor of *New York* magazine, echoes Lalli's sentiment: "In all ways, life has gotten more market-driven."[2] And Larry Green, former executive editor and now vice-president of sales and marketing of the *Chicago Sun-Times*, puts the case this way: "We have to be conscious of who pays the bills, our mortgages, and who makes our car payments and who puts our kids through school."[3] Green is, of course, correct. How can editors do what is in the best interest of their readers when what their readers need to know conflicts with their advertisers' need to sell?

MISTAKES AND MISINFORMATION

The printed word is the most unforgiving form of communication. Once a journalist makes a mistake and commits it to print, the error is out there in the world, where some readers will regard it as a fact.

"Don't believe all you read" is good advice, because the media organizations are run by people and people make mistakes. The following examples prove my point.

One day I got a call from a reporter from *Money* magazine. She wanted to know whether full-service firms were still conducting sales contests after the 1995 Tully Commission (an industry insider group chaired by then Merrill Lynch CEO Daniel Tully) recommended that they be eliminated. I told her that sales contests were prevalent in the industry and most of the major firms conducted them year-round. The reporter was having a difficult time with her story and complained that no brokers would discuss the subject of sales contests with her candidly. Moreover, she thought that sales contests were limited to pushing certain products, like mutual funds, when this is not the case at all, because brokers may win prizes based on their commission output, opening certain accounts, and so on. I was unable to convince her that most firms had sales contests and that brokers were rewarded for more than just pushing certain products.

Despite my efforts, in the March 1998 issue of *Money* magazine, the reporter limited her scope to sales contests that rewarded brokers for selling their firms' own mutual funds. This is only the tip of the iceberg, and such a limited focus might lead readers to believe that firms that don't have sales contests like these might not have sales contests at all. In her article, entitled "Sell Mutual Funds and See the World," she said the following: "In 1995 a Committee of Industry insiders, chaired by Merrill Lynch CEO Daniel Tully, released a report recommending the elimination of sales contests and commission schedules that encourage brokers to push in-house investments. The industry responded by voluntarily adopting these recommendations as 'best practices.' "

She skimmed over the facts and missed a few key points. She neglected to mention that even though Tully chaired the commission, Merrill Lynch, as well as most brokerage firms, still have sales contents year-round. As we already know, full-service brokers are given chances to win fabulous vacations and sporting tickets among other things. Given these facts, why was Tully, a supporter of sales contests, chairing the commission? What does Tully's position say about how serious the industry really was about eliminating sales contests? Furthermore, how was it possible to say that the "industry" adopted the recommendations as "best practices" when some industry leaders still permitted product-specific sales contests at their firms? Either the securities industry adopts certain practices as best practices or they do not. Finally, why did the committee voice concerns about product-specific sales contests but remain silent about sales contests in general? None of the questions I have posed here was addressed in the article, but all of them should have been.

Another example of a factual blunder comes from a popular syndicated financial columnist with an impressive résumé. A graduate of MIT, he makes his home at *The Dallas Morning News,* where he has written thousands of columns. He also writes a monthly column for *Worth* magazine. On his Web site he says, "The basic goal here is to report ways to increase your investment income, reduce risk, and lower fees." I admire his good intentions, but in a January 27, 1998, column, he missed this mark. To this question from a reader—"Is there a significant advantage or disadvantage in which type of mutual fund shares [Class A or Class B] you buy?"—he responded, "Put the money in the MFS Research B shares and there is no commission."

If he had bothered to call the mutual fund company and ask the right questions, he would have discovered a much different story. He would have found that the broker payout—i.e., the commission paid to the broker—was 4 percent. He missed this fact because he was probably under the impression that the absence of an up-front load on the fund meant that the broker was not paid a commission. As we know, this is simply not the case.

He missed other fees as well. Not only is there a 4 percent broker payout, but there is a six-year (4 percent, 4 percent, 3 percent, 3 percent, 2 percent, 1 percent) back-end load as well. The back-end load would penalize investors who decide to liquidate their assets for six consecutive years, starting with a 4 percent penalty the first year.

He concludes his remarks by saying, "Although many investors should give serious consideration to A shares, some are so commission-phobic that their brokers won't recommend A shares even though they make economic sense." Here he's correct, but it is a mistake to imply that B shares don't have a commission that comes out of the investor's pocket. He plays right into a financial consultant's hands, because the easiest way to convince load-sensitive investors to buy a fund is to sell them Class B shares, which may lead them to believe that they are not paying a commission when in fact they are.

There were no factual errors in a *Business Week* article I recently read, but readers may have been left with a false impression. The January 1, 1999, piece concerned Charles Schwab making greater inroads into the IPO market. The writers quote Schwab's co-CEO David Pottruck as saying, "The interest in IPOs is overwhelming, and we've had a difficult time getting enough product to meet the demands." The article also stated that Schwab will soon have the technology to examine all of its 2.1 million on-line accounts to see which customers, based on their profiles, will likely express an interest in an upcoming initial public offering. What is missing? After reading this piece, one might conclude that Schwab makes shares of IPOs available to all of its customers because the firm can examine all 2.1 million of its accounts. But as we have already learned, only Schwab's best clients have access to them. Why wasn't this fact mentioned in the article? Readers have a right to know who gets shares of IPOs at Schwab.

As I make my remarks, do not think that I am beyond reproach. In February 1998, in an article I wrote for *Individual Investor,* I discussed the importance of investors knowing how much commission they were paying so that they could compare it with their overall returns. This statement was in the article: "If you bought 100 shares at $10 a share with a 2 percent commission, the value of your purchase will be listed as $980." Alas, my editor had inserted the example without my knowledge, but I should have asked to review the article before publication.

I thought that the error would be overlooked, but to my surprise a reader caught it and *Individual Investor* published his letter in their April 1998 issue. The reader wrote: "Has the day come when brokers deduct their commissions when you buy shares, or have I died and gone to heaven? Commissions are deducted when shares are sold, but they are always added to the purchase price. If you know any broker who sells $1000 worth of stock for $980, I'd love to do business with him."

NOT BELIEVING MY EARS

When people who are interviewed by the press go unchallenged, and their viewpoints are characterized as facts, it causes me great concern. There can be a multitude of reasons for this, including unalterable deadlines and space limitations, which are not the reporter's fault. The kind of adversarial journalism that is so prevalent in political reporting is absent in the financial press, which makes for good scribes but few thought-provoking reporters. Wall Street needs more journalists who can ask the tough questions and fewer reporters who just write down what their subjects have to say. For example, a September 23, 1998, *Wall Street Journal* article quoted Merrill Lynch's Vice-Chairman John "Launny" Steffens comparing Internet trading to gambling in Las Vegas: "If people turn their account over two or three times a year, they are guaranteed not to make money." He made a case for long-term investing, saying "the do-it-yourself model of trading should be regarded as a threat to Americans' financial lives." He added that the "average" Merrill Lynch customer makes just five transactions a year. Whom is Steffens referring to as the average Merrill Lynch customer? How can the average customer make four or five trades a year, if the company takes in billions of dollars in commissions from securities transactions? Also, could Merrill's fifteen thousand brokers make a living if their average client made only four or five transactions a year?

On November 19, 1998, Merrill Lynch Online held an on-line chat with Steffens and I had a chance to ask him some of these questions. I listened attentively to his introduction, a live Internet broadcast complemented by a slide presentation. Questions from participants are selected by a moderator to forward to the guest. My first question was accepted: "Mr. Steffens, you were quoted in a September 23 article in *The Wall Street Journal* as saying that the average Merrill Lynch customer trades four to five times a year. What did you mean by 'average'?" He replied: "It's obviously difficult to describe an 'average' client when we have seven and a half million of them." My next question, which the moderator did not allow, was, "Well, Mr. Steffens, which definition of average did you have in mind when you spoke with the reporter from *The Wall Street Journal*?" Several other of my questions were also ignored, so I turned off my computer.

Sometime later I revisited Merrill Lynch's Web site and reviewed a transcript of the chat session with Steffens. The question I posed was part of the transcript, as was Steffens's answer, just as I have quoted it above. What surprised me was an additional comment to Steffens's reply that did not make its way to my computer. After his line about it being hard to define the average customer, he added the following: "Our typical household has $350,000 [and] currently has 60 percent of their assets in equities, 30 percent in client fixed income, and 10 percent in cash. And does in fact trade five to six times a year."

Steffens interchanges the word "typical" with "average." Eighty-five percent of Merrill's client base has less than $250,000 in assets in their accounts, so why wasn't this benchmark used instead of $350,000? I don't doubt Steffens's claim that customers in the asset group he mentions trade five or six times a year, but whether these customers are average or typical Merrill Lynch customers is a matter of opinion.

A July 12, 1998, Reuters article also caught my attention. The piece, which was entitled "Securities Industry Pressed to Clean Up Its Act," discussed questionable practices in the industry, from fraudulent stock offerings and insider information to selling risky investments to the investing public. It asserted that a bull market brings scam artists out of the woodwork and warned investors to be careful.

Marc Lackritz, president of the Securities Industry Association, the trade organization for the securities industry, was quoted in the piece. He tried to calm investors' fears and painted a rather positive view of the industry and its practices. He said, "The number of complaints per 1000 transactions has continued to go down over the last five years to fewer than one tenth of one percent. The auto industry would die for a defect rate like that." He acknowledged that there were some problems, but then said, "On the other hand, investors are giving the industry higher marks because of education efforts and improved practices." I wondered which investors Lackritz was referring to. In November 1997, just eight months prior to his comments, the SIA conducted a survey of investors that showed that they had great concerns about the industry. Here are some of the SIA's findings:

- 70 percent of investors believe brokers are more concerned about earning commissions than giving good advice.

- 79 percent think that it is difficult to know how to get a good professional advisor.

- 81 percent think the securities industry should be doing more to educate the public.

Here are the primary issues investors were concerned about:

- 55 percent thought the industry was motivated by greed.

- 52 percent felt brokers put their own interests ahead of investors' interests.

- 47 percent thought the industry was reluctanct to punish wrongdoers.

- 44 percent had a concern about insider trading.

- 39 percent had concerns about internal controls to prevent irresponsible or wrongful actions.

- 38 percent felt there were insufficient disclosures of risks to investors.

When I reviewed the report, I found that in every category investors had greater concerns about these issues than the previous year. These facts were never brought out in the story, but readers should have known about them.

Hardly a week goes by that I don't see a news article that has been tainted by an uncalled-for positive slant. These articles wring out any negative or critical remarks and the reader is left with a fluff piece instead of information that is accurate and useful. For example, a March 22, 1999, article written for Knight Ridder Newspapers caught my eye. The piece was about Arthur Levitt and his role at the Securities and Exchange Commission. The article opens up with this bold headline: "SEC Chairman Pursues Consumer Protection, Education with Zeal." Naturally, I was surprised at the news and my curiosity demanded that I read further to see if Levitt had had a change of heart. The second paragraph had this quote from Levitt: "Investor education is one of the obsessions of this commission." Well, this quote certainly sounds good, but I was surprised that the reporter never included these questions for readers to ponder: If the SEC is so obsessed with investor education, why doesn't the agency take an active role in educating investors? What has the agency done recently to address its obsession, and if the agency is so obsessed with investor education, then why do most investors still know very little about investing basics? Has the agency failed in any way to address effectively the investor education problem? What resources has the agency dedicated to address investor education and should there be more resources dedicated to this effort? None of these questions was posed in the article, but they should have been posed in order to give readers a more balanced view of the SEC's efforts.

Another part of the article also caused me concern. The reporter states later in the piece that Levitt "hasn't been shy about reforming some of the most fundamental business practices of the securities industry." Once again this sounds great, but the statement is free from the necessary critical remarks that would be of the most benefit to readers. If I had been the reporter, I would have made an effort to address these questions in the piece: Why does Chairman Levitt permit sales contests to continue, which jeopardize the interests of investors? Since the securities industry has a fundamental business practice of not stating commissions on brokerage statements, why hasn't the SEC addressed this fundamentally wrong practice? Dealing with both of these questions would have given the piece some balance, but it would have discredited the bold headline and perhaps for this reason the questions were not addressed.

WHEN OPINION BECOMES FACT

One of the criticisms often lodged against journalists is that they make the news instead of reporting it. Every journalist is entitled to his opinion, but when journalists cast their opinions as facts, readers are ill served. For example, a reporter for *USA Today* wrote a November 13, 1998, article entitled "Get to Know Your Advisor." He talked about financial advisors motivated by greed who take advantage of their clients: "Here's some free advice: Make sure your financial advisor has your best interests at heart." Then he wrote, "The overwhelming majority of advisors do" have their clients' best interests at heart. This is only his opinion, which was not supported by any study and was contrary to the findings of the SIA study. Later in the article he wrote: "But most [advisors] are paid by some form of commission on the financial products they recommend. And that can tempt an advisor to recommend high-commission products when cheaper and sometimes better alternatives are available." We are of like minds on this point, and the possibility that advisors are in temptation's way is more fact than opinion, but the critical reader automatically sees a problem in the piece. How can he be absolutely certain that the overwhelming majority of financial advisors have their clients' best interests at heart, but at the same time be uncertain about whether or not most advisors fall to the temptation of selling higher-commission products? This is a problem that simple common sense is all too happy to remedy.

On January 9, 1997, *The New York Times* published a story about a number of stockbrokers who had been charged with fraud. The article talked about fifty stockbrokers from small-to-medium-size firms who were paid as stand-ins for other brokers taking the licensing exam. Robert M. Morgenthau, the Manhattan district attorney, expressed concern about the situation at a press conference and said that "fraudulent examinations threatened public confidence in securities dealers." I don't disagree with this statement, but when Morgenthau is quoted as saying the following, the journalist is reporting Morgenthau's perception, not a fact: "Licensing exams are designed to insure that the investing public is protected from unscrupulous operators. Those who cheat their way to their broker's license prove beyond all doubt that they do not deserve the public's trust." That is Morgenthau's perception, but it reads as if it were the gospel truth in the article. As a matter of fact, the licensing exam's design does not protect the investing public from unscrupulous operators. I have taken the broker licensing exam (Series 7) and I can assure you that it does not in any way ensure that an advisor will not take advantage of his clients. Roger Turner, who stole hundreds of thousands from his clients, passed the exam, and the vast majority of brokers who commit securities fraud have also done so. Whether a broker passes or fails the exam does not shine any light on how he will treat his clients in the future.

Sometimes fact mixes with fiction to quite comical results. When the stock market suffered a downturn in the third quarter of 1998, CNN Interactive (CNN.com) ran a story with this headline: "Wall Street Executives Suffering in Downturn." The article featured a dejected picture of Sanford Weill, the CEO of the Travelers Group, whose company stock options dropped by $785 million, or 50.1 percent. Other top executives who had seen multimillion-dollar reductions in their company's stock were also mentioned. This struck me as bittersweet because these top executives were probably really suffering, but in reality could withstand the pain since most of them had close to a billion dollars in assets.

LOOKING FROM THE OUTSIDE IN

Most reporters write about what companies want them to know, not what companies don't want them to know. For the most part, journalists that report on the securities industry are at a disadvantage because they have never worked inside the industry and their lack of experience shows.

A Reuters article is one such example. Published on December 24, 1997, it was about the results of a study by Prophet Market Research & Consulting Co., a San Francisco–based organization that every year sends a team of anonymous shoppers to call on stockbrokers and then report their findings. The article claimed that almost half of the three hundred brokers in the study neglected to discuss the shoppers' tax situation before they began to pitch an investment to them. The study also found that one in three never asked about the client's financial status and one in four never discussed his or her current portfolio or investment objectives before making investment recommendations.

Up to that point the report was enlightening, but then something convinced me that neither the author nor members of the Prophet Market Research & Consulting Co. had an insider's perspective on the securities industry. The reporter said, "The good news for household names like Smith Barney and Merrill Lynch is that these firms turned up near the top of the list. Merrill Lynch, in particular, told most shoppers that it would be inappropriate to invest before conducting a formal financial plan. National firms seem to have the budget for proper training and it's paying off in more prequalifying of clients by brokers." What the author does not realize (but we already know) is that brokers use financial plans as sales tools to target all of an investor's assets. Many investors have money at a number of different institutions, but they don't tell brokers this when they first meet. When customers fill out a financial plan, they have to note all of their assets and where they are being held. Once a broker knows this, she is in a better position to garner all of the investor's assets under her management. Ultimately, the broker gets paid for doing the financial plan with commission and, in some cases, in contest points. Furthermore, a firm-sponsored financial plan gives third-party credibility to any of the broker's investment recommendations, which makes the sales process go easier. The commissions and fees generated from the sales generally go unquestioned. A broker most likely offers a financial plan to a customer because of proper sales training, not because of proper broker schooling, as the article suggests.

Another case in which an insider's perspective would have helped was a Microsoft Investor article, posted on August 26, 1998. "Five reasons to use a full-service broker" asserted that having a full-service broker was a time saver to investors because it limited investors' choices and saved them from having to wade through all of that time-consuming information. Of course it didn't mention that most brokers don't have time to be professional researchers for their clients.

Next the article claimed that customers of full-service brokers are better off because they have access to IPOs. It says: "The phenomenal success of many recent Internet initial public offerings have once again focused considerable investor attention on new issues. And why not? When you can double or triple an investment in a few days, that's a powerful attention grabber. It's also a powerful reason for certain investors to use a full-service broker." But as we know, only a fraction of clients at full-service firms have access to IPOs. Also, while it is true that with some IPOs, an investor can double or triple his money in a few days, there's no mention that full-service brokers are penalized when their customers sell an IPO in a few days. Lastly, the article doesn't bring up the fact that many brokers try to dissuade their clients from selling because the broker will lose his commission.

The article raved about the advice full-service brokers offer. The broker is presented as a friend to investors who don't want to face the turbulent financial markets alone, and as an objective financial advisor who calms the fears of his clients. When a broker is faced with an end-of-the-month commission hurdle or a mortgage payment, however, a customer might be surprised just how emotional this calming friend can be.

Many times readers only read as far as the headlines, but there is often a lot more to a story than this. An article that appeared on October 26, 1998, in *The Wall Street Journal* is a fine example. The headline reads: "Street Is Sold on Idea eBay Will Lead Auction Market." eBay is an online auctioneer, and on the day before this story appeared, its shares had skyrocketed 46 percent to close at 73⅜. The article attributed the run in part to a research report by Jamie Kiggen, an analyst for the investment bank Donaldson, Lufkin & Jenrette. "Given that eBay is the category leader in the area of person-to-person Internet auctions and has a massive loyal and growing customer base, [Mr. Kiggen] said he believes that eBay shares could get as high as 100 in the next 12 months." Positive remarks about the company also came from Keith Benjamin, an analyst at BancBoston Robertson Stephens. Investors might think from reading the headline that the street was sold on eBay, but they didn't know that Donaldson, Lufkin & Jenrette and Robertson Stephens as well as Goldman Sachs underwrote eBay's IPO, collecting substantial fees for doing so. Readers have a right to know if there is a relationship between the underwriter and the company it recommends. Some in the media make a point of disclosing an investment bank's relationship to a company that it recommends. This is good journalism and an example to be followed by others in the financial press.

All of these examples have one message for investors. Don't take what you read for granted, and don't blindly trust others to inform you. Think about what you read, and critically examine an author's work before you take his word as the truth.

READ THE FINANCIAL PRESS WITH A CRITICAL EYE

• Remember the golden rule when reading today's financial news articles: "Seeing is not always believing." Yes, there are many good journalists, but don't confuse good writing with good information.

• Most news articles tell only part of the story. Deadlines, sound bites, and pocketbook concerns all contribute to modern-day journalism and affect what you read.

• Understand that most journalists have an outside-looking-in perspective, which allows them to report only what companies want them to know—not what they may need to know.

CHAPTER 13

INVESTMENT EXPERTS:
THE PIED PIPERS OF WALL STREET

Independent thought is its own reward, yet many investors gladly give it up to blindly follow the so-called experts. Noah's Ark could not contain all of the experts on Wall Street, even if only one specimen from each category was allowed to enter the craft. The two basic categories of experts today are those who tell investors how to make a lot of money and those who predict the future. They go by a host of professional titles—market analyst, economist, portfolio manager, commentator, or just investment expert. These pundits hand out their opinions and advice on TV and radio, and in magazines.

Investors who blindly rely on experts are committing either an unnecessary act of self-sacrifice or a subtle form of suicide. As I will show you, long live the investor, but may the professional experts suffer an early demise. Let's look at the track record of financial experts in general. We need go no further than CNBC, *The Wall Street Journal, The New York Times,* and *Money* magazine to find today's financial experts. These oracles make their crystal-ball predictions available for millions of average investors. It may be difficult to judge the true value of an expert opinion at the time at which it is made, but historical predictions can be very revealing compared with historical reality.

I could fill an entire book with expert predictions that turned out to be absolutely wrong. They seem funny in retrospect, but at the time they were made many investors took them seriously. Most forecasters share a common optimism about the long-term future, as do the so-called experts who promise to show you techniques that will lead you to riches beyond your wildest dreams. Investors wouldn't invest their money if an expert offered a glum view, and there would be no reason to attend his high-priced seminars or buy his cassette tapes or books. Moreover, what TV network or print publication could draw advertisers to a program that featured experts who consistently painted a negative picture of the long-term future, when the sponsors' livelihood depends on healthy consumer confidence and greater spending? Some of today's experts give investors a false sense of optimism and security. Their predictions are self-serving and based more on what investors want to hear than on the actual facts. After walking investors down the road of personal gain, the Pied Pipers of Wall Street may lead them directly to the water. There are some fine examples of this, which we will discuss later in this chapter.

WHY DO INVESTORS LIKE TO BELIEVE IN EXPERTS?

I know from personal experience what taking the advice of an expert can mean. I was on a winning streak at a Las Vegas blackjack table with winnings totaling $400. It had taken me five hours to win the $400, and on my last hand, I decided to make a name for myself in Vegas and bet half of my winnings. As soon as my hand was dealt, I realized that lady luck had moved to another table and left me with a hand of thirteen and the dealer was showing a seven. I was dealt a three. Should I hit or stay with sixteen? All eyes were on me as I pondered my decision. I asked a stranger next to me for his advice. He was older than I and for some reason I thought that he would make a better decision than I would. Perhaps his white beard gave him the appearance of a seasoned gambler, or the fact that he had a towering column of chips at his side. He said, "If it were me I would hit it." The dealer passed me another card. This time it was a queen and the next motion of the dealer's hand swept my $200 from the table.

The person I deemed an expert was wrong. After I had delegated to him the authority to make my decision, I followed his advice with ease, falsely believing that his judgment was sounder than mine. I didn't inquire about his gambling experience or ask for his credentials. None of this mattered, because in my mind I had decided he was an expert on blackjack, took his advice, and in so doing bet against myself. This same scenario plays out when investors bet on the advice of investment experts. Many investors do not check out the people who have been deemed to be experts. They blindly follow them, discounting their own abilities in the process, when they have no reason to do so. There are a few reasons why investors make such gambles and I have noted them below.

The expert has published a book so he must know what he is talking about. If you walk into most bookstores today, you will find hundreds of books on investing. There may be a multitude of such books, but they generally fall into three distinct categories:

1. How I Made a Million Dollars and You Can Too
2. The Fifty Best Mutual Funds of All Time
3. How to Save and Invest Now for a Wonderful Retirement

Writing a book about investing does not make the author an expert. Most investment books today do not contain any new information. The same material is endlessly rehashed and repackaged under a different name and title. In addition, many of these books are boring and inspire readers to take a nap soon after reading the first chapter. Also, it is very difficult for readers to learn from the achievements of these so-called experts. Even so, investors gobble these books up, hoping that they can duplicate double-digit returns. The numerous variables that went into the author's success may not be present when the reader invests his money, though. Interest rates may have changed, a stock's earnings may have declined, and/or feelings about the stock market in general may have shifted. Financial markets are fluid and books are static, making them ill-suited to the role of good learning tools on how to invest money. In some respects, investing is very much like playing chess, but even the best players, like world champion Gary Kasparov, did not become successful solely by reading chess books. He has played thousands of games and learned from each one. It's best to play, think for yourself, and learn from your mistakes. The same can be said of investing.

The expert appears regularly on TV and radio. The media can help transform an ordinary financial advisor into an expert, sometimes overnight. Investors are generally under the impression that media organizations have chosen their financial experts carefully, checking their credentials among hundreds that are available. In reality, however, TV- and radio-show producers often choose speakers more by who they know than what they know.

Show producers also tend to look more for articulate speakers who are camera- or microphone-friendly than for those who have an important message to share. In these cases, the expert may better serve the station's ratings than the station's viewers or listeners. Most producers look for mainstream ideas, too, and sometimes edit out those that are contrary to popular opinion. For example, when I did a taped interview for CNBC, I mentioned that there was no minimal educational requirement for brokers. I also said that I felt brokers were nothing more nor less than salespeople. Granted my views were not the most ingratiating, but they were hard-hitting and in the public's best interests. Unfortunately, they might have been difficult for some members of CNBC's audience to take, and when airtime came, both statements had been edited out.

Many TV and radio show hosts give cookie-cutter investment advice to callers whom they don't know. Experts who give such advice are like psychics who make predictions for people who call them on the phone. In both cases, the "experts" have only a modicum of information, and the advice is anything but tailored to the individual complexities of the caller because the caller is unknown to them. Whatever credentials these hosts may have are bolstered significantly by the fact that they are on-the-air, but in many cases their main credential is to have been bought and paid for by a sponsor.

In a typical arrangement, the radio or TV station accepts advertising dollars from the host's brokerage firm. The host then uses the show to promote his business and as a prospecting tool for new clients. The impression of legitimacy is heightened because he is on the radio or TV. My message to you is to pay more attention to thinking through your own financial affairs, instead of letting a talk show host do your thinking for you.

The expert has top-drawer credentials and numerous degrees. After reading an article by an acclaimed financial advisor, you might think he knows what is best for you. A seasoned broker, a certified financial planner, and a professional money manager can all give you the impression that they have your best interests at heart. You decide to unquestioningly follow their advice. Mistake! Don't be bashful about questioning an advisor's judgment, and keep in mind that academic achievements do not necessarily translate into good financial advice. We have already seen how different financial advisors can give different investment recommendations in the same set of circumstances. Given the wide range of investment alternatives and the different approaches to investing, how can any investors in good conscience not question the advice they receive?

THE HIGH COST OF SOME EXPERT ADVICE

Wade Cook's life is a classic rags-to-riches story. He worked as a cabdriver in Tacoma, Washington, for some time and then transformed himself into an investment expert. Now he tours the country giving seminars about how he made millions by investing and how other people can profit from his advice. In his book *Wall Street Money Machine,* he wrote, "I make millions. I'll teach you how to do the same. I'm in the foxhole every day—doing what I teach. If all I do is teach seminars, then all I'll teach is 'How to Teach Seminars.' But I am an active investor. My recreation is making $10,000 to $20,000 a day. I do it all the time. I will teach you how to do this, because I'm actively doing it." This is the sort of "expert" you need to be wary of.

According to *The Washington Post*, Cook's professional résumé includes "a bankruptcy (discharged); $405,000 paid in restitution and fines for selling unregistered penny stocks in Arizona, and a cease-and-desist order in three other states for also selling unregistered securities." Yet, in 1997, over 400,000 people attended his seminars in some 379 cities. He has written sixteen books, three of which have made it to the *Business Week* bestseller list. He heads a publicly traded company (Wade Cook Financial Corporation) and in 1997 he made $10.2 million,[1] quite a leap from the standard cab fare in Tacoma.

Cook is so successful because he gives people what they want and tells them what they want to believe. Most of his seminar attendees are novice, middle-class investors who are looking for quick and easy ways to make big money. The cost of attending Cook's seminars and purchasing his products can be staggering, with price tags up to $12,999.[2] He sells videos, audiotapes, an advanced training program, and an Internet bulletin-board subscription. The back of Cook's first book, *Wall Street Money Machine,* suggests that it will help you:

• Double your money every two and a half to four and a half months with rolling stocks.

• Get 14 percent to 34 percent monthly returns—consistently.

• Find the inside secrets to stock options and turn them into a cash-flow machine.

At least half of *Wall Street Money Machine*'s chapters discuss options, which command a large number of stock shares with a relatively small investment. This, I admit, is very appealing to first-time middle-class investors, but the chances of losing money through options far outweigh any reward that a lucky investor might receive. I can't imagine a competent financial advisor recommending option strategies to novice investors if his intention is to do what is best for them.

Over eight quarters, Cook and his seminar speakers lost $167,699 on their securities trades.[3] In an April 2, 1998, press release issued by the company, it was noted the Wade Cook Financial Corporation had paper losses due to trading securities of $804,493 for the twelve months ending December 31, 1997. Gross revenue for the company increased 250 percent from the previous twelve months, totaling $104.9 million. Cook makes his money not by trading securities, but by selling the seminars, books, and tapes that instruct others on how to trade securities.

Many of the people who have attended Cook's seminars have not fared any better. A Web site called Gary's World (www.garywall.com) offers a glimpse into how discontented some of Wade Cook's former believers are. Here are two samples of what they had to say:

> I suffered losses of more than $54,000 in capital, not including interest and related fees. During the same period, I lost more than $6000 in my IRA saving, which I had converted to a trading account at the suggestion of Wade Cook Seminars. And I PAID MORE THAN $6000 FOR THE PRIVILEGE!"
>
> —S. MacGregor, Fresno, CA

> "I lost $3000 in 3 months doing small trades in stock split options and 'news related' options. And it wasn't because I made two or three bad trades at $1000 apiece, my trades were $500 on average."
>
> —Joe in Atlanta

After reading a number of these accounts, I learned that Cook sometimes called on a higher authority to bless his good work. One of the people who made a posting, who referred to himself only as Don, said, "The idea that he was a Christian seemed to add to his credibility in my eyes." Another disenchanted Internet user, one who had lost $4,700, said similarly, Cook "presented himself as a devout Christian who placed God ahead of everything in his life (Lord have mercy on his soul)."

I am not sure if teaching novice investors about complex option plays is doing God's good work. I am also not convinced that telling people that they can make money based on strategies that have reaped the seminar leader losses is in keeping with pastoral practices, either. No matter how much Wade Cook loses or gains, the faithful will attend his seminars or buy his tapes, because he offers a dream. A dream that will not come true.

BEARDSTOWN LADIES

Not many people had heard of Beardstown, Illinois, until sixteen elderly ladies formed an investment club there and became national celebrities. The Beardstown ladies claimed they could beat the stock market and that they had produced double-digit returns from 1984 to 1993. Hundreds of thousands of middle-class investors wondered how these ladies did it. They wrote five books and were popular guests on radio and TV shows all over the country. Their first book, *The Beardstown Ladies' Common-Sense Investment Guide: How We Beat the Stock Market and How You Can Too,* was a bestseller that sold 800,000 copies. The front cover of the book celebrates their eye-catching annual return of 23.4 percent, and the book is filled with warm and friendly pictures of the ladies and even contains some of their recipes. The book's introduction describes the ladies as "religious people, active in churches and volunteer organizations," but I was looking for some evidence of their investment expertise. The book itself was indeed a description of success, but I didn't find much that would give me the tools to duplicate the ladies' spectacular performance. Their confidence in the long-term prospects of the stock market was commendable, but that doesn't explain how they were able to make the 23.4 percent annual returns the front cover so clearly states they made.

Shane Tritsch, former managing editor of *Chicago* magazine, apparently also had some concerns about how successful the ladies really were. In the spring of 1998, he uncovered an accounting error that reduced the ladies' stellar 23.4 percent annual ten-year returns to a mere 9.1 percent. Their actual return did not even keep pace with the stock market, which had enjoyed real double-digit returns during the same time period. The ladies had added into their returns their members' dues, thus inflating the totals. The ladies blamed the mishap on a computer-input error. When the story broke, the financial press had a field day and the ladies suffered a national embarrassment.

Most readers were forgiving, but some felt that they had been duped. In January 1999, the Associated Press reported that Cheryl Lacoff, a resident of Greenwich, Connecticut, was suing the ladies over the error. In her lawsuit she demanded that the $20 that she paid for the book be refunded to her and to all the other people who bought the book. As of this writing, her litigation is pending, but if Lacoff is successful, it could spell dire consequences for the ladies, who might be forced to shell out millions of dollars.

GARDEN-VARIETY EXPERTS

Most experts aren't as notorious as Wade Cook or the Beardstown ladies, but they are out there. As a broker, I often attended luncheons and seminars at which investment experts were guest speakers and I, along with the other brokers in my office, was asked to invite our clients to these presentations. A cautious approach to investing or a negative commentary on financial markets was not welcomed at these presentations, so only positive-minded experts were invited. In addition, the sponsoring firm paid the expert handsomely, and the atmosphere helped persuade clients to invest more of their money. In these situations, brokers hope to generate commissions, while management trusts that the firm's bottom line will improve as a result of the expert's appearance.

Financial services firms sponsor hundreds of meetings like these every year all across the country. The guest-speakers function more as salespeople than purveyors of substantive information. Don't count on a free marketplace of ideas if you are invited to attend one. I object to a sponsor using a paid expert's views to persuade investors to invest more of their money in the stock market. Most market watchers are hard-pressed to speculate about what even the next trading day will bring, and would shy away from making lofty, long-term predictions. This small detail would be glossed over by many who attend these seminars, because to them it would be irrelevant. Most attendees would say that the methods are not worth investigating or criticizing, because to do so might be injurious to the beautiful message that the speaker has to offer. One that has been bought and paid for by those who have a vested interest in having it heard.

THE ONE YOU SHOULD LISTEN TO

It is hard for many investors to imagine that they might be the best experts at handling their own financial affairs. But no one knows you better than you. No one can look out for your interests better than you, and there is nothing that a so-called expert can learn that you, given some time, cannot learn yourself. Don't discount your own ideas about investing and don't think that your ideas are less worthy than a financial advisor's or professional speaker's. I understand that at first you might find financial markets complex and the daily flood of information overwhelming, but this should not deter you from managing your own money. The reason more people don't manage their own money is not their stupidity, but the fact that they have not been taught to do so. There are many things I cannot do. I can't cook a gourmet meal and I can't fly a plane. The list can go on endlessly, but the reason I am not a chef or a pilot is not that I am dumb. It's because I have not had the training. Training is everything, and I assure you that investing is a lot easier than cooking a gourmet meal or flying a plane. To those who say that cooking a gourmet meal is easier than investing, I say that you are making investing more complex than it really is. This is why it is so important to educate yourself about investing so that you can become your own expert. The standard materials on investing can no doubt be at times boring and stale. But don't give up. There is no rush to master the beast because financial markets will be here long after we are all gone. Take your time and learn all that you can before you invest your money.

When you become your own expert, you will have only your interests to contend with. You will never fall victim to the mistakes and misfortunes of others. You *will* make your own mistakes from time to time, but hopefully you will learn and profit from them, instead of letting a so-called expert profit from you. Between now and the time you become self-reliant, learn how to deal effectively with your advisor by following the suggestions I have made thus far and will make in the next chapter. Make managing your own money a goal, if it is not one already, and save the money that you might have given to an expert and invest it in the best company going. The company is you and your financial future, and the prospects look bright.

CHAPTER 14

WHAT EVERY INVESTOR
NEEDS TO KNOW: EXPERT REDEFINED

I can't think of a worthier pursuit than wanting to be your own investment expert. I suppose that you are now settling back in your chair waiting for a barrage of charts, graphs, and investor terms to begin flying off the page. For me to end this book as most other investment books begin would be a great disservice to you. There are many seminars and books that can teach you the basics of investing and I invite you to choose a few that you feel comfortable with. But you should remember, the road to riches will never be found in a book about investment products or vehicles, because such books neglect the real subject of investing: how Wall Street treats average investors and how the securities industry and its regulators neglect to do anything about it. Products, like mutual funds and stocks, the standard focus of investment books, do not in themselves make investors money—people do. People on Wall Street determine who gets personalized attention and what information investors are privy to. People at brokerage firms cater to their wealthy clients while sacrificing the needs of average

investors. People at the SEC allow sales contests and commission recognition clubs to continue, practices that keep the best investment
recommendations from being made. People who work in corporate
America don't provide investor education programs for their employees
and heavily weight their 401(k) plans with company stock. People who
participate in the arbitration process overlook average investors' interests and the injustices done to them. Wall Street is all about how people
treat each other—not the latest investment product or service.

The first step to becoming an investment expert lies not in a classroom or book but in having a well-rounded knowledge of the industry
and its practices. As we have seen, many of the industry's practices
hinder average investors from making the returns that wealthy and
institutional investors have enjoyed for years. The most intelligent and
savvy investor by himself is hard-pressed to overcome these long-
established obstacles. To become an investment expert, you must ac-
knowledge these problems, many of which I have outlined here, and
take steps to remedy them. When it comes to investing, the subject of
greatest concern on Wall Street today should be the average investor.

ROBBING YOU BLIND: THE TRUE COST OF INVESTING

When they calculate the costs of investing, most people restrict
themselves to fees, commissions, and so on, but these costs are minimal
compared with the losses that result from lost opportunities, restricted
information, sales contests, and a lack of investor education. The misdeeds listed below will cost you more than a standard brokerage commission ever will, and it is my hope that once you can recognize them,
you'll make every effort to eliminate some of them.

• *Lack of personalized attention due to internal class structures:* When
a portfolio receives the attention it deserves, it performs better.
Average investors need to attend to their own portfolios even if
they use a full-service broker. The costs of the lack of attention

given to an average investor's portfolio cannot be measured by numbers alone, yet the cost is clearly visible to the naked eye and the effects are long-lasting.

• *Restricted information:* The greatest asset on Wall Street is information, yet the average investor is restricted from getting key information. Selectively informing wealthy and institutional clients costs the average investor dearly because the average investor makes securities transactions based on information that is either out of date or not complete.

• *Sales contests and recognition clubs:* Sales contests and commission recognition clubs motivate advisors to trade unnecessarily and to jeopardize the interests of their clients for the chance of winning fantastic prizes. Both of these long-established practices help brokerage firms make money at substantial costs to their customers, while regulators, like the SEC, stand by.

• *Broker sales training:* Brokerage firms send their brokers to sales boot camps, and investors pay. Brokers are taught to view their clients as "raw material" and to become marketing experts instead of financial experts. The cost to investors that results from such training is staggering and unforgivable.

• *No commission or fees printed on the statement:* Commissions and fees should be clearly noted on brokerage statements so investors can compare the real costs with the rewards of investing. The idea that brokerage statements are too complex for most investors to read and that adding information like commissions might make them even more difficult is bogus. All investors pay a price for being kept in the dark about how much their investments really cost them.

• *Lack of investor education:* There are no minimal education requirements in the securities industry. On Wall Street, sales ability is far more prized than investment expertise. Discount and day-trading firms spend millions in advertising, but little or nothing on investor education, while full-service firms turn their

backs on the importance of educating brokers. The financial illiteracy rate is very high among investors and advisors, and as
long as intellectual capital remains low, investors will pay the
price.

• *The real costs of mutual funds:* The record of success of mutual
funds is not impressive, especially when over 90 percent of them
don't beat the S&P 500. The fees seem so small, but eat away
at returns, often resulting in double-digit losses. In addition to
these costs, most mutual fund companies put their company's
interests first and give special privileges to their wealthy customers. The half-truths and hidden realities in the mutual fund
industry cost average investors dearly and should give them
pause.

• *The unfairness of arbitration:* Investors who have a dispute with
their firm or broker can't count on getting a fair and impartial
hearing. They are forced to air their grievances at an industry-
run arbitration hearing, where the odds are stacked in the securities industry's favor. It's cheaper than going to court, but
the fact that arbitrators don't have to justify their decisions, and
that the hearings themselves are conducted privately, can be
costly. It's time to institute reforms so that arbitration hearings
are fairer to average investors.

• *401(k) tragedies:* The financial futures of millions of people
are at stake with 401(k) plans. Companies need to provide
individual-investor education programs so their employees can
make good investment decisions. The fees of many 401(k) plans,
and the preponderance of corporate stock in these plans, eat away
at overall returns, further harming employees, who may wind
up destitute or having to learn to live on less when they are
elderly. What a price to pay!

• *Journalists and misinformation:* Many average investors base their
investment decisions on information they glean from articles and
news reports in the financial press, but as we have seen, this can
be a mistake. Just because a story is in a name-brand publication

doesn't mean it must be true. Some journalists look at the securities industry from the outside in, and tell their readers only
what the industry wants them to know. Other times, advertising
interests seem to affect what articles are run and what products
are recommended. Sadly, investors wind up paying for information that serves interests other than their own.

• *Experts and more experts:* The cost of letting someone do their
thinking for them is a price that many investors are willing to
pay. Most people like to be told what to do with their money,
but think of all the money that you can save by managing your
own money and doing your own thinking. My message to you
is to be careful when following the advice of a so-called expert.
Managing money is generally not a team sport and the cost of
having your financial advisor not on your team can be danger-
ously high to both you and your family.

• *Political payoffs:* The interests of investors are routinely sacrificed when politicians accept large sums of money from financial
concerns. How can laws to protect investors be written if their
authors are accepting money from institutions that don't want
to see them written? You can find out which organizations contribute money to your representative, however, through the Center for Responsive Government's Web site. This nonpartisan,
nonprofit group based in Washington, D.C., can be found at this
Internet address: www.opensecrets.org.

• *The costs of an uncaring SEC:* The SEC has treated the symptoms
of the industry's unsavory practices for years, but has not effectively addressed many of their root causes. Investors pay the price
for these blindfold tactics, yet ironically they are the ones who
help fund the SEC through their tax dollars. When it comes to
the SEC, investors deserve a refund or at least more for their
money.

STANDING UP FOR YOURSELF: WHAT YOU CAN DO TO FIGHT BACK

The first line of defense against the sins of Wall Street begins with you. Then individual investors must work collectively to safeguard their interests. The following suggestions will help you accomplish this:

1) *Understand an advisor's sales techniques:* The lifeblood of Wall Street is selling and salesmanship. Most investors have little understanding of the sales techniques that advisors use every day to persuade them to buy and sell, but I assure you that knowing these techniques is just as important as the investments you allow your advisor to buy. Once an investor knows the typical ways securities are sold, he has less chance of being duped and a greater chance of safeguarding his own interests. Investors think that product knowledge alone will ensure that they will never be taken advantage of and this belief is far removed from the actual facts.

I wrote my first book, *Tricks of the Trade—An Insider's Guide to Using a Stockbroker,* to educate investors on the standard sales techniques that brokers use. Knowing techniques like "Ask Till They Gasp," "the Ben Franklin Close," and verbal tie-downs will prepare you to deal more effectively with your broker. Other books that might be helpful to you include *The Art of Selling Intangibles—How to Make Your Millions Investing Other People's Money* by Roy Gross, *How to Master the Art of Selling* by Tom Hopkins, and *Conceptual Selling* by Robert Bruce Miller, Stephen Heiman, and Tad Tuleja. All of these books helped me tremendously in my sales career, but if any of my customers had been as familiar with them as I was, I wouldn't have been as successful. I suppose that once a person knows a magician's tricks, the magic wears off and the ability to manipulate an audience by sleight of hand vanishes.

2) *Manage your advisor wisely:* Always think of your advisor as your employee and, as with any employee, make her accountable to you. Here are some tips on how to manage your financial advisor until you feel comfortable managing your own money:

• As often as possible communicate your investment goals and expectations to your advisor through written correspondence. E-mail and well-crafted notes work wonders in teaching an advisor to stop making hasty verbal recommendations. Most advisors will provide talking cures for your investment ills, but be sure not to act on an investment recommendation unless it is supported by a convincing, in-writing justification. Also, the charms of a letter help to cure an advisor's failed memory and will give you future ammunition, should you need to seek legal redress.

• In Sales 101, advisors are taught that the person who asks questions controls the sale and the outcome of the meeting. Many sales-savvy financial advisors will attempt to manipulate their clients through questions that limit their focus on products they want them to buy or sell. Turn the tables on your advisor by asking him as many questions as you like in your initial counseling sessions. Remember, there are no dumb questions and topics for discussion should range from your investments and his professional background and experience to the latest news headlines. Why make the purchase now and for what reasons? How does this investment benefit me? When may I review your professional résumé and past-investment track record? Did you read the article in *The Wall Street Journal* about . . . ? These are all good questions to ask. In this way, you will discover how well informed your advisor really is. Pay attention to the content and tone of your advisor's responses because they will give you clues about his sincerity.

• It is a good idea to have monthly or quarterly account reviews with your advisor, because they will force him to pay attention to your account. At these meetings, have her explain to you all of the terms and values that appear on your statement and ask her to calculate her fees and commissions that do not appear on the statement. Once you know the cost of doing business, compare it with your investment returns, risk tolerance, and future expectations. In addition, you should discuss fine-tuning your portfolio and making adjustments that will keep costs low and investment performance reasonable.

3) *Don't overlook essential paperwork:* On Wall Street the big print giveth and the small print taketh away. Most investors spend more time buying a washer and dryer than they do looking over paperwork that is critical to their financial futures. Victims of securities fraud often fail to ask enough questions about their investments until it's too late. Most investors base their stock purchases on little-researched assumptions, and keep making the same mistakes. To prevent this from happening, thoroughly review all printed materials and pay close attention to what your advisor has to say.

4) *Think about what you read:* Ask yourself if there is more to the story than meets the eye, and check to see if the advertisers and the editorial content seem suspiciously similar. I will suggest one magazine you might want to read: *On Wall Street*. It provides a behind-the-scenes look at the securities industry with updates you will never read about in the mainstream press, such as the latest sales contests at various firms and articles by brokers describing how they get new clients. You can order your subscription by calling them at 800-455-5844.

5) *Learn all you can to become self-reliant:* As I said before, investing is not a team sport. This sweeping statement will be criticized by brokers, financial planners, and all sorts of white-collar professionals who claim to have the average investor's best interests at heart. Some readers may also frown on my position. But I think it is true, since the only person who is rewarded solely on his portfolio's performance is the investor. Brokers, financial

planners, mutual fund managers, fee-based money managers—
all these people have other interests to attend to that compete
with the interests of the investor. While self-reliance is an attractive goal, there are some investors who think that they can
be self-reliant *and* work with an advisor. In their view, the two
should not be mutually exclusive. Other investors throw up their
hands and surrender to an advisor, thinking that they don't have
the time to manage their own money or they can't learn what
investing is all about. I have never known an advisor who wanted
his clients to make their own investment decisions because to
do so would negatively affect his income. And the notion that
advisors, who have thousands of accounts to manage, have more
time than an investor to manage his own money is nonsense.

6) *Believe that you can make a difference:* All change begins with
one person. It will be up to individual investors to seek reforms
in the securities industry that will level the playing field for
them. Hopefully, the SEC will see the error of its ways and weigh
in on the side of average investors instead of catering to the
needs of big business. If you feel strongly about what I have
written here, I invite you to contact the SEC and express your
concerns. You can write them at the following address: 450
Fifth Street NW, Washington, D.C. 20549. Their phone number is 202-942-7040, and you can use this E-mail address—
chairmanoffice@sec.gov—to contact them electronically. The
SEC, I am sure, will be glad to hear from you, since Arthur
Levitt has publicly proclaimed: "I want the tie between the SEC
and American investors to be close-knit, intimate and personal."[1]
Levitt is worth a reported $30 million[2] and he is, of course, a
Washington insider, but I am still counting on him or on one
of the other commissioners to take an interest in what average
investors have to say, and to do something about it. If Levitt
does not, perhaps his successor will.

I have no reservations about telling you that without your help no
reforms in the securities industry will take place. I am also mindful of
the words of my fellow stockbroker Charles Green about middle-class

investors, words I quoted at the beginning of this book, and how unresponsive he thought that they would be about addressing many of these issues. I made a bet with him that investors would care about their financial futures and I still have every faith that they—that *you*—will do just that.

ACKNOWLEDGMENTS

I am very much indebted to the people who took time to talk to me about the various issues that I discussed in the book. I could not have drawn an accurate picture of Wall Street without their professional experience and candor. Each of them made an important contribution and they are as follows: Ted Benna, Thomas Brown, Jeanne Crandall, Lisa Crosby, Tom Fehn, Jeff Ferentz, Brooks Hamilton, Ed Horwitz, Bill Lamoreaux, Tom O'Brien, Terrance Odean, Vivian Palfi, Thomas Southerly, Lynn Stout, Steven Thorley, Robert Uhl, and Steve Watson.

I would also like to thank the librarians at the Dallas Public Library who helped me in doing some of the research for the book. A special thanks goes to the Investment Company Institute, which was very helpful in providing me with information about the mutual fund industry. I am also grateful to the Institute of Management & Administration for providing me with research on 401(k) plans.

Thanks to my literary agent, Margret McBride, who enthusiastically presented the idea for this book to my publisher.

It took me close to a year to write the finished manuscript for *Robbing You Blind* and during much of this time I had the pleasure of working with my editor, Henry Ferris, and associate editor Ann Treistman. Henry's constructive criticism greatly improved the book and I found his guidance very helpful. Both Henry and Ann did a marvelous job in making my work better, and for that they deserve my greatest thanks.

NOTES

1

PITCHING THE AMERICAN DREAM
TO THE MIDDLE CLASS

1 Jeff Nash, "The Year of the Fat Check," *On Wall Street,* February 1998, page 31.
2 Charles R. Geisst, *Wall Street—A History,* page 189.
3 John Leland, "Blessed by the Bull," *Newsweek,* April 27, 1998, page 51.
4 Geisst, page 33.
5 *Ibid.,* page 21.
6 Microsoft Encarta, 1997.
7 Geisst, page 21.
8 *Ibid.,* page 21.
9 *Ibid.,* page 195.
10 Microsoft Encarta, 1997.
11 *Ibid.*
12 *Ibid.*
13 Geisst, page 192.
14 Microsoft Encarta, 1997.
15 Geisst, page 195.
16 *Ibid.*
17 Geisst, page 228.
18 *Ibid.,* page 229.
19 Joseph Nocera, *A Piece of the Action,* page 42.
20 Geisst, page 233.
21 Nocera, page 34.
22 Robert Sobel, "The People's Choice: How Charles Merrill Brought Wall Street to Main Street," *Barron's,* February 17, 1997, page 23.
23 Nocera, page 35.
24 Claire Mencke, "Leaders and Success: Merrill Lynch's Charles E. Merrill," *Investor's Business Daily,* July 21, 1997, page A1.
25 Nocera, page 37.
26 Sobel, page 23.
27 Nocera, page 38.
28 *Ibid.,* page 43.
29 *Ibid.,* page 43.
30 *Ibid.,* page 44.

31 Mencke, page A1.
32 Nocera, page 44.
33 *Ibid.,* page 113.
34 *Ibid.,* page 118.
35 *Ibid.,* page 117.
36 Abby Schultz, "And the Winner Is . . . The Money Markets?," *The New York Times* Online Edition, October 11, 1998.
37 *Ibid.*
38 Nocera, page 76.
39 *Ibid.,* page 77.
40 *Ibid.,* page 79.
41 *Ibid.,* page 46.
42 Congressional testimony of David Gardner, cofounder of the Motley Fool, on September 29, 1998.
43 Nocera, page 248.
44 *Ibid.,* page 248.
45 *Ibid.,* page 248.
46 *Ibid.,* page 159.
47 *Ibid.,* page 160.
48 *Ibid.,* page 160.
49 This was taken from a conversation that I had with a representative at the Investment Management Institute.
50 *Ibid.*

2
RICH MAN, POOR MAN

1 Jeff Nash, "The Year of the Fat Check," *On Wall Street,* February 1998, page 31.
2 "Merrill Makes Mincemeat of Low Producers with New Grid," *On Wall Street,* November 1998, page 10.
3 *Ibid.*
4 Michael Siconolfi and Patrick McGeehen, "Small Investors Face Double Standard from Brokers When Investing in IPOs," *The Wall Street Journal* Interactive Edition, June 26, 1998.
The numerical rankings that are quoted for the mutual fund families come from information obtained from the Investment Company Institute.

3
THE POWER OF INFORMATION

1 Alex Ayres, editor, *The Wit and Wisdom of Mark Twain,* page 5.
2 Phil Serafino, "Dell Comments on PC Prices Were Only Available to a Select Few," *Bloomberg News,* July 23, 1998.

3 Amey Stone, "Commentary: Bad Quarter? Don't Keep Shareholders Guessing," *Business Week* Online, April 6, 1998.

4 Serafino.

5 *Ibid.*

6 PR Newswire Press Release, December 9, 1998.

7 *Ibid.*

8 David Henry, "Companies Hear Investors Say, 'Call Me!,' " *USA Today* Online, July 1, 1999.

9 Elizabeth MacDonald, "SEC Readies New Rules for Companies About What Is 'Material' for Disclosure," *The Wall Street Journal* Interactive Edition, November 3, 1998.

10 Emily Church, "NASD Votes to Expand Trading Hours," CBS MarketWatch, May 27, 1999.

11 Greg Ip, "Soon Online Investors May Be All-Day Traders," *The Wall Street Journal* Interactive Edition, February 10, 1999.

12 Marc Friedfertig and George West, *The Electronic Day Trader,* page 17.

13 Lynn Hume, "SEC Adopts 'Landmark' Rules for Alternative Trading," *NewsEdge* Online, December 3, 1998.

14 Tim Tindall (contributor), "NASD Board Votes to Extend Trading Hours," MSNBC Online, May 27, 1999.

15 Emily Church, "NYSE Delays Expanded Hours to 2000," CBS MarketWatch Online, June 3, 1999.

16 Edward Wyatt, "The Big Board Will Delay Its Decision on Late Hours," *The New York Times* Online Edition, June 4, 1999.

4
SALESPEOPLE, SALES TRAINING, AND SALES CONTESTS

1 Jeff Nash, "Riding the Bear to a Better Job," *On Wall Street,* October 1998, page 48.

2 Jeff Nash, "The Year of the Fat Check," *On Wall Street,* February 1998, page 34.

3 Jeffrey Davis, "E*Trade's Portal Play," *Business 2.0,* Premier Issue, page 75.

4 Tanya Bielski, "What I Learned at Broker Boot Camp," *On Wall Street,* December 1997, page 37.

5 *Ibid.,* page 37.

6 Jackie Day Packel, "We Know What Your Broker Did Last Weekend," *Smart Money,* March 1999, page 116.

7 *Ibid.,* page 37, and editor's note, *On Wall Street,* February 1998, page 8.

8 Bielski, page 38.

9 *Ibid.*

10 *Ibid.,* page 39.

11 *Ibid.*
12 *Ibid.*
13 *Ibid.,* page 40.
14 *Ibid.*
15 *Ibid.,* page 42.
16 *Ibid.,* page 40.
17 *Ibid.*
18 Jeff Nash, "The Big Getaway," *On Wall Street,* September 1998, page 30.
19 *Ibid.,* page 23.
20 *Ibid.*
21 *Ibid.,* page 25.
22 *Ibid.*

5

GOING UNDERCOVER

1 Peter Pae, "NationsBank to Pay Fine for Understating Risk of Funds," *Washington Post,* May 5, 1998, page A01.
2 From the Congressional testimony of Arthur Levitt Jr., Chairman of the SEC, on September 29, 1998.

6

DISCOUNT BROKERS AND DAY TRADERS

The number of online investors and brokers stated in the chapter is based on research conducted by Gomez Advisors and Harris Interactive. According to Reuters, their study projects 8.6 million on-line investors by the first quarter of 2000.
1 Rebecca Buckman, "Brokerages Spend Big Sums on Website Advertisements," *The Wall Street Journal* Interactive Edition, September 11, 1998.
2 *Ibid.*
3 Rebecca Buckman, "Discount and Online Brokers Worry About Investor Suits," *The Wall Street Journal* Interactive Edition, November 25, 1998.
4 *Ibid.*
5 Jeffrey Davis, "E*Trade's Portal Play," *Business 2.0,* Premier Issue, page 74.
6 Terri Cullen, "Why Bother with Online FAQs When Help Is a Phone Call Away," *The Wall Street Journal* Interactive Edition, June 22, 1998.
7 *Ibid.*
8 David Whitford, "Trade Fast, Trade Cheap," *Fortune,* February 2, 1998, page 112.
9 Charles Schwab, *Guide to Financial Independence,* page 90.
10 Whitford, page 112.
11 *Ibid.*

7
MUTUAL FUND MAYHEM

1 Congressional testimony of David Gardner, cofounder of the Motley Fool, September 29, 1998.
2 *Ibid.*
3 James Glassman, "Funds' Lofty Fees Add Insult to Injury," *Washington Post* Online, September 13, 1998.
4 Center for Responsive Politics Web site: www.crp.org/diykit.
5 *Ibid.*
6 *Ibid.*
7 Taken from the ICI's Web site—www.ici.org/issues/fee_html.
8 *Ibid.*
9 Joseph Nocera, *A Piece of the Action,* page 46.
10 Pui-Wing Tam, "Success of Fund Supermarkets Worries Fund-Firm Executives," *The Wall Street Journal* Interactive Edition, December 28, 1998.
11 *Ibid.*
12 Thomas Easton, "The Fund Industry's Dirty Secret: Big Is Not Beautiful," *Forbes* Online Edition, August 24, 1998.
13 *Ibid.*
14 Jason Zweig, "I've Just Discovered Research That Will Forever Change the Way You Think About Mutual Funds," *Money.com.* Printed this piece on September 16, 1998.

8
INITIAL PUBLIC OFFERINGS

1 Robert Barker, "Star Spotting Among Fallen IPOs," *Business Week,* May 25, 1998, page 133.
2 Aaron Lucchetti, "Many High Flying IPOs Are Less Successful Down the Road," *The Wall Street Journal* Interactive Edition, August 20, 1998.
3 Jeffrey M. Laderman, "Wall Street's Spin Game," *Business Week,* October 5, 1998, page 150.
4 *Ibid.*
5 Tony Chapelle, "Regulators Look Closer At Brokers' IPO Practices," *On Wall Street,* page 26.

9
RETIREMENT, SAVINGS, AND YOUR 401(K)

1 William E. Gibson, "Americans Saving Less Money Than Ever Before," *KRTDN Knight Ridder Tribune Business News,* June 4, 1998.
2 Carrie Lee, "The Internet Offers Employees Relief from 401(k) Headaches," *The Wall Street Journal* Interactive Edition, May 17, 1999.

3 Bill Deener, "401(k)s Fall Short for Many," *Dallas Morning News,* November 15, 1998, page 4H.
4 Harris Collingwood and Janice Koch, "It's Going to Cost You," *Worth* Online, September 1998.
5 Lee.
6 Deener, page 4H.
7 *Ibid.*
8 Example taken from Collingwood and Koch.

10
ASLEEP ON THE JOB

1 Center for Responsive Politics Web site: www.crp.org/diykit.
2 *Ibid.*
3 Michael Schroeder, "SEC Turnover Rate Leaves Agency Scrambling in Fight Against Fraud," *The Wall Street Journal* Interactive Edition, October 23, 1998.
4 Kay Vinson, "The Grifter," *Dallas Observer,* September 3-9, 1998, page 18.
5 *Ibid.*
6 *Ibid.,* page 20.
7 *Ibid.,* page 18.
8 *Ibid.*
9 *Ibid.*
10 *Ibid.,* page 15.
11 *Ibid.,* page 16.
12 *Ibid.,* page 16.
13 *Ibid.*
14 Letter written to Judge Joe Fish by Maureen Garbarino, February 4, 1998.
15 Letter written to Judge Fish by Jeanne Crandall, April 30, 1998.
16 Vinson, page 26.
17 *Ibid.*

11
SETTLING DISPUTES WALL STREET'S WAY

1 From a conversation that I had with a representative from the *Securities Arbitration Commentator Newsletter* on February 22, 1999.
2 *Ibid.*

12
JOURNALISTS

1 David Shaw, "Magazines Feel Increased Pressure from Advertisers' Publishing: As More Firms Threaten to Cancel Ads If They Dislike Story Content, Fear of Self-Censorship by Editors Grows," *Los Angeles Times,* Home Edition, March 31, 1998.

2 David Shaw, "An Uneasy Alliance of News and Ads Citing a Need for Healthier Finances, Newspapers Are Breaking Down the Separation of Business, Editorial Departments. Many Fear a Loss of Independence," *Los Angeles Times* Home Edition, March 29, 1998.

3 *Ibid.*

13
INVESTMENT EXPERTS

1 The facts concerning Mr. Cook's background, the number of seminar attendees, and his personal income, etc. were all taken from this article: Jane Bryant Quinn, "Beware Prophets of Instant Wealth," *Washington Post* Online, December 13, 1998, p H02.

2 Anita Bartholomew, "Bull Marketing," *Salon Magazine* Online, August 21, 1998.

3 Quinn.

14
WHAT EVERY INVESTOR NEEDS TO KNOW

1 Kerry Hannon and Julie Schmit, "SEC Chief Levitt Crusades for Investors Ed," *USA Today* Online, March 27, 1998.

2 *Ibid.*

BIBLIOGRAPHY

Ayres, Alex, editor. *The Wit and Wisdom of Mark Twain.* New York: NAL, 1989, page 5.

Barker, Robert. "Star Spotting Among Fallen IPOs." *Business Week,* May 25, 1998, page 133.

Bartholomew, Anita. "Bull Marketing." *Salon Magazine* Online, August 21, 1998.

Bielski, Tanya. "What I Learned at Broker Boot Camp." *On Wall Street,* December 1997, page 37.

Buckman, Rebecca. "Brokerages Spend Big Sums on Website Advertisements." *The Wall Street Journal* Interactive Edition, September 11, 1998.

———. "Discount and Online Brokers Worry About Investor Suits." *The Wall Street Journal,* Interactive Edition, November 25, 1998.

Center for Responsive Politics Web site: www.crp.org/diykit.

Chapelle, Tony. "Regulators Look Closer at Brokers' IPO Practices." *On Wall Street,* page 26.

Church, Emily. "NASD Votes to Expand Trading Hours." CBS MarketWatch, May 27, 1999.

Church, Emily. "NYSE Delays Expanded Hours to 2000." CBS MarketWatch Online, June 3, 1999.

Collingwood, Harris, and Janice Koch. "It's Going to Cost You." *Worth* Online, September 1998.

Congressional testimony of David Gardner, cofounder of the Motley Fool, and Arthur Levitt, chairman of the SEC. Their testimony was given on September 29, 1998.

Cullen, Terri. "Why Bother with Online FAQs When Help Is a Phone Call Away." *The Wall Street Journal* Interactive Edition, June 22, 1998.

Davis, Jeffrey. "E*Trade's Portal Play." *Business 2.0*, Premier Issue, pages 74–75.

Deener, Bill. "401(k)s Fall Short for Many." *Dallas Morning News,* November 15, 1998, page 4H.

Easton, Thomas. "The Fund Industry's Dirty Secret: Big Is Not Beautiful." *Forbes* Online Edition, August 24, 1998.

Friedfertig, Marc, and George West. *The Electronic Day Trader.* New York: McGraw-Hill, 1998.

Geisst, Charles. *Wall Street—A History.* New York: Oxford University Press, 1997.

Gibson, William E. "Americans Saving Less Money Than Ever Before." *KRTD Knight Ridder Tribune Business News,* June 4, 1998.

Glassman, James. "Funds' Lofty Fees Add Insult to Injury." *Washington Post* Online, September 13, 1998.

Hannon, Kerry, and Julie Schmit. "SEC Chief Levitt Crusades for Investors Ed," *USA Today* Online, March 27, 1998.

Henry, David. "Companies Hear Investors Say, 'Call Me!' " *USA Today* Online, July 1, 1999.

Hume, Lynn. "SEC Adopts 'Landmark' Rules for Alternative Trading." *NewsEdge* Online, December 3, 1998. Investment Company Institute's Web site: www.ici.org.

Ip, Greg. "Soon Online Investors May Be All-Day Traders." *The Wall Street Journal* Interactive Edition, February 10, 1999.

Laderman, Jeffrey. "Wall Street's Spin Game." *Business Week,* October 5, 1998, page 150.

Lee, Carrie. "The Internet Offers Employees Relief from 401(k) Headaches." *The Wall Street Journal* Interactive Edition, May 17, 1999.

Leland, John. "Blessed by the Bull." *Newsweek,* April 27, 1998, page 57.

Lucchetti, Aaron. "Many High Flying IPOs Are Less Successful Down the Road." *The Wall Street Journal* Interactive Edition, August 20, 1998.

MacDonald, Elizabeth. "SEC Readies New Rules for Companies About What Is 'Material' for Disclosure." *The Wall Street Journal* Interactive Edition, November 3, 1998.

Mencke, Claire. "Leaders and Success: Merrill Lynch's Charles E. Merrill." *Investor Business Daily,* July 21, 1997, page A1.

Merrill Lynch's Web site: www.ml.com.

"Merrill Makes Mincemeat of Low Producers with New Grid." *On Wall Street.* November 1998, page 10.

Microsoft Encarta, 1997.

Nash, Jeff. "The Year of the Fat Check." *On Wall Street,* February 1998, page 31.

———. "Riding the Bear to a Better Job." *On Wall Street,* October 1998, page 48.

BIBLIOGRAPHY

————. "The Big Getaway." *On Wall Street.* September 1998, pages 23–30.

Nocera, Joseph. *A Piece of the Action.* New York: Simon and Schuster, 1994.

Packel, Jackie Day. "We Know What Your Broker Did Last Weekend." *Smart Money,* March 1999, page 116.

Pae, Peter. "NationsBank to Pay Fine for Understating Risk of Funds." *Washington Post,* May 5, 1998, page A01.

Quinn, Jane Bryant. "Beware Prophets of Instant Wealth." *Washington Post* Online, December 13, 1998, page H02.

Schroeder, Michael. "SEC Turnover Rate Leaves Agency Scrambling in Fight Against Fraud." *The Wall Street Journal* Interactive Edition, October 23, 1998.

Schultz, Abby. "And the Winner Is: The Money Markets?" *The New York Times* Online Edition, October 11, 1998.

Schwab, Charles. *Guide to Financial Independence.* New York: Crown, 1998.

Securities Arbitration Commentator Newsletter.

Serafino, Phil. "Dell Comments on PC Prices Were Only Available to a Select Few." *Bloomberg News,* July 23, 1998.

Shaw, David. "An Uneasy Alliance of News and Ads Citing a Need for Healthier Finances, Newspapers Are Breaking Down the Separation of Business, Editorial Departments. Many Fear a Loss of Independence." *Los Angeles Times,* Home Edition, March 29, 1998.

————. "Magazines Feel Increased Pressure from Advertisers' Publishing: As More Firms Threaten to Cancel Ads If They Dislike Story Content, Fear of Self-Censorship by Editors Grows." *Los Angeles Times,* Home Edition, March 31, 1998.

Siconolfi, Michael, and Patrick McGeehen. "Small Investors Face Double Standard from Brokers When Investing In IPOs." *The Wall Street Journal* Interactive Edition, June 26, 1998.

Sobel, Robert. "The People's Choice: How Charles Merrill Brought Wall Street to Main Street." *Barron's,* February 17, 1997, page 23.

Tam, Pui-Wing. "Success of Fund Supermarkets Worries Fund-Firm Executives." *The Wall Street Journal* Interactive Edition, December 28, 1998.

Tindall, Tim (contributor). "NASD Board Votes to Extend Trading Hours." MSNBC Online, May 27, 1999.

Vinson, Kay. "The Grifter." *Dallas Observer,* September 3–9, 1998, pages 15–26.

BIBLIOGRAPHY

Whitford, David. "Trade Fast, Trade Cheap." *Fortune,* February 2, 1998, page 112.

Wyatt, Edward. "The Big Board Will Delay Its Decision on Late Hours." *The New York Times* Online Edition, June 4, 1999.

Zweig, Jason. "I've Just Discovered Research That Will Forever Change the Way You Think About Mutual Funds." *Money.com.*

INDEX

advertising:
  classified, 74–76
  by discount brokers, 116, 117–18, 122–23
  media dependence on, 215
advisors, financial:
  awards to, 94, 109–10, 111
  bank, 90–98, 106
  evaluation of, 114
  financial planners as, 91, 95, 105–12
  full-service brokers as, 98–106
  guidelines for dealing with, 50–51
  managing of, 246–47
  searching for, 89–114
  understanding the sales techniques of, 245
after-hours trading, 65–69
  NASDAQ and, 68
  on New York Stock Exchange, 68–69
After Hours Trading (radio show), 66
A. G. Edwards, 33–34
  club requirements at, 84

Aidikoff and Uhl, 201
Aim Management Group, 63, 133
Alderman, Jim, 186
Alliance Capital, 45–46
  broker awards from, 94, 109–10
All-Tech Investment Group, 125–29
Amazon.com, stock of, 127, 128
American Century, 133
American Express, financial advisors at, 102–5
American Funds, 43–44, 144
American Home Products, 59
American National Income Fund, 148
American Stock Exchange, 6
Ameritrade, 117–18, 119, 125
Anderson, Kurt, 216
Anderson, Michael, 118
Annable Turner and Company, 190–94
annuities, 96–97, 110, 111, 112
arbitration process, 197–213, 243
  arbitrators in, 202–4
  brokers and, 206–9

arbitration process *(continued)*
  expert witnesses in, 207–9
  guidelines for safeguarding of interests in, 212–13
  judges in, 201–2
  NASD and, 198–200, 206, 209–10, 211
  outsider view of, 210–12
  plaintiff's attorney and, 199–202
  workings of, 198–99
arbitrators, 202–4
Argus, 36
Armstrong, Michael, 35
Art of Selling Intangibles, The—How to Make Your Millions Investing Other People's Money (Gross), 245
asset management accounts, 19–21, 92
Associated Press, 237
ATCO (investment club), 190, 193
attorneys, 197–207, 212
  defense, 204–6
  plaintiff's, 199–202
auctioneers, 5–6
awards, to advisors, 94, 109–10, 111
AXA Financial, 45

Bach, David, 83
back-end loads, 139–41
"Baker, Jim," 126
BancBoston Robertson Stephens, 159, 227
bank investment advisors, 90–98, 106
Bank of America, 188
Bank One, 95–97
banks:
  interest rates of, 15
  investment, *see* investment banks
  1929 crash and, 8, 10
Beardstown ladies, 236–37
Beardstown Ladies' Common-Sense Investment Guide, The: How We Beat the Stock Market and How You Can Too, 236
Benham, James, 16
Benjamin, Keith, 227
Benna, Ted, 168–71
Bennet, Bonnie, 191, 196
Bent, Bruce R., 15
Berkeley, Alfred R., III, 61–62
bestcalls.com, 69
Bielski, Tanya, 80
Blinder Robinson, 201
BOD (broker-of-the-day) calls, 26

body language, mimicking of, 82
bonds, tax-free, 146
bonuses, of brokers, 76, 77
bottom line, making it easy to sign on, 82
breakpoints, 101–2
Britten, Fred, 10
broadcast.com, 61–62
brokerage firms, brokers, 73–88, 93
  advertising as protection for, 215–16
  arbitration and, 206–9
  bonuses of, 76, 77
  business costs of, 102
  in competition with investor interests, 8–9
  in crash of 1929, 7, 8
  discount, *see* discount brokers
  full-service, *see* full-service brokers
  investors' preferences in, 46
  in moves to new firms, 76, 98
  recruitment of, 74–78
  salaries for, 12, 13
  sales contests for, *see* sales contests
  training of, 54, 78–83, 242
  see also specific individuals and firms
brokerspeak, 161–62
Brown, Henry B. R., 15
Brown, Thomas, 154–57
Bryant, Hap, 148
business costs:
  of brokers, 102
  on-line vs. full-service, 124
Business Week, 219, 234
Buttonwood Agreement (1792), 6, 13
Byers, Ernest H., Jr., 192

campaign contributions, 187–89
capital gains taxes, 44
Carhart, Mark, 148–49
"Carla" (day-trader trainee), 126
Carl A. Johnson & Sons, 190
cash management account (CMA), 20, 27, 92
CDs, "Jumbo," 15
Center for Responsive Government, 244
Charles Schwab (firm), 34–38, 68
  investment banks allied with, 159
  IPOs at, 159, 162, 219
  middle-class investors of, 4
  One Source program of, 143
  on-line trading of, 117, 119

on payment-for-order flow, 124
Priority Customer Program of, 35
Priority Gold customers of, 35, 36
Signature Gold of, 36–37, 159
Signature Platinum of, 36–37, 159
Signature Services of, 36–37
Turner's dealings with, 190, 193
Chinese Wall, 155, 163
Citicorp, 188
Class A shares, 137–39
Class B shares, 139–41
Class C shares, 141–42
"client factory," business as, 81
client referrals, 50–51, 97
clients:
　body language of, 82
　facts used in confusing of, 81–82
　high-net-worth, special treatment for, 23–
　　50
　as "raw material," 81
clubs, recognition, 84–86, 242
CNBC, 59, 229, 232
cnbc.com, 69
cnnfn.com, 69
CNN Interactive (CNN.com), 225
Cohn, Roy, 202
Colonial US Growth and Income Fund, 148
commercial banks, in 1929 crash, 10
commission discounts, breakpoints, 101–2
commissions, 37, 73–74, 76–78, 95, 186,
　　207, 242
　for annuities, 96–97, 112
　discount, 34, 50, 165
　fixed, 6, 13–14
　full-service, 33
　maximum, 77–78
　media misinformation about, 218–19
　on mutual funds, 93, 97–98, 101, 102,
　　104–5, 113
　salary vs., 12, 13
　sales contests and, 84
CommScan, 154
compliance managers, 208
computer analysis, 107–9
con artists, 196
conference calls, 35, 58–65, 69
　Internet broadcasting of, 61–63
　of mutual fund companies, 63–64
　restriction of, 58–60
Congress, U.S., 143, 187–89

IRAs and, 21
mutual fund fees and, 132–34
regulation and, 10
see also House of Representatives, U.S.;
　Senate, U.S.
contests, sales, see sales contests
Cook, Cathy, 192
Cook, Joe, 192
Cook, Wade, 233–37
Cotsakos, Christos, 78, 119
Cowen and Company, 59–60
Crandall, Jeanne, 194, 195
credit-card debt, paying off, 92, 93, 95,
　104, 111
Crosby, Lisa, 172–74
CS/First Boston, 36, 159

Dain Rausher, trip destinations of, 86
Dallas Morning News, 74, 218
Datek Online, 66, 118
Dauper, Joseph, 192
"David" (broker), 54
Day, Ray, 83
day traders, 125–29
dealers, 5–6
defense attorneys, 204–6
deferred sales charge, 94, 96
Dell Computer, 59
Desmond, Lael, 118
Dickerson, Beulah, 192
discount brokers, 13, 14, 19, 115–25
　advertising of, 116, 117–18, 122–23
　investor education and, 115–19
　IPOs and, 162
　on-line trading and, 117–22
　payment-for-order flow of, 123–24
　treatment of wealthy investors by, 34–
　　42
Walt Disney, 60, 99–100
　stock of, 127, 128, 129
disposition effect, 121
Domini Social Equity Fund, 143
Donaldson, Lufkin & Jenrette (DLJ), 155,
　156, 227
Dow Jones Industrial Index, 8

eBay, 227
Ebert, Roger, 147
Edgar (Electronic Data Gathering Analysis
　and Retrieval System), 163

education and training:
    of brokers, 54, 78–83, 242
    of day traders, 126–29
    investor, 12, 115–19, 176–77, 180, 223,
        238–39, 242–43
Edward Jones, broker research at, 98–102
A. G. Edwards, 33–34
    club requirements at, 84
Edwards, Ben, III, 34
E. F. Hutton, 190, 191
80/20 rule, 33–34
electronic communications networks
        (ECNs), 66–68
emergency money, 99, 110
Engle, Franklin, 192
Equitable Companies, 188
equity/commission ratio, 208
Equity Value Fund, 104
ethics:
    information and, 61
    of Quick & Reilly, 39
E*Trade, 117, 119, 159, 162
    customer service department of, 120
Evensky, Harold, 132
experts, see investment experts
expert witnesses, 207–9

family:
    of client, 51
    of financial advisor, 102
Federal Reserve, 15
Federated Companies, 94
fees, 186, 242
    of financial planners, 95, 106–12
    media misinformation about, 218
    of mutual funds, 131–34, 137–42
    supermarkets and, 143
    underwriting, 152–56
Fehn, Tom, 204–6
Ferentz, Jeff, 199–202, 205, 206
Fidelity, 17, 144
    analysts at, 156
    Investments' FundNetwork of, 143
    IPOs at, 159, 162
    Portfolio Advisory Services (PAS) of, 39–
        41
    Premium Services Program of, 41–42
Fidelity Magellan, 17–19
financial advisors, see advisors, financial
financial planners, 91, 95, 103, 105–12

Fink, Matthew, 133, 134
First Call, 36
Fish, Joe, 195–96
fixed commissions, 6
    end of, 13–14
Forrester Research, 118
401(k) plans, 168–81, 243
    asking for help with, 172–74
    Benna as father of, 168, 169–71
    company stock in, 177–79, 181, 241
    cost of contributions to, 179–80
    financial future and, 174–77
Franklin Templeton, 63
Friedman Billings Ramsey, 159
friends, investment advisors and, 51
Fujitsu America, 401(k) plan of, 172–74
full-service brokers, 13, 14
    as advisors, 98–106
    as information source, 53–58
    IPOs and, 155, 158–60, 227
    media endorsement of, 226–27
    myth about, 155
    special treatment for high-net-worth
        clients of, 23–50
    training of, 54
fund managers vs. personal money
        managers, 44

Garbarino, Maureen, 192
Garbarino, Robert, 192
Gardner, David, 132
Gary's World (garywall.com), 235
Gau, Tom, 80–83
General Dynamics, 190
General Motors (GM), 60
"Get to Know Your Advisor" (USA Today
        article), 224
Glass-Steagall Act (1933), 10
Goldman Sachs, 188, 227
Goor, Alex, 120
Gramm, Phil, 188
Grasso, Richard, 68–69
Green, Charles, 248–49
Green, Larry, 216
Gross, Roy, 245
Guide to Financial Independence (Schwab),
        122

Hall, Emily, 148
Hambrecht & Quist, 36, 159

Hamilton, Brooks, 175–77
Health Teamm Management, 190
Heiman, Stephen, 245
high-tech companies, 100
    Internet conference calls and, 62
Home Depot, 99–100
Hopkins, Tom, 245
Horwitz, Ed, 207–9
House of Representatives, U.S., 189
    Commerce Subcommittee on Finance and
        Hazardous Materials of, 132
How to Master the Art of Selling (Hopkins),
    245
"Hughes, Mark," 45–46
E. F. Hutton, 190, 191

IBM, stock of, 156
"Improving Price Competition in Mutual
    Funds and Bonds," 132
index funds, 122
    low-cost, 102
    managed funds compared with, 117
Individual Investor, 219
individual retirement accounts, *see* IRAs
information, 52–69, 242
    after-hours trading and, 65–69
    broadcast.com and, 61–63
    conference calls and, 58–66
    full-service brokers as source of, 53–58
    recommendations for, 69
    SEC views on disclosure of, 60–61
Ingle, Kenneth, 192–94
initial public offerings (IPOs), 151–65,
    227
    analysis of, 164–65
    Central Web site of, 163
    of eBay, 227
    fair distribution of, 163–64
    making of, 152–54
    media misinformation about, 219
    offering price for, 153
    opening price of, 154
    payoffs and, 154–57
    penalties and, 160–63
    privileges and, 158–60
    prospectus for, 152–53
    what should be done with, 162–64
Instinet, 66, 67
Institute of Management and
    Administration (IOMA), 177–78

Institutional Investor, 154
institutional investors vs. average investors,
    158
insurance companies, IPOs and, 151
Internet, 30, 35, 116–22
    information disclosure and, 61–63
    investor education on, 116–17
    IPO road shows on, 163
    recommended Web sites on, 69
    recruitment of brokers on, 75
    trading on, *see* on-line trading
Invesco, 64
investing, true cost of, 241–44
investment advisors, *see* advisors, financial
investment banks, 10, 36, 228
    analysts vs., 155–57
    Chinese Wall and, 155, 163
    IPOs and, 151–57, 159
    proposed Monsanto–American Home
        Products merger and, 59–60
Investment Company Act (1940), 143
Investment Company Institute (ICI), 21,
    132–33
investment experts, 229–39, 244
    Beardstown ladies as, 236–37
    book credentials of, 231–32
    garden-variety, 237–38
    high cost of advice of, 233–36
    reasons for belief in, 230–33
    redefining of, 240–49
    top-drawer credentials and degrees of,
        233
    TV and radio credentials of, 232–33
investment research, analysis of, 164–65
Investments' FundNetwork, 143
investors:
    education of, 12, 115–19, 176–77,
        180, 223, 238–39, 242–43
    institutional vs. average, 158
    on-line, *see* on-line trading
    see also clients; *specific topics*
ipocentral.com, 163
IRAs (Individual Retirement Accounts),
    21–22, 168, 192
    Roth, 22, 99–100, 104, 110, 111
    taxes and, 21–22

Jack White, 66
Janus Twenty, 145
J. B. Oxford, 66

"John" (variable annuity coordinator), 96–97

Johnson, Edward Crosby, II, 18

Johnson, Edward Crosby, III (Ned), 18

Johnson, Keith, 83

"Johnson, Matt," 32–33

"Johnson, Mike," 91–95, 107, 109

Carl A. Johnson & Sons, 190

Johnson Companies, 169–70

journalists, 214–28, 243–44
  adversarial, lack of, 220
  advertisers as restriction on, 215–16
  interviewees unchallenged by, 220–23
  lack of financial experience of, 225–27
  mistakes and misinformation of, 216–19
  opinion made fact by, 224–25
  reader guidelines for, 228

J. P. Morgan, 159

judges, arbitration, 201–2

Kasparov, Gary, 232

Kemper, 63, 155

Kemper Blue Chip Fund, 147–48

Kiggen, Jamie, 227

Kiplinger's Personal Finance, 82

Knight Ridder Newspapers, 223

Kobussen, Dan, 148

K-Tel, 63

Lackritz, Marc, 221

Lacoff, Cheryl, 237

Lalli, Frank, 216

Lamoreaux, Bill, 202–4

Large Company Growth Fund, 97

lawsuits:
  against Beardstown ladies, 237
  see also arbitration process

Lehman Brothers, 59–60, 133, 159, 190

Levitt, Arthur, 60, 61, 87, 160–61, 223, 248

Lincoln, Abraham, 55

Lipper Analytical Services, 17, 147, 148

Los Angeles Times, 82

Lusk, Jim, 75

Lynch, Peter, 18

McDonald's, 153, 190

McNabb, William, 132

Magellan fund, 17–19

Maloney Act (1938), 10–11

Manufacturers Acceptance Corporation (MAC), 190–91

Marcelino, Juan, 186

margin:
  buying on, 7–8, 10–11, 30, 118
  defined, 7
  requirements for buying on, 10–11

margin interest, 125

Marino, Dennis, 120

marketing experts vs. financial experts, 81

Market XT, 66

Massachusetts Investors Trust (MIT), 16

Mayday (1975), 13–14

MBNA America Bank, 188

Merck, 99–100

mergers, cancellation of, 59–60

Merrill, Charles, 11–14, 134

Merrill Lynch, 68, 91, 142, 188, 226
  "average" customer of, 220–21
  cash management account (CMA) of, 20, 92
  club requirements at, 84–85
  commissions paid by, 77–78
  compensation at, 28–29
  founding of, 11
  401(k) plans and, 172
  Mayday and, 14
  middle-class investors of, 4, 11–14
  Premier-Plus Households at, 26, 29
  Premier Priority Households at, 26, 29
  Priority Client Program of, 26–29, 35
  sales contests and, 217
  trip destinations of, 86
  Web site recruiting of, 75

Merrill Lynch Online, 220–21

message boards, 129

MFS Investment Management, 16

MFS Investors Fund, 93

MFS mutual funds, 109–10

Microsoft, stock of, 127–28, 129

Microsoft Investor, 226–27

middle-class investors:
  in crash of 1929, 7–10
  Mayday and, 14
  Merrill as champion of, 11–13
  rise of, 3–5, 11–12

"Miller, Karen," 43–44

"Miller, Luke," 106–9

Miller, Robert Bruce, 245

"Miller, Tom," 38–39

Million-Dollar Boot Camp, 80–83
Moine, Donald, 82
Money, 82, 106, 214, 217, 229
money markets, 15–16
Monsanto, 59
Montgomery Funds, 63
Moore, Todd, 196
J. P. Morgan, 159
Morgan Stanley Dean Witter, 74, 133, 188, 200
    classified ads of, 75
    club requirements at, 85
Morgenthau, Robert M., 224–25
Morningstar, 107, 134, 147, 148
"Morris, Katherine," 34–36
Muriel Siebert & Company, 66
mutual funds, 15–19, 40–49, 130–50, 243
    ABCs of, 134–43
    amount invested in, 130
    bank advisors' recommendations for, 91–94, 97–98
    cardinal sins of, 143–49
    Class A shares of, 137–39
    Class B shares of, 139–41
    Class C shares of, 141–42
    closed-door teleconferences and, 63–64
    Congress and, 132–34
    fees of, 131–34, 137–42
    of Fidelity, 17–19, 39–40, 42, 156
    financial planners' recommendations for, 107–12
    firm interests furthered by, 134
    full-service brokers' recommendations for, 98, 100, 101, 104–5
    IPOs and, 151
    IRAs in, 21, 22
    load, 18, 43–46, 101, 131, 136–41
    money market, 15–16
    no-load, 18, 47–49, 94, 101, 102, 107, 109, 137, 142–43
    popularity of, 113
    quality and performance illusions of, 147–49
    sales contests and, 217
    sales kits for, 135
    strategies for selection of, 149–50
    taxes and portfolio turnover and, 145–47
    variety of, 130–31
    as victims of their own success, 144–45
    wholesalers of, 135–36

"Myers, Matthew," 109–12
"Myers, Nancy," 29, 31

nasaa.org/regulators/us/Default.htm, 114
NASDAQ 100, 68
    hours extended by, 68
    information disclosure and, 61–63
nasd.com, 206
Nathan, Silva, 157
National Association of Securities Dealers (NASD), 10, 114, 190, 194
    arbitration and, 198–200, 206, 209–10, 211
    Rules of Fair Practice of, 193
National Association of Securities Directors, 55
National Discount Brokers (NDB), 116–17
NationsBank Investments, Inc., 91–94
NationsBank Money Manager Account, 92
NDB University, 116–17
net worth investment, 99, 100–101
Neuberger Berman, 63
New Deal, 9
New Dimension Fund, 104
New York Curb Market, 6
New York Stock and Exchange Board, 6
New York Stock Exchange (NYSE), 6, 12, 14, 66
    after-hours trading and, 68–69
    Rule 390 of, 13
New York Times, 106, 170, 214, 224, 229
nytimes.com, 69

O'Brien, Tom, 66–67
Odean, Terrance, 120–22, 124–25, 127
Office of the Comptroller of Currency, 132
O'Neil, Mike, 196
One Investor Annuity, 96
One Source program, 143
on-line trading, 117–22, 220
    amount of, 117
    getting the most from, 129
    lawsuits and, 119
    limitations of, 119
    promotion of, 117–18
On Wall Street, 77–78, 80, 247
    on club membership requirements, 84–85
    on trip destinations, 86
opensecrets.org, 244

Oppenheimer, 63
Otiva, 154
J. B. Oxford, 66
Oxford Health Plans, 67
Oxley, Michael, 132–33

PACs (political action committees), 133,
  187, 188
  of Investment Company Institute, 132–
  33
"Paine, Mike," 64–65
PaineWebber, 133, 155, 200
  club requirements at, 85
  commissions paid by, 77–78
  conference call of, 59
  Premier Clients of, 32–33
  trip destinations of, 86
Palfi, Vivian, 195–96, 214
paperwork, essential, 247
payment-for-order flow, 123–24
penalties, IPOs and, 160–63
People, 82
personal money managers vs. fund
  managers, 44
Philadelphia Inquirer, 170
portfolio turnover, costs of, 145–47
Pottruck, David, 34, 219
Prophet Market Research & Consulting Co.,
  225–26
Prudential Securities, 74, 133
  classified ads of, 75
  club requirements at, 85
  commissions paid by, 77
  trip destinations of, 86
Putnam, 63, 144

Quick & Reilly, 38–39
quiet period, 152
Quist, 36

radio, 66, 185–86
  investment experts on, 232–33
Raging Bull.com, 129
recognition clubs, 84–86, 242
Regan, Donald, 20
Regent Investor Services, 46
regulation, 9–11, 143, 185–96
  campaign contributions and, 187–89
  see also Securities and Exchange
  Commission

Regulation Q, 15
Reserve Fund, 15
retirement planning, 166–81
  bank advisors' recommendations for, 92,
  93, 96
  financial planners' recommendations for,
  108–12
  full-service brokers' recommendations for,
  99–100, 101, 104
  getting a grip on, 181
  see also 401(k) plans; IRAs
Reuters, 66, 221, 225–26
Revenue Act (1978), 169
"Reynolds, Mike," 26–29
Ricketts, Joe, 121, 125
RJR Nabisco, 67
Robb Report, 82
"Roberts, Chris," 39–40
"Robinson, Tim," 98–102, 104
Roosevelt, Franklin D., 9
Roper Poll, 9, 12
"Rosenburg, Howard," 46
Roth IRAs, 22, 99–100, 104, 110, 111
Royal Advisory Service, 190
Royal Alliance, 190, 193, 194

sales contests, 83–88, 186, 217, 242
  asking about, 87–88
  for trips, 84–87
sales instruction, 78–83
  Million-Dollar Boot Camp and, 80–83
sales kits, for mutual funds, 135
salespeople, see brokerage firms, brokers
Salomon Smith Barney, 29–32, 59–60, 142,
  155, 226
  classified ads of, 74
  club requirements at, 85
  commissions paid by, 77
  Financial Consultant Fact Sheet of, 31–32
  High Net Worth Fixed Income Program
  of, 31–32
  Preferred Client Services at, 29–30
  Select Client Program at, 29, 30–31
  trip destinations of, 86
Schwab, Charles, 38, 122
  see also Charles Schwab (firm)
Scudder, 16–17
"SEC Chairman Pursues Consumer
  Protection, Education with Zeal"
  (Knight Ridder article), 223

Securities Act (1933), 10
Securities Act (1934), 10
Securities and Exchange Commission (SEC),
    11, 185–90, 244
    after-hours trading and, 67–68
    creation of, 9, 10
    information disclosure and, 60–61, 96
    investor education and, 223
    investor role in reform of, 248
    IPOs and, 152, 153, 158, 160, 163
    media coverage of, 223
    money markets and, 15
    mutual fund fees and, 132
    resource problem of, 196
    sales contests and, 87, 241
    Turner case and, 192–94
Securities Industry Association (SIA), 87,
    133, 221–22, 224
"Securities Industry Pressed to Clean Up Its
    Act" (Reuters article), 221
self-managed accounts, investor education
    and, 118–19
self-reliance, 247–48
"Sell Mutual Funds and See the World"
    (*Money* article), 217
Senate, U.S., 10
    Committee on Banking, Housing and
    Urban Affairs of, 188
Shah, Manish, 154
Simplified Employment Plan (SEP), 99–
    100, 104, 110, 111
Smart Money, 136
Smith, Jack, 35
Smith, Margie, 191–92
Smith, Tommy, 191–92
S-1 filings, 163
Southerly, Thomas, 146
Standard and Poor's (S&P) 500 index, 17,
    117, 148
    401(k) plans and, 178–79
    Magellan and, 18–19
    mutual funds and, 144, 145
Standard and Poor's, 36
Steffens, John "Launny," 220
Stephens, Robertson, 227
stock:
    after-hours trading of, 65–67, 69
    buying vs. holding, 101, 117
    of Disney, 127, 128, 129
    of eBay, 227

full-service brokers' recommendations for,
    99–101
    of General Motors, 60
    Instinet and, 66, 67
    of Microsoft, 127–28, 129
    of Oxford Health Plans, 67
    retirement money in, 99–100
    see also initial public offerings
stock exchange:
    development of, 6
    see also specific exchanges
stock market crash (1929), 7–10
stock quotes, level-one vs. level-two, 126
Stout, Lynn, 210–12
"Street Is Sold on Idea eBay Will Lead
    Auction Market" (*Wall Street Journal*
    article), 227
Stuyvesant, Peter, 5
Sun America, 190
supermarkets, 143
Sweet, Inez, 192

taxes:
    capital gains, 44
    IRAs and, 21–22
    mutual funds and, 145–47
Taxpayers' Relief Act (1997), 22
T-Bills, 15
technology, *see* Internet; on-line trading
"Ted" (day-trader trainee), 126
telephone calls, to investment advisors, 51
television, investment experts on, 232–33
Thompson, Louis, Jr., 68
"Thompson, Mark," 39–40
Thorley, Steven, 122
3Com, 66–67
Tiger Investment Corporation, 155
Tiger Investment Group, 66–67
Towers Financial Corporation, 191
Traulsen, Christopher, 147
*Tricks of the Trade—An Insider's Guide to
    Using a Stockbroker* (Dempsey), 186,
    245
Tritsch, Shane, 236–37
T. Rowe Price, Personal Services Group of,
    48–49
Trzcinka, Charles, 132
Tuleja, Tad, 245
Tully, Daniel, 217–18
Tully Commission, 217

"Turner, Kevin," 95–97, 101
Turner, Roger, 189–96, 225
turnover ratio, 208
12–1 fees, 134

Uhl, Robert, 201–2
Ullman, Chris, 160
Unlimited Selling Power (Moine), 82
Untermyer, Samuel, 9
up-front loads, 137–39
USA Today, 224

vacations, brokers' awards of, 84–87
Value Line, 147
Vanguard Funds, 47–48, 144
   European Stock Index Fund of, 148
   Flagship category of, 47, 48
   Flagship Plus category of, 47, 48
   Voyager Group of, 47–48
Variety, 8

Wade Cook Financial Corporation, 234–35
Wagner, Todd, 62–63
Wall Street:
   brief history of, 5–22
   in crash of 1929, 7–10
   entry of middle-class investors into, 3–5
   information on, 52–69
   origin of name, 5
   regulation of, 9–11, 143, 185–96; *see also*
     Securities and Exchange Commission

   special treatment for high-net-worth
     clients on, 23–50
   use of term, 3
   see also specific topics
"Wall Street Executives Suffering in
   Downturn" (CNN Interactive story),
   225
Wall Street Journal, 37–38, 82, 106, 214,
   220–21, 227, 229
Wall Street Money Machine (Cook), 233–34
Walt Disney, 60, 99–100
   stock of, 127, 128, 129
Washington Post, 234
Waterhouse Securities, 119
Watson, Steve, 209–10
WBZ radio, 185–86
Weill, Sanford, 225
Wertheim, 59
wholesalers, 135–36
"Wilson, Joe," 33–34
"Wilson, Stephen," 48–49
"Wilson, William," 102–5
Wit Capital, 66
Witham, Ken, 186
Women's Equity Fund, 143
Worth, 82, 106, 218
wsj.com, 69

Yahoo Finance, 129

Zacks Investment Research, 157